After the Flames

AFTER THE FLAMES

A Burn Victim's
Battle with Celebrity

JONATHAN R. ROSE

DUNDURN
PRESS

Publisher: Kwame Scott Fraser | Acquiring editor: Russell Smith
Cover designer: Laura Boyle
Cover image: istock/ErinWilkins

All images courtesy of the Hawkins and Philion families, unless otherwise noted.
Image on page 118 republished with the express permission of *Toronto Sun*, a division of Postmedia Network Inc.

Library and Archives Canada Cataloguing in Publication

Title: After the flames : a burn victim's battle with celebrity / Jonathan R. Rose.
Names: Rose, Jonathan R., author.
Identifiers: Canadiana (print) 20230533817 | Canadiana (ebook) 20230533841 | ISBN 9781459753785 (softcover) | ISBN 9781459753808 (EPUB) | ISBN 9781459753792 (PDF)
Subjects: LCSH: Philion, Joey. | LCSH: Burns and scalds—Patients—Canada—Biography. | LCSH: People with disabilities—Canada—Biography. | LCGFT: Biographies.
Classification: LCC RD96.4 .R67 2024 | DDC 362.1/9711092—dc23

We acknowledge the support of the Canada Council for the Arts and the Ontario Arts Council for our publishing program. We also acknowledge the financial support of the Government of Ontario, through the Ontario Book Publishing Tax Credit and Ontario Creates, and the Government of Canada.

Dundurn Press
1382 Queen Street East
Toronto, Ontario, Canada M4L 1C9
dundurn.com, @dundurnpress

For Linda and Mike Hawkins & Joey and Danny Philion

MARCH 10, 1988

THE WEATHER IN CUMBERLAND BEACH, ONTARIO, WAS FRIGID THAT THURSDAY morning. While the thermostat read minus seven degrees Celsius, the icy breath of the nearby lake pulled the actual temperature closer to minus twenty. Less than two weeks earlier, after fixing yet another pipe that had burst from the cold, Mike Hawkins had scrounged together enough money to purchase a new electric furnace for the house he shared with his wife, Linda, and her sons, Joey and Danny. He was sure it would do a far better job heating the home than the old oil furnace they had been using. A few days after Mike removed the oil furnace and purchased the electric furnace (which he was planning on installing himself in order to save money), a home insurance agent told him their policy was being cancelled. Mike demanded to know why. The agent told him a professional electrician had to install the electric furnace. Also, provincial regulations required that for any house to qualify for home insurance, it had to have two secure functioning sources of heat, and with no installed furnace, the house was left with only one source: the fireplace.

At exactly 6:14 a.m., Mike Hawkins woke up. He rolled in the bed, basking in the warmth of his blanket for just a few more seconds before getting ready for work at the Vulcan Hart Industries factory in Orillia, where he started his shift at 7:00 a.m. Always cold, always shivering during the mornings that winter, Mike got dressed in the warmest clothes he had. He didn't bother with a shower, knowing the water would be bitterly cold. Afterward, he went outside to turn on the car: a big, green late-1970s Mercury Marquis. While he left the car running, hoping its engine would make it another day, he enjoyed a cigarette.

Meanwhile Linda, who drove Mike to work, had already woken up and started filling the wood stove and the fireplace with kindling, which she planned to light after returning home to give her and her two sons the warmth they needed. She then checked the wood stove to see if there were any hot coals inside from the night before, but forgot to shut the stove door when she was done.

At 6:35 a.m., the sun had yet to creep up. The drive to drop Mike off at work wasn't going to take long: fifteen minutes there and fifteen minutes back. Linda would be home by 7:05 a.m., 7:10 at the latest, when she would make breakfast for her sons before starting her day.

Just a few minutes after his mother and stepfather left the house, fourteen-year-old Joey woke up to the smell of smoke. He jumped out of bed, but before leaving his bedroom he took off his pyjamas and put on a pair of jeans and a sweater. As soon as he walked into the kitchen his eyes bulged at the sight of thick smoke creeping toward him, pluming from flames growing larger and angrier. He rushed into his younger brother's room and violently shook him awake. Unsure what was going on, Danny initially resisted his older brother's actions, believing them to be just another example of big brother bothering little brother. After a few moments, however, Danny started smelling the smoke and feeling the heat from the approaching flames. Joey grabbed his younger brother, who was dressed from head to toe in pyjamas, rushed him to the window, opened it, and tossed him outside. Joey didn't follow. When Danny asked him why, Joey told him their mother might still be inside.

Joey re-entered the flourishing inferno, desperately shouting for his mother, hoping to hear her voice so he could use it as a beacon to guide him through the thick walls of smoke. He coughed violently. He felt light-headed. The heat from the fire was intense. Moving from room to room, he continued searching for his mother, his shouts of her name growing more muffled as he inhaled more and more black smoke.

When he realized his mother was not in the house, that it was only him and the flames, Joey tried to escape. The first route that came to mind was through the kitchen and out the front door, but that was impossible because the kitchen contained the fiercest flames. That's where the fire had started. A piece of hot coal inside of the wood stove that Linda had failed to find had ignited the kindling she left inside, and by leaving the door open she had given the blossoming fire an opportunity to spread.

Joey turned around and ran to Linda and Mike's bedroom on the second floor of the house, dodging whipping flames along the way. No longer coughing, but choking on the smoke, he didn't have much time. He saw the window and threw himself through the glass. It wasn't Joey that escaped the house, however, but a fireball with a fourteen-year-old boy in the centre. While he was finally out of the house, the fire refused to let him go. It continued relentlessly burning his skin. Meanwhile, his lungs were so full of smoke that, despite the pain, he was unable to scream.

Danny ran over to the house of Lynda Young, who was the closest neighbour. She ordered him to stay in her house before rushing to Joey. He was still on fire. When she tried touching him his skin melted in her hands. She saw that his jeans were the biggest source of the flames still ravaging his body. What she didn't see, however, was that the denim had fused itself to his legs, as had the jeans' metallic zipper, which melted into his thigh. So when she peeled the jeans off, burning her own hands in the process, she also peeled off a great deal of Joey's skin. Afterward, she tossed the jeans onto the seat of a wooden swing set that immediately burst into flames.

Gazing at his deformed, melted hands, Joey pleaded with his neighbour, begging her to help him. That he was still speaking, that he was still alive, that he was still human in those moments came as an incredible shock that Lynda did not reflect upon until much later, when she also reflected on the actions she had taken, questioning if they were right or if they were riddled with costly mistakes.

It wasn't long before other people came to help. Twice they tried to move Joey, but every time they did his still burning body started a new fire. Nearby trees, after feeling the touch or inhaling the heat from his body, were instantly set ablaze. On the third attempt they were finally able to roll Joey over and wrap him in blankets that bravely resisted the urge to combust the moment they touched him.

Lynda ran back into her house and dialed 911. Instead of hearing the voice of a person ready to help, she heard the voice of a groggy telephone repairman. She hung up the phone and dialed zero for the operator. After she had waited several painful seconds she knew were exponentially more painful for Joey, the operator casually asked where she wanted to be connected. Lynda shouted for the fire department, an ambulance, the police, anybody who could help. After she was connected to the fire department, they assured her that emergency responders were on the way. She hung up the phone, told Danny his brother was going to be okay, and ran back outside to Joey.

His body, still tightly wrapped in several blankets, puffed out thick billows of smoke. He looked at Lynda and told her he couldn't feel his legs. She assured him that was a good thing because they were badly burned and, if he could feel them, all he would feel was pain. He also said he couldn't breathe.

The ambulance, along with police and the fire department, finally arrived nearly thirty minutes after the first emergency call was made. It was abundantly clear to everybody present that the paramedics were going to be transporting either a corpse, or a living body that had yet to accept the inevitable fact it was not going to survive much longer. Meanwhile, the fire department started putting out an array of fires from the swing set and the trees to the house itself, which had already started collapsing under the weight of its own suffering.

According to all the newspapers, news broadcasts, interviews, and books, that's what happened. That was the story people read, heard, watched, and talked about throughout 1988 and the years to follow. Except that story wasn't entirely true.

•

Before continuing, it is worth noting that Mike Hawkins, Joey's stepfather, is my biological father. At the time of the fire, I was five years old, living with my mother in Scarborough, Ontario. (My mother and father had separated three years earlier.) The last time I saw him before the fire was in October of 1987, when I visited the house in Orillia less than six months before it burst into flames.

My involvement in the story will come later on, but in the meantime I would like to return to what really happened on the morning of March 10, 1988.

•

The house of Mike and Linda Hawkins and Joey and Danny Philion didn't actually have a second floor, but it did burn down that morning. Mike and Linda weren't home when it happened. Danny escaped the fire unscathed. Joey initially escaped the fire as

5

well, and did re-enter, only to be caught in the grip of its flames, heat, and smoke. He was brutally burned before exploding through a window. Lynda Young did rush over to help. The swing set and the trees did ignite as soon as any part of Joey or his clothes touched them, and it did take nearly thirty minutes for emergency response units to arrive at the scene.

However, there were no hot coals left in the stove, and the kindling did not ignite as a result of Linda's negligence. Joey did not awaken to the smell of smoke, just the same bitter cold he awoke to almost every morning that winter. With Danny still asleep in his bed, Joey woke up, put on his jeans and a sweater, and went to the kitchen. He looked around, heard nothing but silence, saw the time and knew his mother and stepfather weren't home. Shivering from the cold, he went to the fireplace, saw the kindling his mother left inside, knelt down, and lit it with a match. The dry twigs immediately caught fire, but there was no panic, no sense of dread. He added a log. The heat from the small, controlled flames brought instant comfort. He held his open palms above the tips of the crackling flames. He rubbed his hands together. He wondered if he should make his own breakfast or wait for his mother to come back, which, if she was following the same schedule she always did, wouldn't be much longer: twenty, maybe twenty-five minutes.

He turned around, glancing at what food there was on the table and the counter in the kitchen. Before he could identify anything, he heard a louder than usual pop from the fireplace. He spun back around. At first nothing looked out of the ordinary. The fire was still burning calmly, yielding more heat by the second. But when he looked down he noticed that something had escaped the fireplace: a harmless-looking ember that landed on the bone-dry carpet resting at his feet.

In an instant, the carpet was on fire. Joey fell backwards, shocked at the speed and ferocity of the flames. He looked around, desperate to spot something that could put out the fire. What he couldn't have possibly known was there was no way he was going to tame, let alone extinguish the awakened beast. Famished, the fire was obsessed with consuming all it could. Joey ran to the sink and filled up cup after cup of water and tossed the contents into the growing blaze. When he realized he couldn't quell the fire, which at this point had already started producing flames taller than him and smoke thicker than the most oppressive fog, he backed up into the hallway. He couldn't believe his home was on the verge of burning down and there was nothing he could do to stop it. He ran into Danny's room. With the fire not yet reaching the impenetrable strength it soon would, he was able to swiftly walk Danny past the lashing flames and out the front door. Once outside, Danny asked him why he was going back into the house. Joey told his younger brother he was going to search for their mother, but that was a lie. He knew she wasn't there, but he felt tethered to the responsibility for the fire that was destroying their home. He rushed back into the house and valiantly tried to do whatever he could to save it, and that was the last time anybody, including himself, ever saw Joey the same way again.

When it became clear that any hopes he had of putting the fire out were gone, Joey made his way to his bedroom window, but it was frozen shut. Not yet caught by the flames, he smashed the window and tried to clear it of as many shards of glass as possible before making his way through. It wasn't until the upper half of his body was already out of the house, where freedom was so achingly close, that the fire set its sights on him.

Perhaps the fire was incensed at Joey's audacity for daring to challenge it. Perhaps, like Frankenstein's monster, it was enraged that its creator was attempting to destroy his creation. Or, without any feeling, any emotion, agenda, or goal, the fire simply pulsed forward, indifferent to what lay in its path, from a rickety wooden dresser and a small table topped with copies of *Spider-Man* and *Nemesis the Warlock* comics to a fourteen-year-old boy attempting to flee its appetite for destruction.

Looking at the ground beneath the windowsill, seeing the soft snow, feeling the cold air blowing against his face, Joey prepared to push himself through, momentarily putting aside the only dread he thought he had left to consider at that moment: telling his mother and stepfather that he accidently started the fire that destroyed their home. But just as the muscles in his feet and legs started pushing his body forward, his progress was abruptly halted. He kept pushing but couldn't move any farther. He kept seeing freedom right there in front of him but was unable to reach it. He even extended his hands, hoping that somebody might appear, grab his outstretched fingers, and pull him out, but no such person came. He felt the heat from the fire getting closer, but he didn't dare turn around. After several more futile and painful attempts, he realized his torso was caught on some of the loose shards of glass he failed to clear in his rushed attempt to create an escape. After raising his body from the bloodied shards and removing them with his arm there was a moment of relief, followed by a moment of triumph. He believed he was now ready to make his escape, but the fire, cresting in its fury, had already stormed the bedroom. While his eyes were gazing at the peaceful ground below and the snow-covered terrain beyond, a tsunami of heat, smoke, and flames, invigorated by a rush of new oxygen, swallowed him in less time than it took for him to realize what was happening.

How Joey found the presence of mind, let alone the physical strength, to propel himself outside with his entire body draped in a cloak of flames and his lungs filled with smoke is beyond comprehension, but he did, and that's when his journey, and the journey of his mother, his brother, and his stepfather began.

A MOTHER'S LOVE

LINDA DIDN'T HAVE ANY BAD FEELINGS OR KNOTS IN HER STOMACH, NOR ANY premonitions of looming tragedy. During the short drive back from the Vulcan Hart Industries factory, her mind was relaxed. Even when she saw the thick cloud of black smoke looming in the distance and noticed several fire trucks racing past her, she was calm, completely unaware of what was to come.

When she got closer to home, Linda's attention to the black cloud became more intense. Turn after turn, she hoped the cloud would veer off in another direction so she could blissfully leave it behind. But no matter where she turned the car, the black cloud remained directly in front of her, getting larger as she got closer.

As soon as she reached Cleveland Avenue, she knew the source of the black cloud was her house. Her foot pushed heavier on the gas pedal. She saw the inferno. She pulled the car over, not caring where or how it was parked. She rushed out and saw the small gathering of people and the billows of smoke rising from the centre of their circle. She hoped it wasn't a person in the middle, that it was something insignificant, something inanimate, a piece of furniture perhaps, but as she got closer and saw the shock and dread on the faces of the small crowd, she knew whatever or whoever they were surrounding was alive, or had been not too long ago. With a sunken heart, she hoped it was Kelly, the family dog, a beautiful German shepherd and Labrador mix. She loved that dog. Mike loved that dog. So did Joey and Danny. The loss of Kelly, only six years old at the time of the fire, would have been devastating, but Linda knew the family could handle it.

When she got closer, she realized it wasn't Kelly. She looked around, hoping to God to see the faces of her boys and to her relief, she saw Danny in front of Lynda Young's house. But it was just him standing there, alone and afraid. Where was Joey? She turned and saw Lynda kneeling down, talking to someone Linda knew was her first-born son.

She rushed toward him but was told not to touch him. Lynda told her he was too hot, and it would hurt him even more. All she could do was cry. His crimson face was so swollen she couldn't see his eyes. His lips were inflated. All of the hair on his head, his eyebrows, and even his pubescent moustache were gone, burned completely away.

"Try calling the ambulance again," Lynda said, but Linda was unable to turn away from her son. She was upset at being told not to touch him. She wanted to hug him, to comfort him, to take away his pain, to make everything better. She would have sold her soul to put an end to the suffering he was enduring. All she needed was a pen and directions where to sign.

A few moments later, Linda, going against every instinct she had, left Joey and ran to Lynda's house, where ten-year-old Danny continued standing. His face was a mix of dread, fear, and confusion. She hugged him. He squeezed her so tight, she felt paralyzed by his strength.

"Are you okay?" she asked.

"How is he?" he replied. "How is Joey? Lynda told me to stay here. I want to see Joey. Can I see Joey? How is Joey?"

It was clear he didn't want to let go of his mother and he didn't want her to let go of him, but she insisted, saying she had to save Joey. Danny still refused to let go, his hands clenched around his mother's body even tighter, powered by love and fear. Left with no option, Linda took it upon herself to break the embrace. She felt awful for doing so, especially after seeing her younger son's face, so lost, so alone, even though she was right in front of him.

"It will be okay," she said. "I love you so much."

"I love you too, Mom," he replied. "Is Joey going to be okay?"

She grabbed the phone but didn't know what number to dial. So she just pressed zero, got the operator, and frantically asked where the ambulance was. The operator connected her to the paramedics, who told her the ambulance was on the way.

"Hurry!" she said. "Please, God, hurry up. My son needs an ambulance right away."

She hung up the phone and told Danny to stay in the house. Before rushing out to be with Joey again, she saw the same look of isolation on Danny's face, but knew she had to go and knew he had to stay.

Linda didn't feel the cold. It could have been minus fifty degrees Celsius and it wouldn't have affected her in the least. When she reached Joey he was trying to speak but the words were muffled. Soon there were no words at all, just gasps and moans.

When the ambulance finally arrived, Linda saw the faces of the paramedics and knew they didn't know what to do. They didn't want to touch Joey, let alone move him; they weren't even sure if he was still alive, but their hesitation was only momentary before their training took over. Throughout the process of awkwardly and nervously getting Joey off the ground, onto a stretcher, and into the ambulance, Linda was never more than a few feet away from him. Nothing was going to extend that distance.

Once Joey was securely inside the ambulance, Linda jumped in with him, and they made the trip to Orillia's Soldier's Memorial Hospital. Linda stared at her son throughout the ride, telling him she loved him, telling him to hold on, telling him to fight. She gazed into his horribly swollen eyes, conflicted at what she saw. She was happy that, with the fire claiming seemingly every inch of his body, it had chosen to spare her son's eyes, which remained open and functioning. However, the unfathomable pain she saw in those eyes made her question that appreciation. Joey stared at his mother, those same eyes saying what his mouth no longer could. Talking had become too difficult. It was hard enough just for him to breathe. Even though he had the help of an oxygen mask, there was too much smoke in his lungs, clinging to the tissue.

Linda shouted for the ambulance driver to go faster. She shouted at the paramedics to do more for her son but they feared any false move, any negligent touch, would kill him. As upset as she was, she couldn't fault them. She saw what they saw: a fragile, broken boy who looked as if he was on the verge of falling apart like a pile of ash.

When they finally reached the hospital, the doctors and nurses awaiting them were in a state of shock. They had never seen anything like Joey before. His body was starting to swell severely, requiring an immediate incision in his side just to relieve the fluid buildup. It was a small procedure, but it saved his life. After that, several nurses tried cleaning his wounds, but didn't know where to start. His entire body was a wound. Nonetheless they did all they could, knowing it wasn't enough. They knew if Joey stayed in that hospital he would be dead in an hour, two tops. Linda was told that he had to be transferred to the Hospital for Sick Children in Toronto and the transfer had to be done right away.

Linda called the Vulcan Hart Industries factory where Mike worked as soon as she arrived at the hospital, and was connected to the office of Mike's supervisor, Gord. Linda told him about the fire, about Joey, and that she needed Mike to come to the hospital immediately. Gord was about to get up and rush to find Mike but was shocked when Mike appeared at his door. Gord held up the telephone and told Mike to take what was an incredibly important call. Holding the phone in his hand, Mike heard his wife tell him there had been a fire, and that Joey was badly burned, and they were at the hospital. That was all Mike needed to hear. He told her he would be right there. Gord didn't let Mike speak before telling him, "Let's go."

After the short drive to the hospital, Mike rushed in and saw his wife, as well as Lynda Young, who had driven there too, following behind the ambulance. They were both sobbing. Unsure what to expect, Mike opened his arms. Linda rushed over and hugged him. They cried together. Mike started asking questions. What happened? Where's Danny? What about Kelly?

Linda told Mike that Joey was badly burned, that the doctors weren't sure what they could do. She said they told her he was probably going to die. Then she told him they said they wanted to transfer Joey to the Hospital for Sick Children in Toronto because they had the best burn ward in the country and if Joey stood any chance of survival, that's where he had to be. Mike didn't need to hear any more and told her to sign the transfer papers.

Mike and Linda waited for nearly an hour after that, while the doctors and nurses prepared Joey for the transfer. Linda desperately wanted to see her son during that time but wasn't allowed. A nurse came out and told her that it was probably too late, that her son was going to die, and perhaps that was for the best. Linda shouted at the nurse for saying what she considered blasphemy. Her son wasn't going to die and she refused to hear anything that even hinted otherwise.

Linda finally got to see her son after the doctors and nurses completed a partial cleaning. Gone was all the blackness and remnants of scorched clothing, exposing a horribly swollen body that had been burned so thoroughly it looked almost transparent. She could see her son's internal organs struggling to function through what was left of his skin. Meanwhile, his head had inflated to nearly three times its normal size and looked like a grotesque red beach ball, while his eyes had swollen completely shut. She sobbed, and for a brief moment contemplated the possibility that the nurse might have been right, that it might be for the best if Joey didn't make it and his life, but more importantly his suffering, could mercifully end. However, she swiftly and powerfully dismissed that thought. She leaned toward him, resisting every urge she had to touch him, to kiss him, to hold him, and whispered, "I'll always be here, no matter what. No matter how long it takes. No matter what it costs. Nothing matters more to me than you. Keep fighting. I love you and I will see you soon."

After Joey departed for Toronto, Linda and Mike were left having to figure out how they could join him at the Hospital for Sick Children, over 140 kilometres away. They also had to figure out what to do with Danny. They had to figure out how to get clothes. They had to figure out what they were going to do about what was left of their home. They had to get their car. They had to figure out what they were going to do about money.

Luckily, there were friends present, particularly Wayne Cooke, a close family friend and father of Joey's best friend, Wayne Jr. He assured Linda and Mike that this wasn't the time to worry about anything other than Joey, and that anything they needed, he would help them take care of. His words, like his presence and warmth, were a blessing.

When Wayne drove Mike back to his home, Mike was devastated. There was nothing left. He'd had dreams for that house. Before the fire, it was meagre looking. There was nothing special about it. But it was cheap, and it was his. After getting the electric furnace installed, he planned on fixing the place and turning it into a home he could be proud of. He was going to do the roofing, build a deck, and do the landscaping with his own bare hands. He was going to improve that house in every way before selling it and using the money to move him and his family to their ultimate goal: Vancouver Island. But that was all gone. The house, the dream — it was nothing but a pile of charred rubble along with a few stubborn items that bore the brunt of the flames, smoke, and heat, yet refused to collapse.

Mike started laughing. Wayne turned to him and asked what was so funny. Mike looked at him and replied, "Do you think I'll be able to find a clean shirt in there?"

Tears started welling up in his eyes. Everything he had was in that house. He knew there was no home insurance. But there was no time to cry.

"Where's Kelly?" he asked.

Wayne lowered his head and didn't reply.

What was left of the house was blackened by the fire and soggy from the water used by the firefighters to extinguish the flames. Despite the eradication of the blaze, steam still rose from the home's soaked bones in a magnificent cloud that was given extra girth from the chill of the winter air. Mike watched the spirit of the house, of him, of his entire family, rise up to the heavens. But there was no time to cry.

It was a strange thing for Mike to walk through the ruins of a home he had slept in the night before and woke up in that morning. It was like being in two different places at the same time. Stepping on the rubble of the hallway, he saw walls where family pictures once hung. He saw the kitchen where he ate his meals and the living room where he sat to relax. He could see it all as clearly as he saw it just a few hours earlier, but now it was gone.

Mike rapidly made his way through the remains of his home toward what was left of his bedroom. He wanted to fall to his knees and mourn the loss of everything he had, but there was no time. He saw his dresser. It was badly burned. Nonetheless, he opened every drawer, thinking that perhaps some of his clothes may have survived, but none had. His shirts, pants, and underwear were all completely ruined. To his amazement, however, he saw his wallet, which he had forgotten to bring to work that morning. It was resting underneath several burned pairs of socks. Slightly scorched, it was still recognizable, and when he opened it his social insurance card, birth certificate, and other important contents were not only intact but had been left completely unmolested by the flames. He shook his head in disbelief, but that was not the only surprise he found in that drawer. Amidst his ruined socks, he found two candles — the same two candles Linda had received at Joey's baptism several years earlier. They were pristine. It was remarkable. Of all the items in the entire house, those candles should have been the first to submit to the might of the fire. But not only were they untouched by the flames, they had maintained their original shape, seemingly immune to the heat that should have reduced their wax bodies to deformed mounds. Even their elaborate and colourful designs were unaffected by the fire. Mike couldn't believe it, but there was no time to dwell on the mystery. He took his wallet and the candles and left the ruins of his home behind.

"I don't have any clothes," he told Wayne. "Just what I got on."

"Don't worry about it," Wayne replied. "Let's go."

Mike nodded and got in Wayne's car. When they returned to the hospital, Mike saw Linda and Lynda Young in the parking lot. He got out of the car. His wife said that Lynda was going to drive them to Toronto. Linda asked if there was anything left in the house. Mike showed her the candles. She gazed at them in amazement.

"But how?"

He shook his head.

"Are you guys ready to go?" Lynda asked.

Mike and Linda both said yes and walked toward her car, but they were abruptly stopped by a nurse who ran out of the hospital, shouting Linda's name. Her heart sank. She thought that was it. She was expecting to be told there was no point in driving to Toronto, that Joey had died during the trip and was being brought back. She was ready to hear the words but unprepared to believe them.

The words never came. Instead, the nurse handed Linda a very familiar wristwatch.

"We took it off him," the nurse said. "We thought you should have it."

Joey had been wearing the watch the whole time and Linda had never noticed. His body was so ravaged by the fire, so disfigured, it was hard enough for her to cling to the reality that it was even him, let alone have the capacity to pay any attention to what accessories he had on. The watch was badly deformed. The glass had melted into the face, which was completely blackened by the flames, and there were blotches of blood and shards of skin clinging to the band. Yet, in spite of the extensive damage it sustained, the watch was still working. After checking the time on her own watch, Linda was astonished to discover that Joey's watch was right on time; it had continued ticking along as if nothing had happened.

"Linda," Mike said from Lynda's car, "we really have to go."

Linda thanked the nurse, who wished her luck in return, and she got in the car. They were ready to make the trip to the Hospital for Sick Children in Toronto before realizing they had forgotten about Danny.

Lynda drove Mike and Linda back to Cleveland Avenue to the house of Rick and Wilma Sharpe, where Lynda insisted Danny stay when she drove to the hospital to meet up with Linda and Mike. When Linda saw her youngest son, she saw the same frightened and confused boy she had left behind when she got into the ambulance with Joey. He was staring at the burned-down shell of his home. She hugged him and, just like before, she was amazed at how powerfully he hugged her back and, just like before, she had to regrettably break the embrace. Relieved that he was unhurt by the fire, she hoped he would forgive her for having to leave him again.

"We have to go to Toronto," she told him. "Joey is going to the hospital there, and they're going to try to save him."

"Is Joey going to be all right, Mom? Is he going to die? Kelly died. What's going to happen with our house? Are we going to be homeless? What's going to happen to Joey, Mom? I want to come with you."

Linda was on the verge of breaking down right then and there. It took everything she had to defy the emotional gravity aggressively trying to pull her to her knees, but she remained upright.

"I know you do," she said, "and I wish you could, but I need you to stay here. I need you to stay strong, for Joey, for all of us. I need you to do that, Danny. We'll make it through this. We'll be a family again. Can you do that for me?"

After wiping away his tears, Danny told his mom he would be strong. He asked her if there was anything else he could do.

"Just that, Danny," she replied. "I just need you to be strong. We have to go."

Linda thanked Rick and Wilma for watching Danny. They told her that he was welcome to stay with them for as long as needed. Not knowing how to show the incredible amount of appreciation she had for them, Linda, knowing she had to hurry, just thanked them again and got back into Lynda's car. A moment later, they left and in what seemed like no time at all they were on Highway 400, racing south to Ontario's capital city.

Just as they passed Barrie, driving over 160 kilometres per hour, an OPP police car flashed its lights. Lynda pulled the car over to the highway's shoulder. Linda buried her face in her hands, believing every moment they weren't getting closer to Joey was another precious moment wasted. Mike got restless. He knew how fast they were going and he knew from plenty of past experience with law enforcement that where they went from there rested entirely in the hands of the approaching police officer.

While formulating how best to present the story of their predicament in hopes it would convince the police officer to let them go, Mike got out of the car. When he reached the police officer, he was met with eyes of absolute sympathy. It was a relieving sight. After offering Mike a quick glance, the police officer continued listening to Lynda as she calmly but succinctly detailed her reason for speeding. The police officer nodded several times before straightening his body and saying, "Well let's get a move on then. Just follow me."

Mike rushed back into the car and closed the door. Lynda started the car while Linda, whose face had risen from her dampened hands, anxiously awaited a return to the progress toward her eldest son.

Lynda merged back onto the highway right behind the police officer, who raced down the left lane, his sirens blaring and lights flashing. With her foot pushing the pedal of her modest car almost to the floor, Lynda concentrated on little else than the police car escorting her right into the city of Toronto. Meanwhile Mike stared out the window, watching all the other cars passing by in an extended blur that made their colours blend together like a stunning streak of paint.

When they finally reached the Hospital for Sick Children, Mike and Linda rushed through the front doors and frantically asked the receptionist where Joey Philion was. They were directed to the burn unit on the eighth floor. When they got there, the receptionist told them where to go. It was a large room filled with doctors, all of whom were doing something to Joey's body. It was chaos. Lines,

IVs, catheters, monitors, all hooked up to Joey, as if he were a battery providing them with the power they needed to function. Linda gasped after realizing his body had inflated substantially since she last saw him just a few hours earlier. A nurse came out and informed Linda and Mike that Joey's body required several incisions in his sides just to provide it with some relief from the pressure that was destroying his internal organs.

Linda listened. Her face appeared calm but her mind was racing. The nurse made it clear that Joey's condition was grave, and the odds were not good that he was going to make it out of that room. Linda looked past the nurse, through the glass, and into the enormous medical theatre where Joey was the centre of attention. She saw his head, so swollen she could barely see his eyes, which he was no longer able to open. She tried to imagine the pain he was suffering. She tried to take it all on, hoping that if she tried hard enough, if she wanted it enough, she could take it from him and spare him the suffering she knew he was enduring, but it was no use. She was on one side of the glass and he was on the other. Mike held her and told her it was going to be okay. She wanted to believe him, but after yet another glance at Joey she couldn't resist questioning if survival was really best.

Mike stepped away to find a phone. The first person he called was his brother Pat, the next oldest of the four brothers of whom Mike was the oldest. After he told Pat where he was and why he was there, Pat laughed and told his older brother to stop bullshitting him. Mike insisted he was telling the truth but his brother still didn't believe him. After a few painstaking moments of having to convince his sibling that the worst possible thing that could have happened was happening, Pat told Mike he would be right there, along with his wife, Kathy. He also assured Mike that he would call the rest of the family: his mother, Rosemarie, and their other brothers, Terry and Kenny.

•

Ninety-five percent. That was the amount of Joey's body that suffered third- and fourth-degree burns.

First-degree burns sting even after being soaked with cold water
or dabbed with cream. They can sometimes blister, but heal rapidly.
They don't leave scars because they only affect the outer layer of
the skin: the epidermis. Second-degree burns go deeper, affecting
both the epidermis and the dermis, where the nerves reside. That is
why they are much more painful than first-degree. Like first-degree
burns, however, they rarely leave any permanent scarring.

Third- and fourth-degree burns completely annihilate the epidermis and dermis before wreaking havoc on the muscles and ten-
dons underneath. They can even reach the bones. The swelling and
blistering are extreme, and yield a truly horrific sight, as the area
affected — which in Joey's case was his entire body, save for his scalp
and two thin strips of skin on his chest, each measuring less than
ten centimetres in length — looks like fresh meat futilely trying to
restore itself to its original form. When asked about the extreme
swelling, the doctors told Linda and Mike to imagine a small burn
blister swelling with water, and to imagine that was happening with
Joey's entire body. The nerves are also completely severed as a result
of third- and fourth-degree burns. That was a short-term blessing for
Joey as the pain he suffered, while brutal, was dulled by the lack of
nerves to transmit it. However, it was also a long-term curse, as the
nerves would prove to be the fastest parts of Joey's body to regener-
ate, opening him up to an uncontrollable onslaught of suffering that
few people could ever fathom. In the history of Canada, nobody of
any age had ever survived the burns Joey had for as long as he did up
to that point, which had only been about seven hours.

After their grim assessment, the doctors began the process of
debriding. No academic explanation or soothing euphemism could

conceal the bleak truth behind such an innocent, almost unassuming word. "Debriding" is the removal of all dead skin from a severe burn. Imagine a burnt fingertip after touching a hot surface. It hurts. And after the pain's wailing starts to subside, a blister quickly forms. Afterward, when the small patch of dead skin comes loose, it is quickly removed, and a bandage is usually placed over the exposed area. Joey's entire body (save for his scalp and those two strips of skin on his chest) was that fingertip, and while most of his skin had melted into the snow on the ground behind his house, some of it still remained on his body. Because it was all dead it had to be removed, or else it would cause infection. So the doctors used metallic scrub brushes and scalpels, along with cleansing ointments, to methodically remove that skin.

The doctors gave Joey plenty of morphine during the debriding: more than they were initially comfortable giving. They were desperate to spare him from the pain they could only abstractly imagine, but they knew it wasn't enough. They knew no amount of painkiller could dull that level of pain, regardless of his severed nerves. It was too present, too determined. Unlike the fire that birthed it, the pain could not be extinguished by any human solution. Yet, despite overwhelming sympathy, the doctors did not rush their work. It had to be done right, and that took hours. How they were able to thoroughly scrape the surface of Joey's body is as unfathomable as the pain they knew he endured while it was happening. Were they psychotic? And if so, does the possibility of benevolent psychosis need to be extensively studied, if it hasn't been already? Because there is no question about it, those doctors were acting for the sole purpose of saving Joey's life, but any form of conscience or sympathy would have surely given them pause, and pause was not only detrimental but potentially fatal. There was no time for such emotions. Those could, and most likely did, come much later. Those doctors didn't just take the Hippocratic oath, they were pushing it to its limit.

After the debriding was mercifully over, the doctors told Linda and Mike the tale would be told over the next forty-eight hours. They doubted Joey would survive, and they made those doubts clear. They didn't want to stoke hopes that had yet to even become a flicker. Linda sobbed constantly, while Mike held her, telling her he loved her, telling her they were going to get through it.

For the next three days, Linda didn't sleep. She barely ate. She didn't bathe. She didn't even change her clothes. Joey's dried and crusted blood remained on her shirt. Members of her family, her parents, and her siblings, as well as members of Mike's family, all came to the hospital to visit, but she barely registered their presence. When they spoke she heard their words, but was incapable of listening to them. She loved her family but she came to understand that love was finite, and she chose to give all she had to Joey. There was no malice in her decision, she just believed deep in her heart that every bit of love she possessed had to be given to him.

Visitors often asked Linda to take a break but she always refused. Whenever the temptation crept into her mind, it was snuffed out by the possibility of Joey slipping away, dying during the few minutes she decided to spend on herself.

She was fiercely determined to be there for Joey, believing, deep down, that she should have been there when the fire happened, that she should have saved him, sparing him from a moment's suffering. And if anybody should have been lying in that bed, clinging to life, while death pulled with all its might, she was more than willing to convince God that it should have been her.

Joey was barely awake because of the abundance of medication the doctors were giving him. They told Linda that he was rarely lucid, and that was for the best. They told her they had often seen the minds of people in similar situations drift off just to spare them from the suffering. She wondered where her son's mind went. When he was awake, he still couldn't open his eyes because of the swelling, so when Linda was allowed to be in the same room as him, which was almost all of the time, as she insisted on being with him every second, rules be damned, she talked to him constantly, just so he knew she was there. She needed him to know that she would always be there. She tried to comfort him and while he couldn't speak, she still heard him, understanding him through the slight twitching of the corner of his lip. It was the only movement he could make.

Joey survived the first forty-eight hours. That in itself was a miracle. The doctors could not understand how he had made it that far. People typically died after suffering third- and fourth-degree burns on 30 to 40 percent of their body. They had constantly told Linda that her son was on the precipice of life and death, that he could slip away at any moment, but she saw the doubt on their faces and heard it in their voices. They were so sure he was going to die the day he arrived that, when he didn't, they didn't know what to believe, and there was no way she would allow them to convince her of what they themselves could no longer be sure of. Their confusion gave her hope.

When the swelling finally started subsiding, Joey's body had started to shrink to its original size, making the extent of the damage the fire had done much clearer and much more horrifying. His internal organs were ravaged, while his exterior looked necrotic. Throughout those first few days he was given constant blood transfusions and intravenous fluids, but any hope of Joey recovering had nothing to do with healing since there wasn't much left of him to heal. For Joey to survive he had to be completely rebuilt, piece by piece.

•

When you first enter the waiting room of the burn ward in the Hospital for Sick Children in 1988, it initially appears like any other hospital waiting room, though a bit larger. There are the customary chairs and couches and tables topped by magazines. It's only after sifting through the top layer of those magazines that you start to notice a difference. It's under the surface that you find more childish publications, from *Archie* comics to colouring books, almost all of which are filled with a resounding defiance against colouring within the lines.

Nearby there is a room with glass walls, filled with toys. But the room is empty. Where are the children? Meanwhile, the air inside the waiting room feels cold and sterile. There is a moisture in it, very subtle, but it's there, adding to the heaviness you feel weighing on you the longer you're inside.

That unease is swiftly subdued after you see the array of pictures on the walls of the waiting room, most of which are drawn in crayon. There are animals and creatures of all types and all colours. You see purple horses, orange bears, and red dinosaurs, and beside those fantastical creations you see pictures of big-headed stick children, almost all of whom have big eyes, no noses, and wide smiles stretching from one side of their faces to the other. The radiance of these drawings, created by the patients in the ward and compiled and presented by the incredible staff, momentarily make you forget where you are, but the silence reminds you. Like the inside of a discreet church on a major street that people pass without a single glance, the waiting room of the burn ward is ruthlessly quiet. Once inside, you don't want to make a sound, afraid you'll anger the silence.

A large desk rests to the side, occupied by a receptionist who understands the silence better than anybody else ever could. This incredible person had to learn over time how to function in such a unique place. The receptionist never speaks when the silence is in charge, nor do they have to wonder when that is. They just know. Just like they know when not to disturb the people sitting on the chairs and couches, their faces sunken into their moistened palms. Just like they know when to get up and offer a tissue, or direct those grieving, stricken people to the washroom, or the cafeteria, or the nearby vending machine. Just like they know that the one thing you never say is "Everything is going to be all right."

To say that to somebody in the burn ward is to slap them in the face. The receptionist, just like the most experienced nurses and doctors who work in that ward, knows that. However, such weightless expressions are often uttered by visitors unaware of those rules to those strapped to the chairs and couches by their own hurt and worry. Who could blame them? They don't know what else to say. There is an instinct to say something, anything, to comfort somebody in such obvious pain, but there is no comfort there. Whether it is in the waiting room or in one of the many rooms down the long hallway beyond, to be in the burn ward is to suffer in stagnancy. Like death row, relief only comes when you leave one way or another.

When you venture down that long hallway, passing the doors of the rooms where the young patients reside, things change. It's in these rooms that the atmosphere completely shifts whenever a family member enters. It's in these rooms that the emotion is so thick that when it is released, it explodes. It's in these rooms that the silence is not broken; it is ruptured.

Screams, the kind people think only exist in the most intense horror films, can be heard in these rooms at any time, without notice. These screams, these piercing, uncontrollable wails of a family member seeing their child, their brother, their sister, their niece, nephew, or grandchild finally succumb to the burns they suffered, once heard are never forgotten. Each one is unique but equal in the raw despair they convey. These screams are not verbal, but physical. They are not shouted but convulsed. They are not uttered but spewed. And they don't come from the mouth, or the throat, or the chest, but from a place much deeper, much darker: the pit of the soul, where the purest hurt dwells. A person unleashing such screams can never stand straight while doing it. They almost always collapse forward, the weight of their incomprehensible howls pulling them down.

The pendulum of emotion that exists in these rooms cannot remain on only one side, however. It must swing to the other, and when it does, those screams shift to laughter. The laughter comes from seeing somebody you love more than yourself opening their eyes for the first time in days, weeks, even months; when after seeing you their first reaction is to smile warmly and lovingly. You smile back, of course, but a smile isn't enough, and what follows isn't conscious, but a reflex. The body, the mind, the heart, and the soul are filled with so much joy that, like the screams lurking in the depths of those in despair, the emotion must be released, and explodes in a fit of uncontrollable laughter.

The levity that comes when death is unexpectedly denied is truly remarkable. While the first few jokes are almost always good-natured and lighthearted, they quickly make way for black humour — the blackest, most gallows humour you can fathom. It is those kinds of jokes, grimly draped in irony, that are told in these rooms, and it is those kinds of jokes that ultimately inspire the most chest-squeezing, boisterous laughter, the kind that is finally freed from the dungeon of suffering.

But the pendulum never stops swinging in this ward. That laughter will inevitably, at some point, in some room, by some person, shift back to screams, only to shift back again, and on it goes. Sometimes those screams and that laughter can be heard simultaneously in the ward, one in one room and the other in another room. Other times, however, neither can be heard, and the sombre silence once again reigns supreme.

Visiting hours are more theoretical than actual in the burn ward. You can tell a parent they have to leave their child's side at a certain time, but they won't comply. They will bring in and sit on a chair, making it clear a flag has been raised. They will shift their body in that chair, trying to find the best position, knowing that chair will be their world for as long as their child is in that bed. That is exactly what Linda did and the receptionist, the nurses, and the doctors in that ward didn't say a word because there was nothing to be said, and they all knew it.

The silence of the ward was painful for Linda and Mike. It was a dangerous gift, yearned for, but regretted once received. While the chaos that ensued from the moment they entered the hospital was draining, that same chaos was also an inexhaustible engine that kept both of them going. So when the chaos finally, albeit temporarily, subsided, the couple were left with nothing but their own thoughts, their own fears, worries, and speculations. It didn't take long for them to desperately hope for the chaos to return, to keep them moving, and to keep them from having to think about anything else but what was directly in front of them.

Joey was still unable to open his eyes but Linda refused to let him feel alone. She continued talking to him, telling him not to worry about his eyes — that they would open when they were ready and that until then she would be his eyes, and would tell him everything she saw. She refused to let him feel disconnected from the world she begged him to stay in. She pleaded with him to keep fighting. She told him that everybody thought he was going to die but he couldn't, that it wasn't an option to consider, that she wouldn't survive the pain of his loss, that she loved him too much, and if he died, so would she. While he couldn't see his mother or speak to her, he managed to twitch the corner of his swollen lip. It was enough for her to understand that he heard every word and when she asked him if he was going to fight, he responded with a single twitch, meaning "yes." She sobbed, thanked him, and told him he was going to make it out of that hospital.

•

Before Danny was brought to the hospital to see Joey for the first time since the fire, Linda took him to a nearby public library where she showed him pictures of severe burn victims. She wanted to prepare him for what he was going to see. She didn't hold back, showing him pictures that became progressively more graphic. He didn't respond with screams of terror or heaves of sickness or a reluctance to see more. And when he told her he was ready, they made their way to the hospital, but she remained worried, fearing Danny would panic at the sight of his big brother. She was scared he would cry, shout, and run out of the room, crushing what little was left of Joey's fragile spirit. She was scared that Danny, being the young, excitable boy that he was, might inadvertently hurt Joey by touching him where he shouldn't, which was basically anywhere on his body. But Joey was Danny's brother as much as he was her son, and she needed to reconnect them.

Before Danny entered the room where Joey lay, Linda knelt down and talked to her youngest son. He was nervous. His head was down. He was fidgeting. She told him that Joey was in very bad shape but he would make it out of there. Danny raised his head. He smiled. She smiled back, hugged him, and slowly walked him into the room, holding his hand.

As soon as Danny walked in and saw his brother, his mouth gaped open. Linda panicked. Nobody said a word. They all awaited Danny's reaction.

"That's my brother," he said. "That's Joey."

Joey's bed was high, too high for Danny to clearly see him. He turned to his mother. Linda lifted him up, holding him as tight as she could. Danny saw his brother's eyes swollen shut and the extensive damage the fire had done. His brother looked worse than the victims in the horror movies he liked to watch; he looked like

Freddy Krueger, the creator of those victims. He gasped. Linda lowered him. She immediately rushed over to Joey, telling him that it was okay, that Danny only made that sound because he was worried he was going to fall on him. It was a lie, but it needed to be told. She couldn't bear telling him that his younger brother was terrified of how he looked. She then told him that Danny was okay, and that he loved him very much and was happy to see him. Joey, unable to speak, unable to even move his head to the side, curled his lip to the absolute best of his ability, which was barely visible to anybody other than his mother, who saw it for what she truly believed it to be: an enormous smile.

Outside of the room, Linda knelt down again and asked Danny how he was doing. He smiled, though it was clearly forced, but the effort meant so much to her.

"Is he going to be okay, Mom?"

"Yes."

"Is he going to get out of here?"

"Yes."

"When, Mom?"

After Mike drove Danny back to Orillia, it was once again just Joey and Linda, and a team of doctors, led by Dr. Ronald Zuker, and a group of dedicated nurses hoping to rebuild him.

On March 13 and 14, Joey endured two operations, both of which involved putting donor skin grafts on his body. The chances for success were very low, as were the chances for Joey's survival, but the doctors informed Linda they wanted to try. They presented the painfully sleep-deprived woman with the necessary forms she had to sign for the surgeries to commence, and to free the doctors from any liabilities if Joey died during the procedures, which was the expected outcome. Left with little time to think, Linda signed the forms, and the operations were carried out. Joey's body rejected the donor's dead skin, but he survived.

Feeling hopeless, after the second surgery Linda asked the doctors what other alternatives there were.

Joey was still not able to open his eyes. During the brief segments of time when Joey was awake and lucid, and with only the use of the corner of his lip, they were still able to have detailed conversations during which she asked a series of yes or no questions in a constant, patient quest to discover exactly what he was thinking, or what he wanted, or didn't want. He begged his mother to help him see because he could no longer bear the blindness. Linda cried after seeing her son's pleas. She asked the doctors what could be done. They warned Linda that, like the rest of his body, Joey's eyes had been decimated by the heat of the fire and were incredibly sensitive, to the point that even the heat from the lights above could potentially lead to permanent blindness.

So much doubt and so much fear ceaselessly inhabited the minds of the doctors tending to Joey. There was no past experience, no precedent for them to lean on, no prior patients they could refer to, no medical journals to reference, nobody to call in other countries. Their dedication to not harming those under their care sometimes pushed them into moments of fearful paralysis. How can you heal somebody without causing them harm when anything you do to them will invariably cause them harm?

Linda, like the doctors, was in a constant state of worry that any action she made could cause permanent damage to her son. But he persisted. He wanted to see. So as gently as she could, with a doctor present, she rubbed away the thick layers of hardened crust around Joey's sealed eyes. She could see slight spasms on his face. She cringed and apologized profusely. While those spasms may have appeared subtle, even inconsequential, she knew they were akin to agony violently contorting his body. Despite the anguish she felt, Linda continued gently rubbing away the crust until she had cleared the surface of his closed eyes. She then told him to try to open them slowly, and the moment he felt any pain, to shut them immediately. She believed he could survive the surgeries to come, the long recovery, the strong possibility that his body would never be the same, but blindness? The inability to ever see the world around him again? She didn't think he could survive that. So when she saw his thin eyelids rise, she held her breath. At first, he was only able to open one eye, but then the other followed. She asked him if he could see. He twitched his lip twice, gesturing the terrifying response of "no." She gasped, then calmed when the doctor said it would take time for his eyes to focus. A few minutes later she asked him again, he twitched his lip once, meaning "yes." She asked him if he could see clearly. He twitched his lip twice.

"Can you see shapes?"

Twice.

"Can you see light?"

Twice.

"Can you see me?"

Twice.

"Can you see shadows?"

Once.

That was all he could see for the time being: dark silhouettes. But he could see, and that was progress — precious in every rare instance it occurred.

Dr. Zuker was an immensely qualified and equally compassionate plastic surgeon who cared tremendously for those he was tasked with saving. His ambition was to save the young victims of severe burns and to help them get back to who they were, or as close to it as humanly possible. However, in the case of Joey, he knew that he and his team, despite the best of intentions, simply didn't have the resources necessary to save his life, let alone restore him to the boy he was. That is what Dr. Clark, a young plastic surgeon and trusted member of Dr. Zuker's team, told Linda. He told her there was nothing more they could really do for Joey, and if he had any chance for survival and possible recovery, he had to be transferred to the Shriners Burns Institute in Boston, Massachusetts, immediately. If there was any hope for Joey, it was there, at one of the most famous and well-funded burn institutes in the entire world.

Dr. Clark explained to Linda that the medical team at the Shriners Burns Institute had the capability to graft enough skin cultures from the precious little bit of skin Joey had left to cover his entire body. He continued to explain that it took weeks for a skin culture to grow, and because Joey needed new skin on over 95 percent of his body, the process of growing the necessary skin and then applying it would take many months. He also explained that the process would be very hard on Joey, as would the post-surgical care he was going to require, but it was the only path to survival. He needed skin to live, and the Shriners Burns Institute was the only place where he could get it.

Linda had already been told that the ambulance ride from Orillia to Toronto had nearly killed Joey, so she believed there was no chance he would survive a trip all the way to Boston. She also thought about Mike and Danny, who were either on the way back to Orillia or already there. She knew that just coming to the Hospital for Sick Children in Toronto from Orillia, day after day, was going to be an enormous chore for Mike. It was a nearly two-hour drive, depending on traffic. When the question of how he would be able to pay for gas crept into her mind, she panicked. More pressing questions started bombarding her: What were they going to do about their house? Would the insurance company somehow work with them? Where were they going to live? What about all of their stuff? She took a deep breath and closed her eyes, begging the questions to be patient. Pleading with them that she just couldn't deal with them right now.

"Mrs. Hawkins," Dr. Clark said, "if Joey doesn't go to Shriners, he'll die."

Linda gazed into the doctor's eyes. She believed him, and it broke her heart.

"I'm not saying it's a guarantee he will survive if he gets the treatment there," Dr. Clark said, "but what they can do for him is the only chance he has. Shriners has already agreed to the transfer. I need you to sign these papers so we can send him there by air ambulance in the morning."

Linda wanted to talk to somebody she trusted, somebody she loved. She wanted to talk to Mike, but he wasn't there. Nobody was there. She was alone, staring at a doctor pushing her to authorize a transfer she feared would kill her son, and if it didn't, she feared the months of pain and suffering he would have to endure. But if she didn't authorize the transfer, her son would die.

She signed the papers, then went to Joey's room, where she told him what was going to happen. He didn't want to go. Through their usual means of communication he made it clear he wanted to go home. Linda wanted nothing more than that to happen, but she knew it wasn't an option. She didn't bother with the thought that there wasn't a home to go back to, because even if there was, Joey wouldn't have been able to return to it.

Afterward, not thinking about the months of suffering to come, Linda focused on the transfer itself. She was still afraid Joey wouldn't survive the trip to Boston, so she told the doctors that she wanted to join him in the air ambulance. When they voiced their reluctance, she aggressively insisted. When they told her it was against policy, she said she didn't care. When they said no, she said yes. It didn't take them very long to realize that where Joey went, his mother went, so they relented and granted her permission to be by his side during the trip from Toronto to Boston.

While Linda waited for the permission she was hell-bent on receiving to join Joey on his trip to the Shriners Burns Institute, she managed to get a message to Mike, who got right back into his car moments after arriving at Lynda Young's house with Danny and made the long drive back to the Hospital for Sick Children. Mike arrived shortly after the permission for Linda to join Joey in the air ambulance was granted, and they spent what proved to be one of the longest nights of their lives together, in the burn ward waiting room.

Early the next morning, the doctors and nurses prepared Joey for the transfer. They went through a long list of procedures thoroughly, doing all they could to ensure the trip went as smoothly as possible. Meanwhile Linda, who hadn't slept the night before, and had barely slept in days, and wondered if she would ever sleep again, said her goodbyes to visiting family members. She then tightly hugged Mike, who told her that Danny was okay and was staying with Lynda Young, and that as soon as she left he would start the nearly nine-hour drive to Boston and meet her there right in time for dinner. She smiled, telling him that without him she would have never made it to that point, and he replied with a smile of his own before telling her there was no way Joey would have made it to that point without her.

As soon as Linda got into the air ambulance, she looked at Joey. He appeared securely positioned in the bed while the bed itself appeared securely positioned in the helicopter, but she was still nervous, weary of the toll the trip was going to take on him. Once the air ambulance door closed, Linda was immediately uncomfortable. The area inside the helicopter was cramped, even more so with her in it. She could barely move and there was constant jostling between her and the nurse and doctor as they checked, double-checked, and triple-checked the tubes and wires attached to Joey, all of which were crucial to his survival. Linda knelt as close to Joey as she could, talking to him louder and louder, as the noise inside of the helicopter increased as soon as the engines were turned on. She told him all about the helicopter itself, every detail she spotted, every detail she knew he would find interesting.

Joey had always loved flying, and not just the flying itself, but also the vehicles that made it possible, and the people controlling them. That is why he had joined the air cadets before the fire. He dreamt of being a pilot, of controlling those magical machines that ventured high up into the clouds, covering enormous distances in mere hours at speeds that broke barriers people less than a half century before never thought possible. The helicopter ride about to take him to the only place in the world that could possibly save his life was going to be his first-ever flight.

Within the first few minutes of the trip, Joey took a turn for the worse. He was already weak prior to the departure, but after five minutes his blood pressure started dropping, as did the rest of his vital signs. Green discharge and blood started seeping through the bandages covering his entire body. He started shivering. He had a fever and it was getting worse, as was the pain constantly gripping him.

Linda started panicking. She shouted at the nurse, telling her to help her son. The nurse said she was doing her best. Linda told her it wasn't good enough. The nurse told Linda to strap herself in her seat, be quiet, and let her and the doctor do their job. She said that Linda was interfering with their routine, which they had to strictly follow in order to help Joey. Linda seethed. She saw her son suffering and she didn't see enough being done to make him better. She shouted again, telling the nurse that Joey was getting worse by the second. The nurse told Linda to shut up. The doctor, seeing what Linda had seen, asked the nurse for more morphine, but she told him they had only brought twenty cc's and they had already used it all. They had only been in the air for ten minutes.

Linda was furious. How could they have run out of morphine after just a few minutes? How could they be so unprepared? How could they be so negligent toward her son after convincing her to sign off on the transfer? She was blinded by rage, to the point where she wanted to throw the nurse out of the helicopter just to lessen the load to make it go faster. She unbuckled her seat belt, completely ignoring the nurse's orders, and rushed to Joey's side. The nurse grabbed Linda's arm. Linda looked up but didn't say anything. She didn't have to. The nurse let go. She knew Linda was not going to be moved.

Linda started speaking to Joey, softly whispering to him, telling him they were in the air, that he was finally flying, and to relax as best he could, that she knew how much everything hurt but they were almost there. The nurse, while no longer physically grabbing Linda, continued telling her to get back in her seat. Linda ignored her and continued talking to her son, trying to comfort him, and just as the nurse was about to grab Linda's arm again, worried that something could happen, that her actions were making the situation unsafe, the doctor told her to leave Linda alone, that it was okay. Throughout the increasingly heated exchange between Linda and the nurse, the doctor had been staring at the monitors and Joey himself and noticed that from the moment Linda started talking to him, his condition had improved. He was stabilizing. His mother's words, his mother's love, were doing what nothing else inside of the helicopter could.

SHRINERS

AS SOON AS THE AIR AMBULANCE ARRIVED AT THE SHRINERS BURNS INSTITUTE in Boston, the doctors anticipating Joey's arrival took one look at him and said he had to go into surgery immediately. Linda was frantic. Her son had barely survived the trip, and now they wanted to operate on him. She couldn't believe it. She asked the team of doctors if it wouldn't be better if Joey was given time to rest. They told her if they didn't operate on him right away, he wouldn't make it to the morning.

While hearing such blunt declarations about her son's grave condition wasn't comforting, she preferred the determined, confident manner with which the doctors at the Shriners Burns Institute spoke to the trepidation she heard in the voices of the doctors at the Hospital for Sick Children. A series of forms were thrust toward her, forms she was told to sign right away or else they couldn't save her son. Disoriented, well past exhaustion, Linda could barely make out the words on the pages, let alone read them thoroughly enough to understand what she was signing. But she signed them all, believing she, and Joey, didn't have a choice.

After Linda signed the forms, the doctors took Joey into a vast, sterile, brightly lit operating room. His fever remained and he was shaking intensely. His blood pressure and vital signs were steadily plummeting. They immediately got to work by removing the bandages from his body, which were covered in gooey green discharge and blood. They got scalpels, metallic brushes, and an instrument that could only be described as a medically licensed cheese grater and started scraping away all of the remaining charred tissue and eschar (dead tissue). They went deeper and deeper, layer after layer. They were determined to make sure no dead tissue remained, as even the smallest amount would quickly fester and become infected, something Joey's body, which was already shutting down, would not be able to fend off. The odour of the room was fetid, reeking of decay. Throughout the procedure, which lasted ten hours, Joey was hooked up to a series of tubes that pumped him full of new blood, as he was losing a great deal. Meanwhile, Joey was given an abundance of morphine, trapping him in a frightening state between consciousness and unconsciousness.

Throughout those hours, Linda sat in a chair as close to the operating room as she could, waiting for updates that never came, fearing Joey wasn't going to make it, envisioning the doctors putting a sheet over her son's dead body. Her brain was so battered that just raising her head when a doctor finally came out to talk to her was a mammoth endeavour requiring every bit of strength she had left. Luckily, Mike had arrived at the hospital by that point and was right by his wife's side.

Joey survived the procedure. Linda was relieved but too weak to show it. She was too exhausted, too drained, to even comprehend it. Just like her son's, her mind was trapped in limbo. It was hard to focus, hard to hold on to a single thought for more than a second. Talking was becoming a challenge. Nonetheless, she managed to focus long enough to hear the doctor tell her they were going to have to amputate Joey's feet.

Linda and Mike gasped. While Joey's survival remained Linda's primary concern, she also clung to the hope that he would somehow be able to live a life close to the one he'd had before the fire. She hoped for a life where he could see, hear, talk, and touch without difficulty, a life where he could also walk. She pleaded with the doctor, begging him to save her son's feet, that there had to be another way. The doctor listened and compassionately told her they were going to do their best but could make no promises, as Joey's feet were, in his opinion, beyond saving. They had been burned right to the bone. She was then given more forms to sign for the surgeries to come. The purpose of the forms was to empower the doctors to perform emergency procedures in the event that complications arose, which they said would almost certainly occur. If they had to wait for her to sign the forms at the moment those complications happened, those wasted seconds could seal Joey's fate. Linda signed all of the forms put in front of her, then asked the doctor when Joey would no longer be in a position where every surgery could kill him.

"Until his entire body is covered with his own skin. Four months, at least."

It was March 17, seven days after the fire.

•

Established in 1870, the Shriners, formally known as the Ancient Arabic Order of the Nobles of the Mystic Shrine (AAONMS), is a Masonic society with over three hundred thousand members in over 190 temples all over the world. Past members include Franklin D. Roosevelt, Ronald Reagan, John Wayne, Duke Ellington, Harry S. Truman, J. Edgar Hoover, Nat King Cole, and Johnny Cash. They are recognizable from the red fezzes they wear on their heads,

41

but far beyond their choice of hats, what they are most recognized for are the children's hospitals they've established throughout North America, including the Shriners Burns Institute right across the street from the Massachusetts General Hospital in downtown Boston. Acceptance of patients is based on simple criteria: they must be under eighteen years of age (though some exceptions have been made and the age pushed to twenty-one), and the doctors at a Shriners hospital must believe they can be treated. That's it. There are no religious, racial, or economic criteria that need to be met. It doesn't matter if somebody knows every single Shriner in the building or none at all. Furthermore, all of the costs are covered by the Shriners. So, when Joey arrived at the hospital, while Linda was bombarded with more worries than she could handle, the cost of her son's care was not one of them. With an endowment exceeding eight billion dollars, Shriners International has aided thousands of children from around the world who otherwise would have had no chance at survival. While several of the past and present members of the Shriners have divisive reputations, to say the least, the accomplishments of the organization of which they are a part have been and continue to be undeniable.

MARCH 18–20

Three consecutive eight-hour surgeries involved removing all of Joey's remaining skin, right down to the muscles. The doctors also secured a healthy piece of skin, no larger than a loonie, from the thin strips on his chest, which was then placed in an incubator where it was used to cultivate grafts that would become Joey's new skin. The third surgery proved the riskiest, as his body was rawer than it had ever been and was therefore more susceptible to infection.

Prior to each surgery, Joey had to endure the debriding process. After enduring the scraping and brushing on his raw, skinless body, he was then transferred to a large, sterile room with a massive, specially designed tub in the centre. Above the tub was a platform. The tub was filled with diluted bleach and antiseptic water. Joey was transferred from his mobile bed to the platform, his body throbbing from the debriding. The platform was then raised high above the tub before it was slowly lowered inside, submerging his naked body, allowing the bleach and antiseptic water to destroy any possibility for infection.

"To pour salt in the wound." That notion of what it means to add more pain to an already suffering person is not a frightening exaggeration, but a paltry understatement of the reality Joey endured. No salt was poured into his wounds; instead, he was the wound poured into the salt. And despite the powerful anaesthetic he was usually given, which sometimes spared him from the suffering of the debriding process and the dreaded bath, most times the pain proved too powerful. On those occasions he was conscious and able to feel everything, from the scrubbing and scraping to the rising of the platform, to the knowledge of what was coming, to the fear growing more intense as the platform started to lower, to his entrance into the dreaded bath. It was a baptism unlike any other.

A nightmare is but a dream, a fiction of one's own creation, but for Joey it was all too real. He was still unable to talk but was able to scream. Beyond haunting, his screams were the unforgettable wails of a dying person, yet he lived just to scream again. They travelled throughout the entire building, felt by everybody inside.

As soon as the shock of touching that water ran through his body and reached his conscious mind, resulting in those horrendous screams, Joey left. He rose up high enough to look down and see himself submerged in the purifying water. He saw his own body, twitching with spasms as if it were being electrocuted. He pitied that body. He wanted it to stop suffering. He wanted it to die, but it refused. He saw his mother, weeping, reaching out to him, but unable to touch him. He saw her desperately wanting to either pull the body out of that water, or at the very least join it in its suffering.

He saw Mike, standing by, still and stoic, holding his grieving wife, doing all he could to comfort her. His eyes were swollen with pity. Tears welled up but didn't fall. He held them close and tight, in complete awe of what he was witnessing, of the sheer strength that young body was able to muster.

Joey continued to rise toward a light, radiant and pure. It warmed him and comforted him, providing him with a refuge from what the body below was suffering. He didn't want to return. He wanted to stay with the light, to disappear in its lustre, to just fade away, but he looked back down and saw his mother below. He saw her love and he knew he had to return, and he did, as soon as the body, laid flat on the slab, the platform from which it could not escape, was raised up from the tub. Countless razor-sharp droplets slipped from his nude, babyish body, falling back into the torturous pool from which they came. Joey's eyes opened, but he could not turn his head. All he could see were the lights above.

The pain and the copious amounts of medication constantly pumped into his body combined to create hallucinations so powerful that Joey had no idea where he was, or what was going on most of the time. The brief moments of lucidity he experienced were confusing, disorienting, and terrifying. Reality had become the nightmare. It was only the sight of his mother by his side and the sound of her voice whispering to him, comforting him, reassuring him that he would survive, that let him know all was not lost.

MARCH 23

It was Linda's birthday. Joey still couldn't speak, though it was clear he desperately wanted to, but his lungs, like the rest of his internal organs, were severely damaged. To help him breathe, an intubation tube had been inserted into his throat, which made speaking impossible. Nonetheless, she told him it was the best birthday she ever had because she got to spend it with him.

MARCH 28

Linda and Joey started talking about the fire. It was a long conversation, and despite the immense amount of medication Joey was under the influence of, he was nonetheless cognizant enough to recap — with his mother's help and patience — the events of March 10. She softly asked him a series of questions about that morning and, in response, he twitched his lip once for "yes" and twice for "no." Over the course of a few hours, the events of that morning were reconstructed. It was then that Joey stated that he woke up to the flames, proceeded to get Danny out of the house, and went back inside looking for her. He then stated that he got trapped during his search and the fire captured him. It is incredible that Joey, despite the pain and medicinal haze, was mentally strong enough to lie. He must have known there was no way his mother wouldn't have forgiven him for starting the fire. But he was still a young teenager, and he didn't want to tell her the truth if that truth led to her disappointment in him.

Linda had no reason to disbelieve her son. And while the doctors warned her that after eighteen days of heavy medication Joey's mind was affected, she refused to believe he was being anything but honest with her. Meanwhile, just as Joey's mind was affected by the medication and sheer, blinding pain, Linda's mind was affected by her lack of sleep and food, and the constant worrying. But the story she received was the story she believed, and ultimately became the story she relayed to those interested in hearing it.

MARCH 29

Operation to amputate all of Joey's toes. Started at 2:30 p.m. and finished at 7:00 p.m.

The doctors, heeding Linda's pleas throughout that week, compromised by believing they could, at least for the time being, save Joey's feet, something Linda was immensely relieved to hear. But they made it clear that his toes were too far gone, that there was nothing they could do to save them. The same ten toes a doctor joyously confirmed were all there when Joey was born, a team of doctors fourteen years later sombrely confirmed were gone. She wept at the news but understood it, and found solace in knowing that her son had survived yet another operation.

APRIL 1

Cleaning of Joey's legs. Started at 8:30 a.m. and finished at 1:30 p.m.

After the cleaning, which Joey was luckily not awake for as the anaesthetic proved especially effective that morning, Linda sat beside him, staring at his heavily bandaged feet. She knew his toes were no longer there but Joey didn't. She couldn't stop staring at the truth but believed if she told him that truth, it could tip the scales against his already fragile will to keep fighting, so she didn't. The only way she was able to bear her decision was resolving that if he asked about his toes, she would not lie to him; then, and only then, would she tell him the truth.

Following Joey's debriding and subsequent surgeries, a dressing called "Biobrane" was put on him. Made from a knitted, nylon mesh that is bonded to a thin, silicone membrane, Biobrane is placed on burned areas of a body as a barrier against possible bacterial invasion and water vapour transmission.

APRIL 3

The Biobrane placed over Joey's body was removed because the doctors were preparing to put on new skin in an extremely risky surgery set to take place a few days later. It was like having his skin removed all over again, except where the fire had melted it off quickly, the doctors removed the Biobrane slowly and methodically, knowing that any errors could potentially lead to fatal complications. Staring up at the bright lights above, Joey was conscious throughout the entire process. He felt everything.

Joey was always tired, even though he was rarely awake. While he often passed out, he rarely, if ever, got REM sleep. As a result, he was severely sleep-deprived, but because he couldn't speak, and it was something nobody even thought to consider, he suffered in silence. The surreal mixture of intense pain, powerful drugs, and sleep deprivation fertilized even more hallucinations that became so intense and visceral that when Joey succumbed to them, which was quite often, he was in a state that few human beings could ever reach, no matter how many drugs they took or the desperate lengths they went to. His out-of-body experiences were no longer happening only during the disinfecting baths. They also started happening when he was in bed and the pain made sleep impossible. So, he floated above himself, seeing his body and the doctors and nurses tending to it or consulting with each other, seeing his mother weeping over it and his stepfather comforting her as she wept. He ventured down the hallways and even into other rooms, areas of the institute he had never seen, yet he would be there, a projection of himself that nobody else could see. He saw other children suffering as he was. He heard their cries, their screams. He saw their scars. He saw them awake, staring up, just as he was, and believed, on some occasions, that they saw him too. When he returned to himself, he yearned for sleep. He daydreamed about actual dreams. He wondered what he would see. He became afraid, horrified at the thought of returning to the fire, feeling the heat of its flames and the suffocation from its smoke. He questioned if dreaming was denied to him by his mind for its own good because the nightmares sure to come would be too much for him. But he still yearned for sleep.

Luckily, his mother was always there, leaning over him. She was always covered from head to toe in medical garments. The risks her body presented, the same body that cultivated him for nine months before giving birth to him, were so high that even the slightest cough or gentlest touch could kill him.

Linda and Joey had a song during those days: "Where Do Broken Hearts Go" by Whitney Houston, released a month before the fire. She often played it for him at a volume he could tolerate. While sleep was too far away to attain, he was at least able to cling to those four and a half minutes.

"Would you like me to play it again?"

Joey twitched his lip once, and four and a half minutes became nine, then thirteen and a half, then eighteen, until the pain became too powerful, snuffing out Whitney's voice, and he floated away again.

APRIL 5–8

Eight-hour operation to put freshly cultured skin grafts on Joey's thighs, right arm, and the sides of his torso. The operation was extremely risky. Linda was informed of the 0 to 10 percent possibility of success when she signed the forms before the surgery. She was told it was experimental, that they had never grown so much skin from so little and had never replaced such large areas of a body. They said death was highly probable but that they would learn a great deal from the procedure, which would allow them to help countless children in the future.

Joey lost a lot of blood during the operation and required several transfusions, but he survived.

•

The Halcyon House was a large brownstone in Boston. It was a gorgeous building that acted as temporary housing for the families of patients at the Shriners Burns Institute and Massachusetts General Hospital. The walk toward the house along Boston's Commonwealth Avenue was stunning, particularly during spring and autumn when the trees lining the lovely street colourfully flanked the collection of towering brownstones. The walk was also very peaceful. However, the closer you got to the Halcyon House, the more that peace was shattered by the piercing sound of sirens, all day and all night, blaring from the nearby hospitals.

The house was enormous, with ten-foot ceilings and many rooms. Families from a variety of countries including Colombia, Brazil, Peru, Puerto Rico, England, several Eastern European countries, and so many more called it home. Many of those families stayed in the house for days, some for weeks, some for months. It all depended on the outcomes of their children's treatments for everything from meningitis and cancer to severe burns and calamitous injuries from war.

As grand as any upscale hotel, the house was spotlessly maintained by a diligent staff, all paid by the Shriners. During the day the house was sombre and silent, as if the walls were padded with muted compassion. While there weren't any specific rules or guidelines for guests written anywhere, the house was nonetheless very strict in its unspoken policies. When people talked, their words were almost always uttered in a soft whisper. Nobody raised their voices. There were never fights, or arguments, or squabbles. It was a hallowed building where everybody knew why everybody else was there. And while they might not have known the specifics, it didn't matter because everybody inside respected the suffering everybody else felt because they were feeling it too. The result was an environment of tremendous friendliness that was as subtle as it was poignant. Nobody acted as if they were better than anybody else, regardless of where they may have stood economically, or for any other reasons. Everybody in the house was enduring the worst life had to offer, and there was a powerful solidarity in that.

When night came, that's when the crying started. Too loud, too uncontrolled to be contained in an assigned room, it echoed throughout the hallways, but nobody dared to silence it or speak ill of it. Everybody knew there was a good chance that, at some point during their stay, they too would unleash the same primal wails after receiving bad news. When that happened, because of the limited space, families were given that night to grieve before they had to leave, making room for others facing the same results: they would either be leaving the house with tears of joy as they returned to their homes with their child healed and alive or leaving with completely different tears as they returned to their homes with the memory of a dearly departed child.

In the mornings, the families gathered in the most spectacular room in the house: the kitchen. There was a giant book right there at the entrance, and page after page was filled with thank-you notes written in every language imaginable by past guests. Once you walked in, you saw a well-equipped kitchen.

The rules of the kitchen were simple. Guests could use whatever dishes or appliances they wanted but had to provide their own food, which they also had to mark to prevent any confusion. There was one exception however, one item of food guests at the Halcyon House never had to purchase for themselves and never had to worry about running out of: ice cream. The cavernous freezers were always filled with every flavour you could want, donated by a nearby restaurant. It was during the days in the kitchen, especially at dinnertime, that joy and laughter could be seen and heard, especially from the young siblings of the children receiving the best care possible in the nearby hospitals. Those kids, overwhelmed by the reality of having all of the ice cream they could ever want, something they thought only existed in their dreams, were often a source of pure life to the grieving adults. Those kids' jokes, stories, smiles, and hugs brought warmth to a building where the bitter cold was always just around the corner. No matter how broken somebody felt, it was virtually impossible to not crack a smile when a child, who had just eaten four bowls of chocolate ice cream smothered in every topping they could muster, said with the utmost sincerity, "You can't die from eating too much ice cream, right?"

A room that was just as popular as the kitchen was the chapel. Rarely did a day, but especially an evening, go by when somebody was not in the quiet, dimly lit, serene room, almost always kneeling down, hands clenched, head bowed, quietly praying.

During this period, Linda spent a lot of her time turning to religion, mainly with the help of Father Michael Medus. He was a priest from Boston who, not long after Joey's arrival at the Shriners Burns Institute, heard about him and about Linda and Mike and visited them often. While quite young, not even thirty, he nonetheless embodied a calm wisdom that far exceeded his years and provided them with something they truly needed: an ear that listened without judgment.

In addition to Father Medus, there were other memorable people who showed tremendous kindness and compassion to Mike, Linda, and Joey, perhaps none more than the receptionist of Joey's ward, Anne Driskol. She was an older woman who stopped at nothing to make Linda and Mike feel not just comfortable, but welcome. No matter how angry, stressed, sad, or tormented they felt, Anne was always there to console them, and whenever they needed something, from an extra blanket to directions around Boston, she always accommodated them.

Meanwhile, Joey's anesthesiologist at the Shriners Burns Institute always reminded Mike of the character Hawkeye from the television show *M*A*S*H*. Beyond looking just like the character Alan Alda made famous, the exceptionally capable anesthesiologist also shared the character's biting sense of humour and would often lighten up the most devastating of moods with a well-placed sarcastic joke.

There was also an old man named Tommy, who Mike and Linda met at a bar where everybody from the Shriners Burns Institute went to escape, grab a drink, and, if lucky, catch a laugh or two. Tommy ran an antique shop on Charles Street. It was a beautiful cellar in an old brownstone that carried an abundance of treasures, from eighteenth-century ship steering wheels to fifteenth-century Spanish conquistador armour. He also helped Mike get weed whenever he needed it, something Mike appreciated very, very much.

Tommy wasn't the only person who helped Mike procure his most trusted means of relaxing and coping. There was also a kindly janitor at the Shriners Burns Institute named Mac who got weed for Mike and liked to enjoy a joint or two with him in the basement of the institute. One day, Mike was looking for Mac in the halls of the first floor of the institute to get more weed. After a few minutes he thought he had found him and gestured for him to come over. When the man did, Mike playfully whispered, "Hey, hey, do you have any more of that stuff?"

"What stuff?"

Mike laughed and replied, "Come downstairs with me, to the basement."

Mike, the janitor, and Linda went to the basement of the institute. When they got there, Mike said, "Hey, so do you got more of that good weed?"

"What? What the hell are you talking about, man?"

Mike looked at Linda, who started laughing before she said, "Mike, that's not Mac."

"Really?" Mike said, "But he looks just like him!"

Mike and Linda started laughing, while the janitor gazed at both of them with utter confusion and a hint of annoyance.

"Oh shit, I'm so sorry about that," Mike said. "No hard feelings?"

The janitor shook his head and went back upstairs. Meanwhile, Mike and Linda, alone in the basement, weedless, continued laughing. Mike asked if she wanted to see a movie at the theatre in the mall behind the institute. An hour later, after enjoying a Philly cheesesteak at their favourite restaurant in the same mall, they watched *Beetlejuice*, which had just premiered days earlier.

When they came back, Mike and Linda passed through the institute's long walkway that led to the medical buildings and sat on one of the benches near the garden. They talked for a while, cherishing the night together for as long as they could. Before they left, to commemorate the evening, Mike approached a wall and with a key, he chiselled his and Linda's names. Together, they looked at the names carved in the cement and wondered how long they would last before eroding.

APRIL 7

Operation from 9:00 a.m. to 2:30 p.m. The doctors cleaned Joey and took muscle from his left leg. They initially planned on putting metal pins in his fingers because they were starting to deform. The doctors feared if they didn't straighten them, the fingers would have to be amputated, but decided to postpone that procedure.

Linda had horrifying nightmares the night before. She woke up very early, with darkness still blanketing the sky, fearing her eldest son

wouldn't survive that day's surgery, but he did, and while she was relieved, she was too stricken, too exhausted to feel it, let alone express it.

Linda became angrier and angrier over the next few days. She
started noticing that several nurses were not treating Joey as carefully as she wanted them to, and felt no compunction about openly,
loudly, and aggressively challenging them whenever she felt it was
necessary. One nurse, Cathy, was particularly rough with Joey in
Linda's opinion, a view that was seconded by Joey himself. Linda
reported what she deemed to be inexcusable behaviour on Cathy's
behalf to the head nurse, who in turn reprimanded Cathy. After
Linda told Joey that Cathy got into trouble, Joey made it as clear
as he could that he felt bad about that. Linda told him his only job
was making himself better, and her only job was ensuring that he
was treated properly, and he should not waste his energy worrying
about Cathy, or any other nurse for that matter.

APRIL 11

Emergency operation required to fight off infection that started
spreading in Joey's left leg. At the conclusion of the operation,
which was successful, doctors informed Linda they might have to
amputate both of Joey's legs below the knee.

APRIL 12

Extensive operation to put fifty postage stamp–sized squares of
freshly cultured skin on Joey's back. The doctors were cautiously
optimistic, but unsure if the new skin would be accepted by Joey's
body. To maximize potential success, they informed Linda they
were going to paralyze Joey for several days prior to the surgery as a
means of calming his body down. It was failing in a variety of ways,
from his internal organs to its increasing susceptibility to infection.

She asked what exactly paralyzing her eldest son entailed. They told her he would be able to feel and hear everything but would not be able to move in any way, including his lips, making him unable to communicate at all. At first Linda begged for the doctors to come up with another option, but they said it was absolutely necessary. She reluctantly agreed to it.

APRIL 14

Extensive cleaning operation, followed by a thorough check of Joey's legs for infection. Following the procedure, the doctors told Linda they had done all they could but they didn't believe Joey was going to live through the weekend. They told her his lungs were in terrible shape and his other vital organs were all showing signs of steep decline. Linda, with tears in her eyes, gazed at her son, who was unable to even consciously twitch. She wondered if him passing away would be for the best, but she couldn't hold on to the thought, not out of denial or fear, but pure inability. She simply could not imagine her life without him.

APRIL 19

Cleaning operation. The doctors were at a loss. They didn't understand what was keeping Joey alive. They made it clear to Linda and Mike they had never, in all of their combined years of experience at the Shriners Burns Institute and other hospitals, seen anything like it. When asked how much longer they thought Joey would continue surviving they were unable to offer an answer, because they were convinced there was no way he should have lived as long as he already had.

As a result of the constant blood transfusions that Joey required from the barrage of surgeries, the institute ran out of Joey's blood type, O-negative, so they had no choice but to give him O-positive blood following his surgery on April 14. Linda and Mike had to call a local radio station asking them to ask the public for more O-negative blood. It was the first act of public outreach made on Joey's behalf.

APRIL 20

Lengthy and delicate operation that took skin from the top of Joey's head and put it on both of his arms, except for his hands and shoulders. Following the operation, the doctors decided to start weaning Joey off the abundance of different painkilling drugs he was on because his blood pressure was steadily rising.

APRIL 22

Three-hour operation to clean and check Joey's legs. His body was starting to swell again.

The next day, finally able to move, Joey started gesturing to the best of his extremely limited ability, but nobody could figure out the reason for his movements. Linda soon understood that Joey was complaining about the lights above, which he had been forced to stare at during his paralyzed state because he was unable to move his head, and it was driving him mad. As soon as Linda told the nurses and doctors what was wrong, they gave Joey a pair of sunglasses that had to be stretched in order to fit his still severely swollen head.

After seeing her son crack what looked to be the faintest of smiles, a wave of joy overcame Linda. In that sliver of a smirk, she saw hope. After leaving the room, she approached Cathy the nurse and apologized for her outburst several days before. She told her she knew she was doing all she could, and she noticed how much better she had been treating Joey over the last few days. Cathy started to cry, while thanking Linda for her words. Linda hugged her before telling her that Joey trusted her.

APRIL 25
Operation to put grown skin on the backs of Joey's legs from the knees up, and some on his lower back.

APRIL 28
Four-hour cleaning operation.

MAY 2
Another cleaning operation.

MAY 5
Joey asked Linda for a mirror so he could see his face. Since arriving at the Shriners Burns Institute, he had not received a clear reflection of himself, only the blinding, blurred version he saw thrown back at him from the light fixtures above, as well as the feverishly distorted versions he saw when he left his body and gazed back down at it. Linda hesitated and asked him several times if he was sure. He affirmed his request every time. She worried the sight of his face would shock him, or terrify him, or, even worse, affect his will to live. Nonetheless, she provided him with a mirror and positioned it so he could see his entire face. She held her breath, anxious and frightened, anticipating his response to his own reflection. A few seconds passed and Linda's anxiety decreased exponentially when he showed no signs of panic or fear. When they communicated,

Joey expressed that he thought it was going to be much worse, but in the reflection, while he saw the massive damage caused by the flames, he still saw himself. Linda was relieved. He then asked about the Biobrane on the top of his head. Linda explained that was where they were getting the original skin needed to grow the grafts they were slowly putting on his body.

Joey gestured for his mother to lower the mirror so he could see the rest of his body. She really started to panic at that point, knowing that while the state of his face was bad, the state of his body was much worse. She stepped back and dimmed the lights before returning and placing the mirror in front of him and slowly moving it down so he could see his entire body. He told his mother he didn't like the way he looked, that he looked like a monster. He then asked about the lights and why they were so low. Linda told him it was so he wouldn't see every scar and that it was best to get used to his body slowly.

Later that day Joey was moved to a new room because the doctors believed the room he was currently occupying, room number 1, which was assigned to the patient in the worst condition in the ward, was too risky in terms of possible infection. However, the new room was unsafe, as nobody could hear the alarm go off whenever Joey started choking, which happened often. He was returned to his old room with a plastic tent set up around him to help prevent infection. Linda hated the tent and made that hatred quite clear, as it prevented her from touching her son or even seeing him clearly.

MAY 10

Drastic operation in which the doctors decided to put pig skin on the areas of Joey's body that still had no skin on them, while new skin continued to grow in the incubators. They had taken skin from Joey's head seven times, and believed that was the absolute maximum they could do without causing damage. Like a mine stripped of its silver, there was nothing more to take. The doctors made it clear they had to get new skin on Joey's body as quickly as possible, and that involved getting creative. Linda found the procedure grotesque.

MAY 11

Five-hour operation that continued the process from the day before of putting pig skin on Joey's body.

MAY 13

Operation that started at 8:00 a.m. and ended at 2:00 p.m. to continue putting pig skin on Joey's body.

The following day, Joey complained about pain in his left knee. The doctors discovered the knee was badly dislocated but there was nothing they could do about it, though they worried if the joint got infected, they might have to amputate it.

It was yet another amputation scare that Linda was getting more and more accustomed to. She remained every bit as devastated as when she heard about the possibility of amputation several weeks earlier, but it had become so commonplace she just accepted the possibility, while hoping it wouldn't come to pass.

The following day, Joey discovered his toes were gone after catching a glimpse of his foot when his mother held the mirror lower than she intended. Joey asked why she didn't tell him. She replied that he was in such bad shape and required so much drugging that if she told him he might forget, and she would have to tell him again, and have to see his face after hearing the news for what he believed was the first time. He said he could still feel his toes, even though they had been removed. He told his mother he wanted to know everything from that point forward, that he no longer wanted to be kept in the dark about anything. Linda briefly argued that he should focus on getting better, not on trying to take on all of the horrors he had been spared to that point, but he was resolute, and she chose to respect his wishes. She proceeded to tell him their dog Kelly had died, something he had not known up until that moment.

Linda started visiting the chapel in the Halcyon House more during that week. She had always believed that God never put a person through more pain than they could take, but she started questioning that concept.

MAY 16

Operation from 12:00 p.m. to 4:00 p.m. to remove the pig skin from Joey's body after it got infected. Joey was in extreme pain, as a large portion of his body was once again completely raw.

The doctors decided to go in a new direction when it came to the constant fight against infection. They chose to implement dressings that involved applying a great deal of special ointments before wrapping his body with several layers of gauze. The process took approximately three hours and had to be done three times a day, every day. They also decided that because of the atrophy starting to take hold of Joey's increasingly weakened body, in addition to the extremely painful process of turning him from side to side to avoid bedsores, he would also have to endure at least one hour of exercise every day.

The exercises, which involved the movement of all of his limbs and were extremely painful, were carried out by Kelly Conte, a physiotherapist at the Shriners Burns Institute. Joey often pleaded with Kelly to either limit the exercises or to abandon them completely, but she always insisted he do them, making it clear they had to be done to keep the possibility alive that, if he were to recover, his limbs would be able to move normally.

Meanwhile, Linda's erratic state was getting out of control, and she knew it. She regretted it more and more when she snapped at anybody who said anything she deemed wrong, and that anger often fell into a state of grief, only to return to anger. She was breaking down and it was becoming impossible to conceal. She started smoking more cigarettes than ever, going through at least two packs a day. To dull the edges of the relentless stress, she also increased her drinking, giving her a means to escape from her world of hurt, if only for a short time. Meanwhile Mike matched his wife cigarette for cigarette, but instead of alcohol, for which he never had much of a taste or tolerance, he preferred his weed.

MAY 18
Operation to put fresh human skin cells on Joey's legs and back.

MAY 20
Operation to take more skin from the top of Joey's head, even though the doctors believed no more could be harvested.

As a result of taking so much skin from Joey's scalp, the doctors ended up removing many of the hair follicles as well, preventing any new hair from growing. Linda immediately offered to give Joey as much of her own hair as he needed since they shared the same hair colour.

The following day, the doctors decided to put Joey to sleep while they applied his dressings as a way to spare him from the pain it caused, but told him and Linda they couldn't do that every time. They said it was too risky, since putting him to sleep too often could lower his blood pressure and complications could arise in an instant. The doctors also hooked Joey up to a methadone drip because he was showing signs of withdrawal after his doses of painkillers had been lowered.

MAY 25

Operation to remove even more skin from the top of Joey's head. The doctors told Linda it was definitely the final time for a while. She was skeptical, as was Joey, who went so far as to question if there was even anything left up there.

It was Linda and Mike's third wedding anniversary, but there was no time for celebration, and while they did manage to enjoy a dinner together with some wine and time alone, their minds couldn't have been further away from themselves.

MAY 27

Three-hour operation to completely clean Joey's body and check to see if there were any signs of possible infection.

Three days later, Joey was put on antidepressants. He was becoming more withdrawn, barely communicating. He had become listless, just going through the motions like a victim of torture who finally accepted there was never going to be anything else. Through their constantly evolving means of communication that involved not just the twitching of his lip but also the blinking of his eyes and mouthing of phrases, he told his mother that he was sick of lying on his back, sick of the pain, sick of the lights above, of the smell of his own decay, of the doctors, of the nurses, of the tormenting baths, of the cleanings, of the dressings, of the exercises, of the hallucinations, of the new procedures, the failed procedures, the successful procedures. He was sick of everything.

In an effort to make her son feel better, Linda asked what he wanted for his birthday, which was coming up on June 4, when he would be turning fifteen.

"To go home," he replied.

On the night of June 5, Linda had a dream where she was looking through the glass roof of her old house while it burned. From above, she could see all of the rooms filling with smoke. She saw Joey frantically running through the house. She started banging on the glass, screaming for him to get out, but he couldn't hear her. He kept running through the house, looking for her, screaming for her. Linda slammed her fists against the glass harder and harder but it wouldn't crack, let alone break. She screamed his name, hoping he would stop, look up, see her, and get out of the house, but he just kept yelling and searching before he disappeared into the smoke. She woke up, crying. She was unable to go back to sleep that night.

The very concept of time had changed for Linda. Each hour had become a day and each day went by slower than the last. After less than three months, she had aged tremendously. Wrinkles severely cracked her face, while her voice had become hoarse and rough. Her eyes appeared permanently glazed, while the bags underneath them were pitch-black.

JUNE 8

Seven-hour operation to harvest more skin from the top of Joey's head, which was then put on his back. The doctors believed enough time had passed to do the procedure safely. However, his head had become completely raw after they took far more skin than they initially intended, or even thought they could. His face swelled after they scraped it extensively during a cleaning session in the operating room.

Three days later, Joey made it clear he didn't want to be touched by anybody — not nurses, not doctors, not even his mother. He just wanted to sleep.

The next day, worried about her son's mental state, Linda fought desperately with the doctors and nurses to have them install a television in his room. They told her they would look into it. That wasn't enough for her and she loudly and angrily told them not to look into it but to do it. She fought hard for the television, making it abundantly clear that Joey needed something to occupy his mind immediately, that the depression was hurting his mind just as much as the pain was hurting his exposed flesh. She refused to drop the issue until they relented, which they did that same day, allowing him to be distracted by an onslaught of daytime television, from game shows to soap operas.

JUNE 15

Operation to check the skin grafts the doctors had applied to various parts of Joey's body. They looked good, no signs of infection.

Two days after receiving that encouraging news, Linda left Boston and went back to Orillia for a few days. She was resistant right to the end, but it wasn't until Joey told his mother to go home that she felt confident enough to do it.

Back in Orillia, Linda spent all her time with Mike and Danny. They were both overjoyed at finally seeing her, especially Danny, who constantly begged Mike and Linda to let him come to Boston; however, knowing he would receive no quality time and would be left to his own devices in a place where childish antics could prove dangerous, they refused. During the daytime the three of them took walks together under the summer sky, talking, reminiscing, and remembering why they all loved each other so much. At night they continued spending nearly every waking moment together, but instead of walking, they sat together in front of a campfire.

Almost immediately after seeing the flames and hearing them crackle, Danny expressed his shock to his mother that she was able to sit so close to the fire, something he couldn't do. Linda told him that as long as he respected the flames and didn't act carelessly around them, he would be okay. Danny remained unconvinced and maintained his distance. Later that night, Mike's brother Terry arrived. Not long after his arrival, Terry got drunk, tossed some of the camping equipment into the fire (scaring Danny in the process), and then hit his girlfriend, Connie.

Mike punched his younger brother out, then told him how inappropriate his behaviour was, believing it was best to show how seriously he felt about the words to come, as opposed to reinforcing them after the fact. After that, Mike threatened more blows unless his brother left the site and slept in the truck, which Terry did, along with Connie, once again leaving Mike, Linda, and Danny alone together, a family incomplete.

Two days later, Linda was scheduled to return to Boston. It was a bittersweet departure. She was anxious to see Joey again so he could hear her voice and see her face, but it also meant having to leave her youngest son behind, as well as her husband of only three years. But she knew she had to go.

JUNE 22

Operation to put new skin on the back of Joey's legs.

On the night of June 27, Linda had two dreams. In the first dream her father died, and the ambulance brought his body to her mother's house. After arriving, he started to move before turning into a child, and that's when Linda prepared a baby bottle of milk for him while he sat on the couch watching television. Her second dream involved Mike's death. After his burial she was in a church, wearing her wedding dress. The priest was going to marry her and

Mike but because Mike had died, she stood alone at the altar, cried, and ran away to her mother's cottage, where she continued crying, unable to accept what had happened. Then she woke up.

JUNE 28

Five-and-a-half-hour operation to check Joey's new skin grafts, as well as to remove the Biobrane from his back and legs. Things went well. Seventy percent of the new skin on Joey's back was accepted, while 100 percent of the skin on his legs was accepted. As a result of Joey's steady improvement, Linda was able to touch her son's body more often and with less fear, as there was finally skin for her to touch. She used those opportunities to massage his face and body with vitamin E cream, which he enjoyed every time.

At the end of the month, when Mike arrived in Boston, he went to the Halcyon House, where he always stayed with Linda in a room with no locks, which they both found unusual until they were told it was a policy so that nobody could be locked in their rooms if there was a fire.

While Linda spent nearly every waking moment in the hospital with Joey, Mike, who spent the majority of his time in Boston by her side, did make some time for himself. It was something Linda told him he needed to do. During that time, he often walked around downtown Boston, appreciating the architecture and scenery. Both activities appealed to him because he had always been an explorer, but also because he had little money to spend and those activities were free.

Since March, Mike had befriended several families in the Halcyon House, almost all of whom were from El Salvador. Most of them were there because of the civil war that had left countless children burned and maimed. Once they arrived, like the other families there, they were scared and disoriented. Almost all of their time was spent either at the hospital with their children or in the chapel in the Halcyon House to pray for their children. They also prayed for their other family members still suffering through the war in their homeland, which they knew they would be returning to.

Many members of those families, especially the adults, didn't speak English, and Mike didn't speak Spanish, yet they still spoke to each other, understanding few words, but understanding so much more through the emotions expressed. They connected, those families and Mike. And after so much time spent together, especially in the Halcyon House's enormous kitchen, Mike soon learned enough Spanish, and several members of the Salvadoran families, particularly the fathers, learned enough English, for their conversations to expand, further solidifying their shared bond.

When Mike received three baseball tickets from the Shriners as a gift, his first thought was to invite a Salvadoran man named Pedro, with whom he had grown close, and his daughter. Pedro's son was receiving extensive treatment at the Shriners Burns Institute for injuries he had suffered back in El Salvador. At first Pedro graciously refused Mike's offer, but Mike persisted, telling him the tickets were free and it would be a lot of fun, especially for his daughter. Pedro soon relented, smiled, and warmly thanked Mike for the offer.

It was a beautiful summer day. The crowd, all walking to the same place, started swelling. The energy was palpable. Pedro's daughter, seeing the excitement all around, started smiling and tugging at her father's arm, wondering what magic they were going to witness. Meanwhile Pedro smiled back at his daughter, telling her they were going to have fun. Seeing the joy on the family's faces warmed Mike's heart and momentarily made him forget about his current circumstances, a feeling he hoped the family joining him were enjoying as well, even if it was only temporary.

Once the stadium came into view, highlighted by the legendary wall nicknamed the "Green Monster" looming over left field,

Mike felt like a little boy. A long-time baseball fan, he had always wondered what it would be like visiting the most famous stadiums in the sport, from Wrigley Field in Chicago and Yankee Stadium in New York to Fenway Park in Boston. However, his bubbling excitement immediately shifted to utter shock when he saw Pedro standing frozen, seemingly unable to take another step.

Pedro's face was stricken with an expression of horror. The man's eyes immediately welled up before tears spilled out. He started trembling. Mike looked down at Pedro's hands and noticed every single knuckle had become stark white. One hand was clenched into a fist, while the other was squeezing his daughter's hand so tightly she started wincing. Surrounded by so much enthusiasm and carefree fun, the sight of this man, looking like an eternally suffering ghost, shook Mike to his core. He used the little Spanish he had to ask what was wrong. In equally limited English, Pedro told Mike Fenway Park reminded him of the soccer stadium in San Salvador, the capital city of El Salvador. Mike asked why that was a bad thing, and why he was so afraid of it. Pedro looked Mike in the eyes and coldly whispered that was where the army took people to be tortured and executed.

The succinctness of Pedro's words, amplified by his loose grip on the language from which he summoned them, only added to their impact. Mike turned toward the stadium, and while he knew he would never be able to see what Pedro saw, the man's face, the man's words, made it as clear as it was ever going to be. Mike glanced at Pedro's daughter and was relieved that, despite wincing, she was still smiling, still staring at the stadium with the same sense of wonder the countless other children streaming toward it had. Her appearance assured him she had been spared the memory her father would never forget. Seeing Mike's relief, Pedro nodded, saying without words that his daughter's smile and her youthful energy was the victory he had managed to tear away from the bloody grip of civil war.

Mike apologized, telling Pedro he didn't know, and if he had known he would have never brought them. Pedro told him it was okay, but he needed to leave. Mike turned around and took a single step before Pedro told him he should still go to the game, but Mike said there was no way he was going to do that. Pedro smiled, and together they returned to the Halcyon House, where they went back to their respective routines while the children they loved fought for their lives.

Mike and Pedro took many walks together during that summer when they continued teaching each other their respective languages. And as their ability to communicate verbally grew, so did their friendship. They confided in each other, mutually learning that suffering, pain, and loss transcended languages, cultures, and borders, and that while the circumstances often differed, sometimes wildly, there was a connection to be found, a purely human bond that could be shared and cultivated, where empathy and compassion could grow.

Mike learned about Pedro's son. He had lost an arm, while the rest of his body was terribly mangled by shrapnel from an explosion. Despite the tremendous damage his tiny body suffered, the child had miraculously survived not just the explosion and the risk-filled trip to the Shriners Burns Institute, but also the treatment he had received. He was one of the lucky kids who got to leave the institute in much better shape than when they arrived, and with his father and sister, he returned to El Salvador. Mike and Pedro soon lost touch, but he thought about Pedro and his family often, hoping they were okay.

Mike had bonds with other people in the Halcyon House and the Shriners Burns Institute, but over time those bonds weakened. He started limiting his interactions, preferring small talk, or no talk at all, as a means of shielding himself, as many of those bonds led to tremendous pain when some of those people, mostly children, died.

That happened on several occasions, including one time when he bought a fishing rod for a young boy he had gotten close to only to discover the boy had died before he could give it to him.

JULY 5

Operation to take more skin from Joey's scalp and put it on his back. The skin on his head had become very thin and the doctors were not able to harvest any more for at least two weeks. The doctors remained positive, however, believing that after another three, possibly four more operations, Joey's body would be completely covered by grafts grown from his own skin.

A few days before the operation, Joey started complaining about not wanting to do the exercises he was supposed to do, making it clear they were too painful. However, trusting Kelly Conte, Linda insisted that he do them despite the pain. She made it clear that with his body beginning to look better with every passing day, there was more hope than ever that recovery was not just possible but plausible. But if he didn't do the exercises now and continue doing them for the next two years, which Kelly had made clear was essential, all of that recovery would be for nothing because he wouldn't be able to utilize his limbs properly. The muscles would be too weak. Joey responded like the fifteen-year-old boy he was and reluctantly went along, while making his dissatisfaction obvious. His mother accepted that, as long as he did his exercises.

The day before the operation, the nurses altered the schedule for Joey's dressing so he could watch the Fourth of July fireworks on the television. He enjoyed the show but told his mother he wanted to see things like that in person. She told him he would, soon.

It was also during this time that the intubation tube, which had been inserted into Joey's throat shortly after his arrival and had remained there for months, was finally set to be removed. He had been looking forward to its removal the moment it was inserted, but whenever the possibility was mentioned, it was always followed by a delay for fear he would not be able to talk if it were removed because his vocal cords might have been too damaged.

JULY 12

Three-hour operation to remove Biobrane from Joey's legs, followed by a thorough cleaning.

Two days later, a baby that had been brought into the institute the day before died at 11:00 a.m. The young woman who caused the fire that ended up killing the infant was charged with one count of murder and two counts of attempted murder. Linda never ceased being awestruck at the amount of good done at the Shriners Burns Institute but was equally astonished at the amount of tragedy that entered the building with just as much frequency.

So many kids arrived and died within hours to make room for more that it was difficult to attach faces to the names of the deceased. Seeing them come and go was like being in a bizarre alternate universe where you saw nothing but numbers and names moving in every direction, making it impossible to focus on one before it disappeared and another raced by. It was a dizzying experience, made even stranger the longer you were there. And after nearly five months, Linda felt more plugged into the world of constantly revolving sadness, joy, pain, fear, anxiety, and celebration found within the walls of the Shriners Burns Institute than she did to the world outside of it.

Her experience did not go unnoticed by parents of other children at the Shriners Burns Institute. They saw Linda's seeming ability to handle what they believed they never could and clung to her for support, believing her strength could help them endure. That clinging often added even more stress to Linda's already overwhelmed psyche. One mother in particular, Lee Sorenson, who had arrived with her young son, Brett, who had been terribly burned in an accident about a month after Joey, somehow got Linda moved out of her private room at the Halcyon House into a shared room with her. At first Linda was angry about having to share the room, but she understood why Lee did what she did. She knew she would have done the same thing if she believed it would help her be in a better position to help her suffering child.

JULY 20

Doctors finally took the intubation tube out at 8:00 a.m., but Joey's breathing was laboured following its removal. He had to keep his breathing above 90 percent or else the tube would have to be re-inserted. Linda spent the entire day and night doing breathing exercises with him. She treated 95 percent as if it were 90, just to keep Joey going. By 9:30 p.m. Joey fell asleep, but when his breathing dipped below 97 percent, Linda woke him up to do more breathing exercises. Finally, by 4:00 a.m., Linda watched her son sleeping soundly, breathing at 100 percent. She left the hospital and returned to the Halcyon House but, unable to sleep, she called the institute at 5:00 a.m. just to make sure Joey was still breathing well. One of the nurses assured her he was, and she fell asleep at five thirty.

A few hours later Linda woke up and rushed to the institute to see how her son was doing. He was still breathing well and was finally able to eat solid food. His first dish was chicken soup for lunch. For dinner, he had macaroni and cheese along with a milkshake and chocolate pudding. He said it was the best meal he'd ever had in his life. Hearing her son speak again filled Linda with joy and hope. However, the voice she remembered so vividly was not the voice she was hearing. Joey's new voice was low and raspy. He sounded like an old smoker who had lived through many hard years.

JOEY'S DOING GREAT!

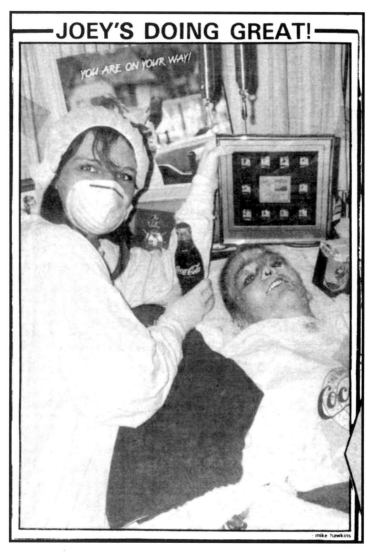

Linda visiting Joey at the Hospital for Sick Children in Toronto, Ontario, in 1988, in a photo taken by Mike that appeared in the *Packet and Times*.

JULY 27

Cleaning operation.

As more skin grafts were accepted by Joey's body, the doctors realized the new skin had to breathe. So, in order to provide the new skin with sufficient air, particularly the skin on his back, they had to turn Joey onto his stomach three times a day for two hours each time. It was incredibly uncomfortable and he hated it, but it had to be done.

Two children arrived at the Shriners Burns Institute not long after Joey. They were both younger than him and both suffered severe burns on their bodies, but at a much lower percentage than Joey. While he took an interest in the condition of both kids, he really focused his attention on Billy, the older of the two. He always asked nurses for updates on how Billy was doing, as they often moved between him and Joey. Things looked promising for a while but on August 2 Billy died. It affected Joey tremendously, confusing him as to why he was still alive despite suffering far worse burns than Billy had.

AUGUST 10

Operation to put more skin on Joey's back. Afterward, the doctors said there wasn't any more skin left on Joey's head that could be harvested. The skin on his scalp had become too thin, and the little bit of skin they found on his armpits and chest had been used once and couldn't be used again. They informed Linda they had to wait another ten weeks, maybe longer, before they could take more skin from his scalp, but that was okay because they still had the cultured cells, which meant they could grow more skin. Unfortunately for Joey, his feet remained skinless and the risk of infection remained high.

The skin graft from that operation was not accepted by Joey's body and had to be removed the next day.

AUGUST 30

Operation from 1:00 p.m. to 7:00 p.m. that involved putting metal pins in Joey's legs to keep them straight, while also putting new skin on them. After the operation, his legs were hoisted upwards with a rope, while he remained on his back.

The next day, with Joey's appetite steadily improving since the removal of his intubation tube, he was genuinely hungry for the first time since he had arrived. He started by eating ice chips, then ice chips covered in chocolate sauce, then lemon pie, then chicken soup. After he finished, Linda asked him if he wanted to eat the fork too. He smiled and told her that depended on how much chocolate sauce she covered it with.

On September 10, six months after the fire, Linda and Mike were invited to enjoy a cruise around Boston on a yacht called the *Sequoia*, which was a former presidential yacht used during the administrations of Herbert Hoover right through to Jimmy Carter. Mike recalls being told at one point in the evening that Linda was sitting in the exact same spot where Marilyn Monroe had sat during one of her visits with John F. Kennedy. It was one of the few celebratory evenings they got to enjoy together and, while they did have fun, though their bodies were there, their minds were focused solely on Joey and how he was doing.

On September 13, Linda heard from some doctors at the Shriners Burns Institute that scientists were starting to clone the cells of sick and dying animals. That made Linda think it was possible that in time, possibly even ten years, they would be able to develop a new type of skin that could help Joey look just like he did before the fire.

Linda had known for months that Joey was a guinea pig. In the beginning, the concept of her teenage son being used as an experiment for medical procedures that up until that point had only existed in theory offended her. It made her angry. She wanted her son to get better, not to be a means of study to help other kids in the future. But as time went by her stance softened. Just as she saw the crushing disappointment in the eyes of the doctors when a procedure failed, she saw their unbridled excitement when another procedure that had never been done before succeeded. Joey was on the brink of death for months on end, so if there was a way to prevent other children from suffering that same fate, should it not be explored?

It was a concept Linda wrestled with constantly. The idea that her son might die to save thousands of other sons and daughters was always in her mind, followed by a resentment she couldn't resist that those other children weren't hers. Joey was, and he was the one she cared about most.

SEPTEMBER 16

Five-and-a-half-hour-long operation to clear Joey's lungs after he contracted pneumonia and was no longer able to breathe on his own, giving the doctors no choice but to reinsert the intubation tube. It was removed less than a week later.

SEPTEMBER 21

Operation that took much longer than expected that involved inserting a feeding tube into Joey's stomach that bypassed his digestive tract. His stomach was no longer functioning properly because of the staggering amounts of pain medication he had taken and was continuing to take. Linda was initially furious when she found out the reason behind the risky surgery but understood the uncharted waters that was Joey's pain. The doctors and nurses were completely unsure as to how much pain medication they were supposed to give him because nobody had ever been given the amount he'd already taken. And while they were aware that giving him too much medication could damage his organs, or potentially kill him, the pain was so intense he often needed more than they were willing to give.

SEPTEMBER 27

Operation to put skin grafts created from the cultured cells on Joey's feet and parts of his legs and elbows. When the grafts were accepted, 90 percent of his body was covered by freshly grown skin. He and his mother were no longer told he had between a 0 to 10 percent chance of surviving surgeries. However, with his improved condition, and the possibility of him having a life to live in the future becoming more believable, self-consciousness started taking over.

Like any fifteen-year-old, Joey constantly focused on his own reflection, but he wasn't worried about pimples or patches of awkward-looking facial hair; instead, he was concerned that he would forever look like a freak. He was terrified that people would see him and gasp or laugh. And when he voiced those concerns to his mother, she stuck to her stance of not lying and said that, yes, some people were going to laugh at him, some would even say hurtful things, but they would get through that together.

Puberty and all of the chaos it entails is a nightmare for every teenager, but for Joey it was a nightmare subjugated by a much bigger one that compounded every aspect of it. The situation didn't extinguish Joey's sense of humour, however, as he jokingly said he had the deepest voice of anybody his age, and he didn't care if hair grew in strange places, just as long as it grew.

On October 10, seven months after the fire, Joey started doing walking exercises. They were extremely painful and he often begged his mother to not make him do them, but she knew they were important. While Kelly Conte was strict with Joey when it came to his exercises, she was also keenly aware of what his limits were, sometimes even more than he was, and never caused him more pain than was absolutely necessary.

OCTOBER 24

At 11:30 a.m., against all odds, Joey was transported by air ambulance from the Shriners Burns Institute back to the Hospital for Sick Children in Toronto. Initially, he wanted to wear a flight suit given to him by the Snowbirds, the aerobatics flight demonstration team of the Royal Canadian Air Force, who had heard about Joey's ordeal and offered a great deal of support, but in order to make the flight suit fit properly, the doctors said they had to cut it. Not wanting to see his beloved gift tarnished, Joey said that was out of the question and wore a Boston Bruins shirt given to him by the *Toronto Sun* newspaper instead.

The circumstances surrounding Joey's departure from the Shriners Burns Institute could not have been more different from those of his arrival. When he got there he was a burned, broken boy; a lost cause who probably wouldn't make it through his first day. Two hundred and twenty-one days later, he was leaving as a courageous survivor, not just of the fire that should have claimed his young life but also of the subsequent horrors and torturous medical procedures that came with that survival. He had endured the unfathomable torment of the disinfecting baths and the constant dressings and turnings and exercises. He suffered not one but two bouts of pneumonia, both of which could have, and should have, killed him. He had a series of blood infections, contracted a methicillin-resistant *Staphylococcus aureus* (MRSA) infection, which was not uncommon in the burn unit of the institute, and had calcium deposits in the joints of his legs that caused him excruciating pain.

He overcame all of it.

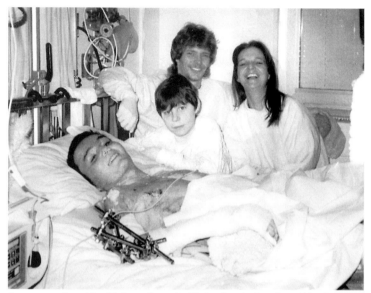

Joey recovering at the Shriners Burns Institute after doctors fused his elbows.
Mike, Linda, and Danny sit at his bedside.

INFECTION

IN THE 1980S, BELL CANADA SAID IT WOULD COST ANYWHERE FROM FIFTY thousand to several million dollars per community in Ontario to install an emergency 911 number. They said it depended on size and population, and it would have to be paid for by the municipalities. The enormous gap in projected costs prevented local Orillia officials from agreeing to the installation, which it was closest to authorizing in 1987, just a few months before the fire. Meanwhile several surrounding areas already had the 911 emergency number, including Mississauga, Toronto, London, Waterloo, Windsor, and Halton, while Sudbury, Sault Ste. Marie, Ottawa, Peel, and Niagara Region were on the cusp of having it installed.

While there was some concern from members of the Orillia community about the decision to forgo the installation of the 911 emergency number, that concern was muted and did little to force the hands of their elected representatives. What did exist was the Traffic Operator Position System, known as TOPS, which tied all nearby operators together and routed calls to operators in the areas from whence the calls came, unless the line was busy, in which case those calls were routed outside the calling area. Norma McCall, the local Orillia office manager at the time, believed TOPS was quite good, while Simcoe East MPP Al McLean publicly stated on several occasions it was not good enough.

On the morning of the fire, after constantly seeing the emergency 911 number referenced in newspapers and on television and believing it was functional throughout not just the province but the entire country of Canada, Lynda Young dialled it and was connected to a telephone repairman. She then had to hang up and dial 0 just to be connected to an operator who wasn't located in the Orillia area, forcing them to spend several moments searching for the correct emergency phone numbers to call. This was all taking place while Joey smouldered on the ground outside of his burning home. Those seconds, which grew to minutes, cost him his skin.

In June of 1988, with nobody wanting to be another Joey, a local community task force was assembled, vowing to see change. They conducted a survey of 520 people living in Orillia and the results spoke volumes.

Ninety percent of the people surveyed said they didn't know the correct number for the fire department or ambulance service.

Eighty percent of the people surveyed said they knew what 911 was for.

Ninety-eight percent of the people surveyed said they were in favour of having a direct 911 line installed in Orillia.

After showing the results of their survey to various elected representatives, local officials requested that Bell install an emergency 911 number, believing it was within the budget, since a similarly sized area, Sault Ste. Marie, was only being charged fifty thousand dollars to get it. But to their surprise and annoyance, Bell Canada quoted them an inflated cost of three hundred thousand dollars. A lengthy negotiation took place, but eventually Orillia did get a 911 emergency number installed.

Joey's story, which was seeping into more and more newspapers and newscasts throughout the country, was proving to be much more than just a story, and he was proving to be much more than just a burn victim.

As soon as the helicopter arrived from Boston at the Toronto Island Airport on the morning of October 24, 1988, Linda saw a mob of reporters. She was shocked at how many of them there were, all armed with cameras and microphones. She told Joey but he didn't seem too concerned. He was finally out of the hospital, finally able to feel, smell, and taste the fresh air. That was all he cared about.

When the paramedics and nurses wheeled Joey out of the air ambulance, the reporters kept their distance, but when Linda exited, they swarmed her. She was blinded by the flashing lights of their cameras. With so many questions fired at her from every side, she was unable to distinguish one reporter from another. Shouts of "How is he?," "What are your plans now that you're home?," and "How does it feel to be the mother of a hero?" were all she could hear.

Despite feeling overwhelmed, Linda became fiercely protective of her son. She worried that one of the zealous reporters would get too close and possibly stumble and accidently hit him. It was a thought she couldn't stand considering. She started getting angry about something that hadn't even happened. She put her anger aside, however, when she saw that the reporters maintained a safe distance from Joey. They were showing respect. She calmed down. It was only when she saw Danny and Mike, along with several members of his family including his brother Pat and Pat's wife, Kathy, that she finally smiled. She wanted to hug her husband but the crowd of reporters was too thick and he couldn't get through. But when they locked eyes, regardless of the distance and obstacles in the way, they told each other, without having to utter a single word, how much they loved each other. Linda looked back at Joey, who she felt beyond blessed to still have.

Meanwhile Danny, wearing a cap given to him by one of the paramedics that was too big for his head and an equally oversized smile to match, showed none of the restraint the reporters did, and dashed through the horde as if it wasn't even there toward his mother and brother. After hugging his mother, he leaned close enough to Joey to feel his breath. They started speaking while the reporters pressed their microphones as close as they could, hoping to capture the kind of precious, personal, intimate family moment they knew would make the evening news. Not liking the interference, Danny, standing well below five feet tall, spoke like a giant and demanded that the reporters stand back, telling them they were too close and he couldn't hear his brother. The reporters laughed at first, but after realizing the young boy was serious they obeyed and took a collective step back. After that, the paramedics and nurses, who were running out of patience and wanted to get Joey to the hospital, moved him through the crowd of reporters and into a waiting ambulance that took him to the Hospital for Sick Children.

Joey was glad to be back in Canada. It was important to him, just as it was for Linda and Mike, to be back home, even if the notion of "home" had become more of a concept than a reality. While being homeless certainly weighed on Linda and Mike, they weren't afforded much time to dwell on it, since all of their attention and energy remained focused on Joey.

Thinking the blitz of attention was a one-time thing, Linda, Joey, and Mike were shocked that the reporters who met them at the airport followed the ambulance all the way to the hospital. Moreover, another group of reporters had already gathered at the hospital awaiting their arrival. Combined, the two mobs created a frenzied swell of eager journalists, all trying to get a word from the boy they couldn't stop referring to as a hero.

While Joey was at the Shriners Burns Institute, Linda had felt like she was in a bubble. The outside world didn't exist to her. She rarely, if ever, read the newspaper, didn't have time to watch the news, and never bothered asking anybody about anything beyond what was happening in Joey's room. She liked the insulation. She preferred it. She didn't want any distractions and had neither the inclination nor the energy to bother with them anyway. She spent all of her time either in the Shriners Burns Institute or her room at the Halcyon House. Everything else in the world could have ceased to exist for all she cared.

When it came to media attention, the amount Joey's story had gotten while he was in Boston was minimal. While a few reporters from Boston and Toronto did come to the institute after hearing about Joey, they did so in a cursory manner. They usually arrived in the morning or afternoon, politely asked Linda a few questions, and then left. Sometimes they asked for some words from Joey, which they knew they would not be able to get themselves as they were not permitted to see him in his room or to enter the ward. So they asked Linda if she was willing to ask him a few questions on their behalf. Believing Joey would welcome the distraction, she usually agreed to the requests.

One visiting reporter from CBC's program *The Fifth Estate* asked Linda to ask Joey what happened during the fire, to recap the events of that frigid March morning. That was when Joey told his mother that he had run back into the house because he thought she was still inside, not to put out the fire he had accidently started. It was the same lie he had told his mother when they reconstructed the events of that morning together less than three weeks after they occurred — a lie she believed to be the truth, a lie she repeated to the reporter, who then returned to Canada and repeated that lie to the entire country. In no time at all, that lie started making headlines around the world, gracing the front pages of newspapers in England, Singapore, the United States, and many other nations. Linda was completely unaware of the spread, and the brief interview offered no hint at the enormous impact it ultimately proved to have.

Linda and Mike started realizing the impact of Joey's story not through newspapers or television, which they continued to ignore in favour of being with, thinking about, worrying about, and obsessing over Joey, but through the mail. As the months passed in Boston, Linda and Mike were made aware of fan mail for Joey. At first, they thought it was a few letters, kind gestures from a few people who had heard about him and wanted to express their sympathies and offer words of encouragement. However, they discovered from the post office near the Shriners Burns Institute that there were several large sacks full of letters for Joey. When they went to the post office they were shocked to see not only the size of the sacks, but how full they were. After they grabbed the sacks, which were much heavier than they looked, they thanked the workers at the post office and were about to leave, believing they had everything. That's when the workers started laughing.

"What's so funny?" Mike asked.

"That's not all of them," one of the workers replied.

"There are more?"

The worker nodded.

"How many?" Mike asked.

"No idea."

Mike was confused, as was Linda, but before they could ask for an explanation, the postal worker provided it.

"After a few dozen we stopped counting and just put them in a mail truck, which is full, and we need to clear it out, so if you don't mind helping us out that would be great."

Mike was shocked. Linda was shocked. But when they actually saw the truck, that shock turned to utter stupefaction. They couldn't believe it. The truck was absolutely stuffed with dark brown sacks, all of which were filled with letters for Joey.

The Boston post office assisted the family by sending all of the mail to Toronto, where it awaited Joey, Linda, and Mike's arrival.

Joey enjoyed reading the letters sent to him from thousands of people he never met, encouraging him, telling him that his fight to survive inspired them and his heroism in saving his brother and trying to save his mother was beautiful. Linda was speechless. Meanwhile Joey, while overtaken with gratitude to those who wrote to him, also realized his lie was no longer his, and like most lies that grow beyond the person telling them, it had become too big to take back.

After the first few hundred letters had been opened, it was also becoming clear that in addition to words of encouragement, many people had sent financial gestures as well, and those gestures added up. Seemingly overnight, the amount of money sent had risen from hundreds of dollars to thousands, necessitating a level of organization that neither Linda nor Mike were prepared to handle, considering how much of their attention Joey required.

Back in Toronto, Linda started to worry after seeing Joey's face. She knew he was exhausted from the journey and needed a rest. But that was the last thing in the world the reporters seemed willing to grant him. She was also aggravated at how loud and frantic the reporters were inside the hospital, a place where she believed the doctors and nurses were meant to be heard as clearly as possible. She started getting angry when the reporters turned their attention to her and constantly asked her to speak into this microphone or that microphone and to focus on this camera or that camera. All she wanted to focus on was Joey, and they were getting in the way of that. That's when her anger grew even more intense. She no longer wanted to see them, hear them, or talk to them, but like ravenous mosquitos, they weren't going to go away on their own. Something had to be done. So she decided to hold a press conference that evening, hoping it would be the first and last time she would ever have to do it.

Resting in front of Linda like a collection of rifles aimed at her head were over a dozen microphones, each with their news station's insignia. There were CFRB, CFTR, Citytv, Global News, and more. The barrage of flashing lights and bombardment of shouted questions was dizzying. Linda started to panic. She had become so accustomed to the respectful quiet of the Halcyon House and the tense silence of the ward at the Shriners Burns Institute that the sudden explosion of noise gave her what could be best described as media shell shock. Nonetheless she persevered, answering as many questions as she could.

They revolved around the donated money the family had been receiving and what they were planning to do with it, what their plans for the future were, and her thoughts on reports of a house being built for them — something Linda had never even heard about so was unable to comment on. Most frequently, she was asked whether or not she believed Joey was a hero. She replied, more than

Mike, Linda, and Danny preparing to give a press conference in a photo from the *Packet and Times*. Photo by Vik Kirsch.

once, that she was just happy he was still alive. Fed up with repeating the same answer to the same question, she elaborated by saying she didn't understand why her eldest son was being propped up to such a lofty position. She continued by saying she thought it would be more interesting for them to speak to the people who thought Joey was a hero than to speak to her, or even to Joey himself for that matter. After the reporters got their fill, and the press conference finally, mercifully ended, Linda was given time to breathe.

Joey didn't understand his ascendance to celebrity status. He wasn't an actor who had just starred in a critically acclaimed block-buster film, nor was he a beloved athlete who had just finished leading his team to a successful championship. He wasn't a soldier returning home with a bevy of metals or a politician fresh off an election win. He was a teenager who had survived a fire. He didn't see what all the fuss was about. But regardless of how he felt about why he was a celebrity, the fact that he *was* a celebrity, especially in Canada, was undeniable. By the end of 1988, the *Toronto Star* confirmed that Joey had received the second highest percentage of media attention in Canada after Ben Johnson, the Jamaican-born Canadian sprinter who won the hundred-metre gold medal at the 1988 summer Olympics in Seoul, South Korea, with a time of 9.79 seconds. It was a new world record at the time, although his medal was stripped away from him three days later for doping.

Prior to the press conference, when Linda had some time to re-acquaint herself with the staff of the Hospital for Sick Children, she was greeted by Dr. Clark, who was unable to hide his shock at how different Joey looked. He couldn't believe it. None of the doctors or nurses in the ward could. He was blown away by Joey's will to survive all the medical procedures he'd had to endure. It was now his responsibility, and the responsibility of those working with him, to continue pushing the momentum. They were determined to do the job. However, they were determined to do it their way.

Arriving at the Hospital for Sick Children with Joey, Linda, Danny, and Mike were a physiotherapist and a nurse from the Shriners Burns Institute. The purpose of their presence was to instruct the various therapists and nurses in Toronto as to how they believed Joey's care should continue, based on their own experience over the last several months.

There was a meeting that took place in a conference room not far from the burn ward. Linda and Mike were present along with the therapist and nurse from the Shriners Burns Institute, in addition to the team of therapists, nurses, and doctors who would be caring for Joey at the Hospital for Sick Children. The therapist from the Shriners Burns Institute began by making it clear that the splints on Joey's feet were not to be removed. They were essential in keeping his feet in a stable, upright position, ensuring they could heal properly, keeping the hope alive that he could walk on them. The therapist strenuously emphasized the importance of not removing the splints, making it clear that if they were removed, Joey's feet would regress rapidly to a point when they could not be saved.

The therapist then explained the types of exercise Joey had to do. She made no effort to conceal the fact that they were painful. She even showed a video of a particular exercise in which Joey's legs were repeatedly raised as high as possible before being lowered, just to be raised again. Throughout the exercise, Joey was screaming in agony. The therapist thought it best to show things as they were, and needed to be, as opposed to how others may have wanted or hoped for them to be. She knew the techniques used at the Shriners Burns Institute were considered unorthodox by other institutions, but they worked. There was a proven track record, and she did her best to emphasize that point.

She also made it clear that the pain Joey was experiencing during the exercises was a necessary price to pay. The exercises, if done correctly, would strengthen his muscles so that they could hold his weight when the day finally came when he was in good enough condition to walk. But if those exercises were not strictly adhered to on a consistent basis, his body would not be strong enough, regardless of how much he had recovered. It was a critical time and if things were not done the way they had been done at the Shriners Burns Institute, she believed the consequences would be irreversible.

Linda and Mike keenly watched the reactions from the nurses, therapists, and doctors from the Hospital for Sick Children, and were not encouraged. They had been there during every single one of Joey's exercise sessions and they knew how painful they were for Joey, but they also knew how important they were, and seeing doubt on the faces of those who were going to be responsible for Joey's care from then on was incredibly worrisome. Linda, in particular, was not pleased with the lack of enthusiasm.

It didn't take long for Linda and Mike's apprehension to prove prescient. Just a few days after the therapist and nurse from the Shriners Burns Institute left Toronto, a decision was made to remove the splints from Joey's feet. Linda and Mike were furious. They kept questioning why the splints were removed when it was made abundantly clear they were to be left on, and the only answer they received from the doctors at the Hospital for Sick Children was they believed, in their professional opinion, that it was for the best.

Knowing the removal of the splints could have enormous repercussions for Joey's recovery, Linda and Mike immediately turned to somebody they could not only trust, but somebody who genuinely cared about Joey's well-being: Cherie Tuohy. She was the head nurse in Joey's ward at the Shriners Burns Institute and had spent more time with him than anybody not named Linda or Mike.

When Linda called Cherie and told her that the doctors at the Hospital for Sick Children had removed the splints from Joey's feet, she was livid, but not surprised. She had been told by the therapist from the Shriners Burns Institute that the reception she got from the staff in Toronto regarding her instructions and the video she showed them was not what she would have liked. Linda asked Cherie what she should do, that she was at a loss, that she trusted the staff at the institute, Cherie most of all, but the staff in Toronto were insistent on doing things their way. They kept telling her they didn't want to cause Joey more pain, that he had been through enough and they wanted to focus on making him feel better. Cherie did her best to comfort Linda, who was terrified that the progress Joey had made, as painful and arduous as it was, would be undone.

Cherie made it clear to Linda that she was just as concerned about Joey, something Linda would not have believed if anybody else had said it. Cherie also made it clear that the staff at the Shriners Burns Institute who cared for Joey for so long would be just as livid as she was at the news of the splints' removal. Linda asked Cherie what could be done.

"I'm coming there," Cherie replied.

On her own dime, Cherie flew to Toronto from Boston a few days after that phone call. As soon as she arrived, Linda and Mike wanted to march her into Joey's room, but were warned it wouldn't be that easy. Cherie told them she couldn't just walk in and identify herself as a nurse from the Shriners Burns Institute who wanted to see her old patient.

"Why the hell not?" Mike asked.

Cherie understood what Linda and Mike didn't: that while the Shriners Burns Institute and the Hospital for Sick Children were both in the business of helping others, as in any business there were enormous benefits from being "the best." And with both institutions known worldwide as titans of the industry of child medical care, Joey's case was of particular value.

Prior to Joey's arrival, the Shriners Burns Institute was already well ahead of the pack when it came to skin grafting for burn victims, especially young ones. That was why Dr. Clark, just days after the fire, had insisted that Joey's only chance for survival was to go there. He wasn't thinking about competition at that point, because there was no competition. The Shriners Burns Institute was the best for what Joey needed and like any good doctor, which Dr. Clark definitely was, his primary goal was the survival of his patient. And after Joey left the institute, they were so far ahead of everybody else their only competition had become themselves. As a result of the opportunity Joey provided them, progress they initially believed would take years had been achieved in months. Joey's body provided them with a means to test things they would have never otherwise had the chance to test in a real-world scenario, enabling them to establish procedures that could, did, and continue to help thousands of children around the world. Joey was a guinea pig, of that there is no doubt, but in the realm of medical science without the guinea pig there can be no progress, and with no progress there are no breakthroughs.

While the Hospital for Sick Children had no illusions about their shortcomings when it came to groundbreaking skin-grafting procedures, they were confident in their well-earned reputation as a top-tier care centre for children. If the Shriners Burns Institute was the lab where boundary-pushing medical science was created, the Hospital for Sick Children was where the patients who got to receive the fruits of that science went to take the final steps needed for a full, miraculous recovery. In theory, the coalescence between the two life-saving institutions should have resulted in a seamless transition for Joey, since they both shared the same goal of not just saving his life but also seeing him recover enough to enjoy that life. However, despite sharing a common and beautiful goal of saving the lives of children, the two peerless institutions became hardened in their respective stances that they alone knew what was best for Joey's recovery. This resulted in a tense, precarious peace maintained by an unspoken agreement not to step on each other's toes.

If Cherie were to announce her presence in an official capacity, that peace would be threatened. And while Linda and Mike could not have cared less about the two institutions' feelings, or any petty, pointless squabbles that could arise from just walking Cherie into Joey's room with her Shriners Burns Institute identification dangling from her neck, they nonetheless heeded her warnings. So they snuck her in, listing her as a family friend who just wanted to visit Joey. There was no mention of the institute or even that she was a nurse.

Once inside Joey's room, as if she were committing an act of espionage, Cherie looked around to make sure nobody saw her, pulled out a camera, and took several pictures of Joey's feet, minus the splints, from as many angles as she thought necessary. After the pictures were taken, she swiftly put her camera back into her bag and started talking to Joey, who was overjoyed to see the one nurse he trusted above all others. She asked some questions about his exercises and lack thereof along with other inquiries about the care he was receiving, but they mostly just reminisced about some of the jokes they shared back in Boston and the time they had spent together. She truly liked Joey. He was her friend. She cared about him just as she cared about Linda and Mike, whom she also considered friends.

As soon as Cherie returned to Boston, she developed the film from her camera, brought the photographs she had taken back to the Shriners Burns Institute, and showed them to the doctors who had taken care of Joey. They were furious. Almost immediately, precarious peace be damned, they called the Hospital for Sick Children, angrily asking why they had removed the splints they had explicitly stated were not to be touched. The response from the staff at the Hospital for Sick Children was equally hostile. They took offence at having their methods of care questioned. Eventually, after the hostilities between the two institutions diminished, an agreement was made to send Joey back to the Shriners Burns Institute. Linda and

Mike were overjoyed at the news. Joey was not as enthusiastic. He liked being back in Toronto and he liked not having to do the excruciating exercises all the time. Linda tried to console him as best she could, telling him the pain he felt in the present was going to help him in the future, but he didn't see things that way, which wasn't all that surprising considering he was still a fifteen-year-old kid.

After the agreement between the two institutions was made, Joey was flown back to Boston, transferred back to the Shriners Burns Institute, and brought back to the same room in the same ward he'd left not too long ago. The doctors immediately saw for themselves what they had seen in Cherie's clandestinely taken pictures: Joey's feet minus the splints. And just as they had feared, the damage done had been as rapid as it was irreversible. After some brief deliberation, the doctors concluded Joey's feet were too deformed and would never reach a point when they could be used for walking. There was no other option: his feet had to be amputated.

When the doctors told Linda and Mike about what had to be done, they were torn between heartbreak and rage. Saving Joey's feet had been a goal of Linda's since the first weeks they had arrived at Boston. She had pleaded and pleaded with the doctors at the Shriners Burns Institute to save his feet unless there was absolutely no other option, and they had done that, but it was all for nothing. When the doctors told her Joey's feet had to be amputated, she knew they knew how much saving them meant to her and to him, so if they were saying they couldn't be saved, she knew it was the truth, and she had no choice but to begrudgingly accept it.

Mike, however, was enraged. He couldn't get over the fact that right in front of his face, the therapist from the Shriners Burns Institute had implored the therapists, the nurses, and the doctors at the Hospital for Sick Children not to remove the splints, and yet they had done it anyway. He wanted something done. He wanted accountability. Mike and Linda considered filing a lawsuit for negligence against the Hospital for Sick Children, but they didn't have the money it would have cost to put it together. They were also told by a lawyer that it would be virtually impossible to win such a case, since all the administration at the hospital had to do was state that the staff was doing what they believed was best for the patient and that would be that. So the case was closed before it was even opened.

Meanwhile, Joey was doing quite well back at the Shriners Burns Institute despite the amputation of his feet, and while he hated doing the exercises, had almost immediately started showing amazing results. In less than two weeks Joey was actually walking, albeit with prosthetics, but still moving in a manner nobody thought possible.

The return to Boston and the Shriners Burns Institute was never meant to be very long, nothing like the time spent from March to October. If it weren't for the issue with the splints and subsequent amputation of his feet, Joey wouldn't have returned at all. Linda and Mike didn't want to return to the Halcyon House either. While they forever felt indebted to the kindness they had received in that hallowed building, being away from it made them realize it was only for those who needed it most, and that no longer included them. They wanted to rebuild their lives back in Canada, something they had been putting off ever since the fire because all of their time and all of their attention had been focused on Joey's recovery. They also had to think about Danny, who was going through his own personal issues during that time. The problem with their goal of rebuilding their lives, however, was they still had no home to come back to.

That's where Hans Gerhardt came in. Son of a German immigrant family, Hans was the general manager of the upscale Sutton Place Hotel, located on Bay Street in the heart of downtown Toronto. The hotel was a favourite with Hollywood's elite, from Meryl Streep to Michael Caine to Sophia Loren and many more. It

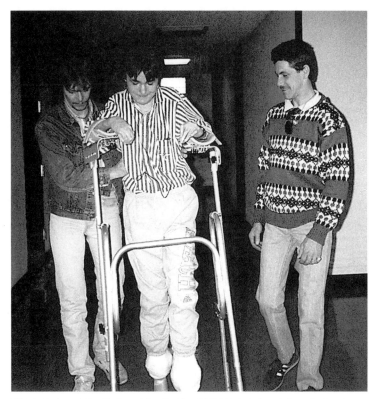

With help from Mike (left) and family friend Cliff (right), Joey takes challenging steps following the amputation of his feet at the Shriners Burns Institute.

was the kind of exclusive place people immediately imagined when they thought of luxury hotels. It had marble floors and enormous glistening chandeliers.

Hans had first heard about Joey and the fire in the same manner most people throughout Canada did: through the newspapers. But it was after seeing Linda's press conference that he was convinced he had to help. So the day after the press conference, October 25, he contacted Linda and Mike and offered them a room in the hotel, free of charge, for three months, knowing the hotel was close to the Hospital for Sick Children. Linda and Mike couldn't believe it. They thought it was a joke, a sick prank somebody was playing on them. When they realized the offer was real, however, they were nervous to accept it. They didn't want to be charity cases. Mike was determined to find work so he could once again support his family, but he also knew it would take at least a month, probably longer, before he could save up the money necessary to find them a cheap apartment in the city. After a long conversation, Linda and Mike decided to accept Hans's offer. While they stayed at the hotel, Mike planned on working as much as he could so that at the end of the three months they could find a place of their own, while Linda spent all of her time with Joey.

With nothing more than two bags and the clothes on their backs, when Linda and Mike saw the room they were going to be staying in, their initial disbelief grew tenfold. They would have been happy if they had been taken to the maintenance closet, sleeping with the brooms, mops, and buckets; instead, they were led to a beautiful room with a big bed in the centre and a fantastic view of the city. It was the kind of room neither of them had ever seen before, let alone spent a single night in. They couldn't believe such a room could ever be associated with words like "economy" or "low-end," but according to Hans, that was the type of room it was.

They thanked Hans profusely and told him he was an angel of a man, and that he was helping them more than he could ever know and more than they could ever express. Hans told them he was happy to help a family in need and left them to their room. Linda and Mike spent about a week resting in the comfortable room, which they found out would have cost them over $250 a night, before leaving for Boston to be back with Joey until he was to be released from the Shriners Burns Institute.

About a month later, after the doctors at the institute said it was safe for Joey to travel, he returned to the Hospital for Sick

Children, where his treatment once again did not align with the suggestions of the staff at the Shriners Burns Institute. The staff in Toronto continued insisting on a less aggressive approach. Linda and Mike did not agree with this but decided to stay out of the way and see how things went. In just a few days Joey's overall mood had improved tremendously. He was in less pain and even began rediscovering his old self. For the first time since the fire, he started acting like the teenage boy he had always been. While the price of that improved mood was that he would never be able to walk on his own feet again, Linda, riddled with conflict as to how to view the situation, decided that if Joey felt better at the moment, that was worth cherishing, and when it came to the future they would deal with that when it came. Meanwhile, back at the Sutton Place Hotel, Hans informed Linda and Mike that their room was no longer available because it was being used for paying customers. While they completely understood the situation, considering they had been gone for several weeks and were incredibly grateful for the week or so they got to spend in those beautiful quarters, they were worried. Hans didn't owe them anything, and he was the general manager of a business, and they both believed his initial commitment to house them for three months at no charge was too good to be true anyway. Ready to leave the hotel and find a new place to stay, they were shocked when Hans told them that because their previous room was booked, they had been moved to a penthouse suite.

"Wait, what?" Mike said. "Are you serious?"

Hans laughed. "Of course," he replied. "I told you that you could stay in this hotel for three months. I didn't say it would be in the same room."

Linda and Mike laughed harder than they had laughed since before the fire. That laughter was a warm blanket, a soft pillow, and a hot shower. It was a gentle embrace to spirits that had been through hell, and it proved not only cathartic for the couple but also showed them how powerful, how helpful, and how necessary it was.

When they entered the room with Hans, Linda and Mike gasped. It was unlike anything they had ever seen. It was enormous and beautiful. Mike told Hans the bed was bigger than the bedroom he grew up in at 6 Glamorgan Avenue in Scarborough. When he went into the washroom, he said it was bigger than many apartments he had in his early twenties, eliciting more of that beautiful laughter from himself and his wife. Exploring the suite was like consciously walking through an exquisite dream. When they approached the window, they couldn't believe the view. From the top floor of the hotel, the city of Toronto looked magnificent. They couldn't believe where life had taken them.

"Yeah," Mike said, "I guess it's okay."

More of that beautiful laughter.

One of the biggest adjustments for Linda and Mike in their new penthouse suite was seeing members of the cleaning staff come into their room every day to change the towels and bedding, while also ensuring the room looked as pristine as it did the day before. It made them uncomfortable. They knew they were staying for free in a room that surely must have cost over a thousand dollars a night, and the last thing they wanted to do was take advantage of that by occupying the time of the cleaning staff.

The second day in the suite, Mike told one of the women who came into the room to do her customary cleaning that she and her co-workers didn't have to clean the room, since they were going to be staying there for several weeks. He told her they should take the time they would have spent cleaning the room to enjoy a break, but the young woman just smiled and told him they didn't mind at all. After she and the other woman had finished cleaning the room, doing so with remarkable speed and efficiency, Mike went to the perfectly made bed and saw a chocolate resting on each of the two plush pillows. He grabbed one of the chocolates, looked around as if he was stealing it, opened it, and ate it. It took everything he had to not eat the other one but through sheer force of will he managed to resist the urge and give it to Linda, who immediately smiled, saying it was one of the most delicious chocolates she had ever had.

The following day, when the same young women came to the room, Mike told them they didn't have to change the towels every day or clean every part of the room, something the women agreed to, albeit reluctantly. He then said rather mischievously that if they insisted on leaving those tasty chocolates on the pillows, he wouldn't be opposed to that. The young women, along with Mike and Linda, laughed, and after the cleaning was finished and the women left, Mike went into the bedroom and saw not one, but two of those delectable chocolates on top of his pillow and two more on top of Linda's.

The Sutton Place Hotel was not just a great place for Linda and Mike. While he didn't get to spend nearly as much time there as his mother and stepfather because of school, when he was there, Danny got to enjoy it, too. Along with exploring the majestic building with the same joy and sense of adventure as if he were in a palace, Danny also made some interesting friends during his brief time there. He formed a bond with Arkansas-born-and-raised country and rock musician "Rompin' Ronnie" Hawkins (no relation to Mike and his family), along with other celebrities who stayed at the hotel whenever they were in Toronto. But the closest friendship Danny made while he was staying at the hotel during that Christmas season of 1988 was with actor Mark Hamill, who gave Danny his phone number. He told Danny he could call him if he ever wanted to talk, which Danny did on several occasions, allowing him to live the dream of countless children: being able to talk to Luke Skywalker.

Spearheaded by Hans, an enormous Christmas Day feast was prepared for Joey in the hotel's banquet hall. Linda and Mike couldn't believe it. The assortment of food was vast, with every new course seemingly competing for the title of most delicious. Everything from juicy turkey, cranberry sauce, and potatoes to a wide selection of pastries and pies, with wine and champagne to wash it all down. The meal, and the elaborate manner in which it was presented, was something out of a feel-good Christmas film. Unable to contain themselves, and encouraged by Hans, Linda and Mike, along with Danny, ate and ate until they could barely move. It wasn't long before they started wondering if they would end up exploding like the man who decided to eat one last wafer cruelly offered to him by John Cleese's waiter in *Monty Python's The Meaning of Life*.

The party was incredible, made even better by the presence of Joey, who was brought to the hotel by ambulance and cared for by nurses volunteering their time. He finally met Hans and thanked him for helping his mother, stepfather, and brother have a place to stay near the hospital. And while he couldn't enjoy nearly as much of the food as everybody else, he nonetheless did get to taste several of the dishes.

Along with the great food and company was also an assortment of gifts presented to Joey and his family. While there were a number of wonderful, often sentimental gifts, one gift stood out most of all, not for what it was, but for the joyous laughter it yielded. Members of the Toronto Fire Department presented Joey with a brand new, top-of-the-line mountain bike. At first, Linda and Mike looked at each other quizzically, unsure how to react to a gift that Joey had absolutely no use for, but it was Joey himself who destroyed the brief moment of awkwardness by openly speculating how hilarious it would look riding the bike without any feet. The laughter started slowly and nervously before erupting into a glorious roar as everybody in the enormous room started picturing, with Joey's enthusiastic urging, the image of him in his current state riding the bike through the city's snow-, slush-, and ice-covered streets. Even the members of the fire department, who had purchased the bike well before finding out about the amputation of Joey's feet, joined in the laughter.

The mountain bike given to Joey was just one in a long list of gifts he received from people throughout not just Canada, but many other countries. Almost all the gifts he received were accompanied by letters wishing him well and congratulating him on the incredible acts of heroism the senders had read about in newspapers or heard about in news broadcasts.

Here are just a few examples of what Joey received:

- a printed letter from the royal family at Buckingham Palace wishing him well
- a letter from the prime minster of Canada, Brian Mulroney, stating how proud the country was of him
- a letter from the Satan's Choice Biker Gang offering to take him for a ride
- a plaque from the Kiwanis Club of Lindsay
- a signed photograph of several pilots from the 425 Tactical Fighter Squadron
- a signed photograph featuring all of the Snowbirds pilots, who, along with sending him the flight suit he cherished, had created a flight manoeuvre called the "Philion Roll" that they performed at their air shows
- a photograph of the 1989–90 Toronto Maple Leafs hockey team
- an enlarged photograph of Bobby Orr's famed 1970 Stanley Cup Final diving goal against the St. Louis Blues, with a signature and the message, "Way to go Joe, your friend, Bobby Orr"
- a signed photograph of singer Elton John with the message, "To Joey, Best Wishes"
- a patch from the 434th Tactical Fighter Wing

- a photograph of CBC sportscaster Brian Williams with his signature and the message, "Get Well Soon"
- a photograph of singer Anne Murray with her signature and the message, "Joey, Get well soon, I'm thinking of you, Anne Murray"
- a photograph of stock car racer Gary Elliot in front of a race car with his signature and the message, "To Joey, Jesus Loves you #36"
- several autographs from other celebrities including Bill Cosby, Larry Bird, Christopher Reeve, Michael Jackson, Billy Joel, the Italian Flying Team, the Thunderbirds, the cast of *Les Misérables*, the cast of *Cats*, Phil Collins (who along with Robert Plant from Led Zeppelin and Rod Stewart sent their best wishes via a short tribute video), Bryan Adams, members of the band Strange Advance, and members of the band Rush, who also sent a number of cassettes of their music and signed posters
- sportscaster Don Cherry sent an entire box of gifts including a number of signed hockey pucks, photographs, and hockey cards along with a number of his popular "Rock'Em Sock'Em" videos
- the Department of National Defence's Cadet Award of Bravery
- a song, "Soaring Free," written for Joey by Paul Dick and Michael Racioppo and sung by Marek Normal
- an award-winning benefit concert in February 1989, "Stars Shine for Joe Philion," to raise money for him and the family, organized and headlined by the Jeff Healey Band and Joey's favourite band, Glass Tiger, along with other bands
- a book, *To Live Again: The Medical Miracle of Joe*

Philion, written by Martyn Kendrick and published by
Random House Canada in 1990
• an official letter from the Ministry of the Solicitor
General, dated November 29, 1988:

Dear Joe:

On behalf of the 6,000 officers and employees of the
Ontario Provincial Police, I wish to extend our most
sincere wishes for your speedy recovery.

Nothing I can say adequately expresses our deep re-
gard for you and our admiration for the courage you have
demonstrated during these long and painful months.

Please accept this small token of our esteem and best
wishes for you. We hope the collage of photographs
presented to you will bring a few moments of enjoyment and will serve as a continuous reminder that we
are thinking of you and eager to see the day you leave
the hospital.

Thomas B. O'Grady
Commissioner

Nia Herhily lived on a farm in Shelburne, Ontario. She was a teenager in 1988, a few years older than Joey. As soon as she heard
about the heroic boy who saved his brother and attempted to save
his mother and was clinging to life as a result, she felt compelled
to write to him.

Nia wrote Joey several letters while he was at the Shriners Burns
Institute and the Hospital for Sick Children. The letters were very

sweet, as almost all of the letters he received were, but there was something different about Nia's. They were more personal and vulnerable than the thousands of other fan letters he received from people around the world. Almost immediately, Joey felt a connection to the girl he had never met.

In one particular letter, Nia wrote a poem for Joey about the legend of the phoenix. She described the mythical bird that died in a bed of flames only to rise again from the ashes. She told Joey that he was just like the phoenix. The sentiment resonated with him. He loved the poem and had Linda read it to him many times. Nia's letters kept coming almost every week, and Joey always looked forward to receiving them.

After several months passed, Linda asked if he wanted to meet Nia. He was nervous, worried that his appearance might scare her or he wouldn't live up to the image she had cultivated of him from afar. But Linda insisted that he had nothing to be nervous about, that Nia would be happy to see him. He agreed to the meeting, set up by a *Toronto Star* reporter named Jim Wilkes who sought out Nia at the request of Linda, who thought meeting her would be a great source of joy for Joey. When Jim found her, Nia was nervous about actually meeting the boy that she had only seen on screens and read about in print, but with her parents' blessing she agreed to the meeting at the Hospital for Sick Children, where she and Joey immediately hit it off, laughing, talking, and flirting as if they had known each other for years. Nothing pleased Linda more than seeing her son smile, and when Nia was around, he couldn't do anything but smile.

As the early months of 1989 passed, Joey continued improving, the relationship between him and Nia kept blossoming, and rumours of a house being built for him and his family continued growing.

THE HOUSE THAT LOVE BUILT

KEN MCCANN NEVER MET JOEY PHILION. HE NEVER MET MIKE, LINDA, OR DANNY. He never asked any member of the family what they needed, or what kind of help would serve them best. But after hearing about the fire that nearly claimed Joey's life, the electrician and Orillia resident felt compelled to do something. It was early autumn of 1988 when Ken started focusing on the plight of Joey and his family. He learned about the loss of the Hawkinses' family home. He learned that Joey was at the Hospital for Sick Children in Toronto, recovering from the many surgeries he had endured. And he learned that throughout Joey's recovery, he wanted more than anything else to get out of the hospital and go home, but there was no home for him to go to. Sending money to Joey wasn't enough for Ken. He wanted to do more. After several discussions, his wife, Dellsi, proposed an idea that was as simple as it was audacious. Joey needed a home to return to when he was released from the hospital, so why not build him that home?

Ken knew he could not build the house himself, but he knew that once the house was being built he could happily perform all the electrical work free of charge. That sparked the notion that if he were willing to volunteer his expertise for Joey's new home, maybe others would too.

Before a single nail was pummelled into a single piece of wood, Ken got to work by picking up his phone and making call after call, seeing if what he imagined in his mind was even possible. He didn't ask, but challenged other contractors to follow his lead, to take their expertise and their time and put them toward a cause that could benefit a boy, a fellow Orillian, who was in desperate need of more than just thoughts and prayers.

The challenge was also proposed in the local Orillian newspaper, the *Packet and Times*. Almost immediately, several contractors not only agreed to what Ken suggested to them, but often surpassed his requests by offering to do much more than was expected, always completely free of charge.

Once word got out about the plan to build Joey a new house, calls offering help swiftly started flooding Ken and Dellsi's home. Those calls, and the offers that came with them, soon became abundant to the point when Ken and Dellsi had to start graciously turning people away. They feared that too many hands could lead to confusion and possible difficulties once construction was underway.

The pieces were in place. Ken was going to spearhead the construction of the house, coordinating things with designers like Ivan Cobbe and a number of different contractors. Meanwhile, Dellsi would be in charge of coordinating all of the volunteers, in order to keep things as efficient as possible.

Ken and Dellsi's plan was not symbolic. It was not created to be a heartwarming gesture, or a beacon of hope. It was a tangible mission. It was to be a house, a home, a place where Joey and his family could live without worry. But a regular house wasn't enough for Ken. He knew that in order to accommodate all of Joey's needs it had to be uniquely constructed. Ken consulted with different designers along with various medical professionals who were familiar with what Joey would need following his release from the Hospital for Sick Children. They informed him that Joey required a large, specially built Jacuzzi-sized tub in order to bathe, an elevator so he could move from floor to floor, hallways to fit a large wheelchair, special toilets, an intercom system that could enable easy communication throughout the house, and a top-of-the-line fire-and-smoke-alarm system, along with many more items that had to be designed and specially built.

When the question of where the house was going to be built came up early in the planning process, Ken felt the only logical place was on the same plot of land where the old house burned down. The charred bones of the old home had already been cleared away, so the land was ready to accommodate a new one. Furthermore, building a better home on the same ground where the older one died just felt right to Ken.

One of the biggest difficulties in the project had to do with something that neither Ken nor Dellsi, nor any of the people offering their help, could control: the weather. It was already late autumn by this point, and while the beauty of the changing leaves often brought smiles to the faces of the Orillia residents who got to admire them, for Ken, Dellsi, and the contractors and volunteers, those changing leaves were a ticking clock.

Like in most of Ontario and the better part of Canada, winter in Orillia operates entirely on its own schedule. It has been known to arrive as early as Labour Day, the Monday after the first weekend of September, while extending its stay well past Easter, belligerently postponing the arrival of spring. Orillian winters are also notoriously cold and windy due to its close proximity to Lake Simcoe. There is no way to know from year to year whether or not the winter will be long or short, bitter or mild, full of snow or light on precipitation. One certainty though, regardless of the temperament of winter, is that construction work during Canada's most famous season is extremely difficult. That is why many large projects are often paused until the spring, when they kick back into high gear until the end of autumn. However, Ken knew his project could not enjoy that luxury. Joey needed a home, and if he waited to start construction the following spring, the house would not be completed until late summer or early autumn at the earliest. That was far too late. Ken was determined to have the house completed by the spring of 1989.

The transition from idea to the gathering of people necessary to manifest that idea to the breaking of ground was miraculously fast. In what seemed like no time at all, detailed blueprints were drawn up by skilled designers, while the delegation of who would be doing what was conducted thoroughly and respectfully. And when it came to the number of people and companies that chose to volunteer their skills, materials, and time to the project Ken and his wife came up with, the list, compiled by Ken and Dellsi and printed by the *Packet and Times*, was as staggering as it was inspiring. It included the following names under the title "A Salute to Joe's Army":

> William Walters Construction – Site Foreman, Mastertoll – John McNeill, Rob and Janie Davies, D.&D. Pumps – Dave Fulsom, Westmount Church Marg Goodchild, Moly Maid, Duro Pumps – Paul Henderson, Jim Beavis, Donna Walters, Rod Young Architect – Ivan Cobbe, Glen Rest Sheet Metal Limited – Bill Colyer, Scott Hamlin, Doug Hembly, Spencer and Ruth Potter, Dave Derbecker Plumbing, Bill Hopkins, Greg Mulligan – Bourne, Jenkins & Mulligan, Mary Ellen Mulligan, D&S Contracting – Don Ferris, C&R Short Construction, Mike Sinclair, P&D Wells, Roward Pipeline Company Ltd. – Mike Stevens, Keith Mills,

Aknor Construction, Ron Kolbe, McGill Sanitation, K&S Cranes – Ken Watling, Ken Rogers Plumbing & Heating, Trillium Cable, Econo Air – Bill and Paul Tolland, Custom Gas – Roy Coneybeare, Orillia Township, Orillia Health Unit, Bill Temple, Lock, Stock & Barrel – Ed Ansdel, Woodhead Plumbing, Lindsay Electric, Jane Grant, Elaine McCreith, Nedco Electric (Barrie), Solar Industries, A&D Interiors, Tim Lauer, Complete Building Contractors, Home Building Supplies (Staynor), Brockwell Motors (Staynor), Tom Daikoff, James Bull, Dick's Floor Specialists, Ramca Tile, Olympia Tile, Darden & Stanton – Land Surveyors, Uniplant Industries Inc., Joe Mattwee, Jack Blackwell, Champlain Overhead Doors, Lori Powel, Bill Tiffin, Bancroft Windows – Matt Ireland, Gail Reeves, Renkema, George James, Peter Vriezbma, Dave Deval, Triangle Supply, E.L. Hamlen, Complete Rentals, Ron Simmons, Warren Doner, Satellite Specialist (Orillia), Tom and Yvonne Ruff, Bruce and Catherine Gallivan, Conrad Martin, Can-Save Insulation, Northland Floor Supplies – Chris Lalonde, Bill Lalonde, Rob Murphy, Ted Lawrence, Shamrock Chimney, Jack Ferguson, Air Built Industries (Markham), Camvoy Masonry, Mrs. Montgomery, Waggs Laundry, Banks & Flemming, George Evans, R&B Installations, Nelson Gravel, Burman and Fellows Electric (Toronto), Jon Burman, Warren Vause, Scott Anderson, Don Mazepa, Shawn Richter, John Fellows, Kevin Parsons, Dianne Jackson, Kathryn Weller, Andrews Lighting (Toronto), Nedco (Toronto), Westburne Electric (Toronto), Ruddy Electric (Toronto), Revere Electric (Toronto), Main Electric (Toronto), Danbel Industries (Toronto), Union

Electric (Toronto), Paul Wolf Lighting (Toronto),
Lindsay Electric (Toronto), Chrus Family, Chrus
Plumbing Employees, Sterwyn Electric (Toronto),
Hygrade Fuel (Toronto), Filet of Sole (Toronto),
Nuroc Plumbing (Toronto), Neelands Refrigeration
(Toronto), Oakwood Mechanical (Toronto), Marksbury
Construction (Toronto), Imperial Tobacco (Toronto),
Fred Dumais, Lease a Sign Company, Friends of the
Mal Fellos Fund (Toronto), McPhee Painting, Marvel
Painting – John Arsenov, Dusk to Dawn – Sandra
Heiriman, Ron Gableson, Roger Poirer, Simcoe
Coating, Barry Morrow Roofing, Joyce Skinner, North
Ridge Contracting Ltd., Georgian Heavy Equipment
– George Thompson, Morris Shelswell, Bob, Gerry
and Ron Barkey, Terry Hubbell, Mariposa Roofing,
Electrolux Canada, Al Cook Aluminum Siding,
Stan Boyell, Cabinet Tree – Gary & Dan Stanford,
Champlain Concrete, Bob Hewitt, Barrie Trim and
Mouldings, Tony Mercado, Shriner's, Atlas Block, Taps
Whole Sale Company, Housser's Paint, Mike Cooper,
Stewart Construction, Mrs. Hurst, Bill Grant Decorator,
Dean Chisholm, Country Produce, Randy O'Connel,
Barrie Plumbing, Cathy Miller, Allen Robertson, Chris
Clark Diesel Company, Barrie Glass and Mirror, Gord
Morrison, Joe Naughton, Archie Denne, Ian Brunck,
Beaver Lumber, Sarjeant Company Limited, R.C.
Fire Systems – Ron Chidwick, Novus Engineering,
Emco Supply, Scepter Manufacturing, Orser Electric
– Bill Bundy, Mr. & Mrs. Clements & Sons, Orillia
Steel Roofing, Steel Tile Co., Mrs. James Sleightholm,
Canada Windows – Don Mills, Wiles Haulage,
Frank McMillan, Reme M. Van Belt, Paul's Sealing

Service, Annis Way Signs – Don Mayor, Beaverbrook Estates Inc. – Bruno Nazzzicone, Barrie Lumber Yard, United Home Centre, Barb Christie, Ontario Hydro Inspection Dept., Washago Lumber, Filter Queen, Success Safety Products, Mrs. Linda Taggart, The Traditional Hardwood Floor, Peter Rayfiled, Mr. & Mrs. Ken Emery, Jim Wood, Walter Iles, Frank Orr, Imants Kitchen Cupboards, Michael Monteith Enterprises Limited, Norweld Steel Co., Al-Can Building, Jim Brand, Alcan Action Trusses, Motorola Cellular Phone, Beverley Ketelaara, Phil Murray, Kathey Bull, Martha Bull, Cellro Communications, Butch McClintock, Bob Ween, Weldwood of Canada Ltd. – Bill Ewert, Future Trend Kitchen Designs, Beech Builder & Suppliers, Mike Proctor, J.S. Contracting, Johnson Construction, Ken Manogold, George and Anne Pellett, Mid Town Disposal, Beam Vacuum, Carol Fernie, Lauer's Restaurant Equipment Ltd., Designer's Alley – Gord Cook, Tony Colangelo, Severn Lighting Centre, Culligan, Switzer Buildall, Doug MacDonald, Colin Sheridan, Anglo Contracting, Universal Drapery, Woolworth Co. Ltd., Best Buy Buildall, Steven Rope Stencil, Hitch House, Mr. Wenn, John Dawson, Fred Allin Construction, John Kerteston, Ace Fire Sprinkler, Hytrac Elevator Co. Ltd. – Hubert Houben, Glen Forsyette, C.T.E. Telephone, G.I.T. Fire Security Systems, Peniston Industries – Ben Westlaken, Tim Lovering, Century Kitchen Cupboards, Frank Provenzano, Ontario Hydro Linesmen, Mariposa Wood Products, Canada Door, Spatek – Wally Wray, Gordon & Soskin Co., Margo Construction, McKenzie Financial – James O'Donnell,

Bill Thorburn, Arris Craft Corp. – Walter Muxworthy, Junior Stairs, Colin McMillan, Mike Stevens, Guardian Angels Church, Marv Plant, Phil Anderson, The Silk Nursery, Mary Matthews, Al Clark, The Brick, Don Shave, Rennaissance Marble – Len Biggart, J. Koza Interiors, Beaver Lumber – Leo Tucker, Ken Casey, Neil Reid, B.B. Bargoons – Diane Smith, D. & D. Central Systems, Tim Horton's, Kentucky Fried Chicken, Frank & Melita Miller, Derlyn Valley, Central Supply Toronto, Chubb Fire Security, A&B Galleries – Art McClary, Pat Pringle, Carrie Pethick – Miss Orillia Fall Fair, Martin Walsh, Weller Tree Service, Peter and Nancy Clare, Charles Quinn, St. James Anglican Church, Garry Scandlin, Dominion Lumber, Federal Pioneer, Stewart Forest, TPA Administrative Services Ltd., Orillia Y's Menettes, Bogdon & Gross Furniture Co. Ltd., Meryl Stewart, Todd Bradley, Steve Bradley, Roy Bradley, Troy Bradley, Ed Sears, Ross Quinlan, Gary Poole, Paul Elam, Stan Cowie, Wally Rainbow, Ross Wilson, Bille Bette, Paul Debattista, Dave Tully, Bernie Morash, Bing Priest, Seal Taping Service, Dutch Touch Cleaning Service, Tupperware Barrie, Glen Archer, Len Shular, Gerry Revell, Todd Iles, Jan Brunch, Archie Denne, Morley Brechin, Brian Seaward & Co., Murray Taylor, Gerry Walters, Stephen Walters, Greg Walters, Mike Carpino, Frank Reda, Bill Hopkins Jr., Tom McGill, Ross Rabbitts, David Coward, Bill Pepper Haulage, Ram Satellite Systems, Neil Weller, Dave Dawson, Bruce Bingham, Bruce Barnard, Jack Crosby, John Derko – Oak Railing, Harding Carpets, Mrs. Peterson, Stewart Forest, Colin & Willma McMillan, Helen Cherrett – Mess Enders,

Craig Reading & Educational Services Inc., Studio Two, General Electric, Ideal Supply, Foster Appliance Ltd., Dial Delivery, Forsco Inc., Bill Jones, Thomspon Leisure Equipment, CKVR T.V. Orillia, Raney Fuel & Building Supplies, C.G.C. Drywall, Westrock, C.E. Shnier Co. Distributors, Richmond Carpet & Harding Vinyl Floors, Yolande Gysberg, American Standard Products, Moyen Faucets, Fiat Products, Jacuzzi Canada Ltd. – Clarence Renehard, Franklin Electric of Canada Ltd. – Gord Forrest, Moonstone T.V. & Satellite Systems, Linda Young & Doug Ciccarelli, Apple Computers, Sandra Dunning, Wilma and Rick Sharpe, Joe Brown, Jacques & Janine Maltais, Rita & Tony Ketelaara, Chamber of Commerce, Nicholson and Shelswell Insurance Brokers, Murray Cooper.

They concluded this long list with a disclaimer: "We would like to extend our appreciation to all people who wanted to remain anonymous and our apology to anyone we have overlooked. Ken and Dellsi McCann."

It didn't take long for headlines to accompany the construction of the house, most of which came from the *Packet and Times*. One of those headlines, "The House that Love Built," really struck a chord with people throughout Canada. And as construction continued throughout December, one headline called it "A Christmas Miracle." It was followed by several others that shared the same sentiment.

Ken McCann was even named Orillia's citizen of the year.

People throughout the country paid close attention to the construction of the house, and as the date set for completion, April 3, 1989, approached, the public's anticipation grew even more intense. They looked forward to seeing what they believed was the perfect ending to what was being framed by a series of newspaper articles

Photograph from the *Packet and Times* on February 3, 1989, of Ken McCann (left) accepting the award for Orillia Citizen of the Year for 1988, along with his wife, Dellsi McCann, and the *Packet and Times* publisher, Jack Marshall (right). "The house that love built," still under construction, is visible behind them. Photo by Mike Dodd.

and news broadcasts as a beautiful, touching story. It was a story presented with an abundance of wonderful photographs and interviews of hard-working men and women in thick coats, toques, and gloves building a house in the middle of an especially frigid winter. Together, they released a cloud of breath that hovered over the site just as a cloud of smoke had hovered over it less than a year earlier.

While the house was being built, all of the money that had been given to Joey was starting to build as well. Soon the donations had exceeded one hundred thousand dollars and were on the way to two hundred thousand dollars, in what had become a substantial trust fund. Donations to the fund came from a myriad of sources, all of which showed incredible generosity on behalf of the donors. Just a few examples include the following:

- A "Jazzamatazz" show at Park Street Collegiate led by Ted Duff raised $476.82.
- At Twin Lakes Secondary School, students participated in an auction, bidding on everything from concert tickets to running shoes, raising $2,400.
- Ten thousand dollars was donated by Speedorama, a custom car and motorcycle show held in Toronto each year, on behalf of musicians who appeared at the show.
- "The Stars Shine for Joe Philion" concert generated approximately $40,000.
- The proceeds from the Bridal Show 1988–89 that was held at the Highwayman Inn on September 25, 1988, went to the fund.
- Alex LeGard put on an organ concert in October 1988 at the Orillia Opera House, using equipment from Keenan's Piano and Organ Centre, and donated the proceeds to the fund.
- At an Orillia McDonald's, during McHappy Day on October 19, 1988, 1,728 Big Macs were sold, as well as balloons, raising $2,079.
- There was a "Joey Philion Day" at the Huronia Regional Centre with the goal of raising $1,000.
- The Orillia Township Firefighters raised $6,000 at a benefit dance.
- A dance was organized by Rick Sinotte, the owner of RIX, a teen dance club, that raised over $250.

The only time Linda and Mike met Ken and Dellsi was in a conference room in Orillia, where Ken outlined the details of the new house just as construction was set to begin. Still not sure if they even wanted to continue living in Orillia, Linda and Mike had questions and concerns, mainly about the decision to build the house on the same site where the old house was. They made it clear they were uncomfortable living on the same plot of land that had already taken so much from them. They also expressed their concern about the psychological effect living in the same spot where he was nearly killed would have on Joey. In response, Ken made it clear that the construction of the house was going to proceed as planned and if they opposed it, construction would cease.

'Christmas miracle' builds new house for burn boy

Burn victim Joey Philion's mom Linda Hawkins and brother Danny, with stepdad Mike, watch construction of their new house in Orillia yesterday — being built free by the community — as Joey (inset) recovers in a Toronto hospital. Michele Mandel's report, with photos: Pages 90, 91.

Linda, Danny, and Mike in front of "the house that love built" during its construction, from a *Toronto Sun* article. Photo by Tim McKenna.

It was an offer Linda and Mike couldn't refuse. They didn't have a home to go to and didn't have any money to rent one, let alone buy one. So they accepted the offer as graciously as they could, knowing that despite the heavy-handed manner with which they were told they were getting a free house, they were still getting a free house.

As the firm grip of the winter season started loosening, the house was nearly complete, and it looked beautiful. However, much more work needed to be done, and the deadline Ken had in mind was fast approaching. There were questions as to whether or not the house could be finished by the time Joey was set to arrive on April 3, but Ken was insistent it would.

With April 3 just a few days away and the house appearing finished, Ken was overjoyed at what he, his wife, and the volunteers had achieved. However, that joy was abruptly muted by a complication: the bathtub wasn't the correct size. Ken was shocked. He believed the five-foot-deep Jacuzzi that had already been installed was the right size, but he was told by a medical advisor that a bigger, more specially designed tub was required. Before Ken could start formulating how to fix that issue, another problem arose: the size of the elevator. Ken was told it wasn't big enough to accommodate Joey's brand new electric wheelchair that cost the hefty sum of twenty-five thousand dollars, paid for from proceeds from the fund. Ken frustratingly said that Joey wouldn't even be using the elevator the first year anyway, since he would just be going from the bedroom to the bathroom and back. More issues came up and Ken's goal of April 3 was deemed no longer feasible. The date was pushed back to April 17, much to his disappointment.

Joey was anxiously looking forward to moving into his new house, just as any other teenager would be. However, for Joey, moving into a new house wasn't as simple as it would be for any other teenager. He was going to require a great deal of care from a number of different people, including the following eleven professionals:

- primary nurse
- physical therapist
- plastic surgeon
- bacteriologist
- dietician
- recreational therapist
- school teacher
- psychiatrist
- occupational therapist
- public health nurse
- psychologist

Finding, hiring, and organizing these people and their schedules was proving more difficult than originally thought, and was not going to be done by April 3, so even if the house was ready by that date, Joey wouldn't have been. There was also a growing belief amongst many doctors, as well as Mike and Linda, that it might not be a good idea for Joey to move into the new house at all. Instead, it was suggested by several doctors, particularly those who treated him at the Shriners Burns Institute, that Joey should be transferred from the hospital to a rehab centre where he would receive the kind of intensive and focused care they believed was critical to his recovery.

As moving day approached, several doctors at the Hospital for Sick Children, along with many at the Shriners Burns Institute, remained concerned, based on the information they had about the house, that Joey's long-term care issues had not been sufficiently resolved. Those concerns were refuted by Dr. Walter Ewing, the associate medical officer of health for Simcoe County, where Orillia was located. Despite Dr. Ewing's assertion that there were no issues and Joey's long-term health was not at risk, the Hawkinses' family doctor, Dr. Tibor Harmathy, refused to care for Joey once he had moved into the new house. He insisted that he didn't believe Joey was ready to leave the hospital and didn't want to be held responsible for any future problems stemming from what he deemed to be an irresponsible decision.

The concerns of the doctors who didn't believe Joey should leave the hospital to move into the new house were not baseless. Parts of Joey's body weren't yet completely covered by new skin, including several holes the size of loonies and some even larger than that. On Joey's buttocks there was an uncovered spot the size of an adult palm, while on his shins there were uncovered areas that were approximately two centimetres wide and twenty centimetres long. But despite all the concerns expressed by some doctors, and the subsequent rebuttals by other doctors, and the public pressure to get the perfect ending to the story with which they'd become obsessed, the final word as to whether or not Joey was going to be discharged and allowed to move into his new house rested with one person, and one person only: Joey.

Should Joey have been allowed to make such an enormous decision that ended up having equally enormous repercussions in the future for both him and his family? The answer doesn't matter because he did make the decision to go home, and with the help of Ken McCann, Ken's wife, Dellsi, and the hundreds of volunteers who helped, there was now a home for him to go to.

•

On April 17, when Joey was finally discharged from the Hospital for Sick Children, he was transported back to Orillia where he was finally going to begin living in the house built for him and his family. He did not go straight to the house, however. Instead, at around 8:30 a.m., he was transported to the parking lot of the Cumberland Beach Public School, where he was welcomed by a crowd of people who had been anxiously waiting for him. It was raining, but none of Joey's fans seemed to care. There were over two hundred kids cheering for him as soon as he was slowly taken out of the ambulance that brought him from Toronto. They shouted, "Welcome home, Joey," while many of them held up signs with the words, "Welcome Home, Joe" written on them. It took mere seconds before the crowd swallowed Joey. Countless hands and fingers grazed his body, while the warm breath of the crowd pelted him from every side. Throughout it all, Joey smiled, truly appreciative of the adoration and congratulations he was receiving, while his Boston terrier puppy, Yoda, looked around nervously from his lap.

There were dozens of cars lining the streets along the short trip from the school to the new house. People poked their heads out of open car windows, shouting, smiling, and waving their hands at Joey. On the sidewalks were a horde of onlookers, waving at Joey, applauding, some even crying as he slowly passed them, offering slight waves of his hand.

Once Joey and his family reached the new house, which none of them had seen up to that point, they gasped. Despite the swamp of mud formed around the house after intense rain, Joey, Mike, Linda, and Danny couldn't believe what was resting in front of their eyes. The house was big and beautiful. It was painted sky blue, and the trees standing in front of it and around it were the same trees that had stood there before March 10 the year before, despite several of them catching fire that morning.

Joey and his family were only able to venture a few feet before a blockade of reporters and cameramen sprung up all around them, as if they rose from the muddy ground. There were representatives from a number of news outlets, including the *Globe and Mail*; the *Toronto Star*; the *Toronto Sun*; *CTV National News*; CFTO-DT, Toronto; CKCO-DT, Kitchener; CKVR-DT, Barrie; Citytv, Toronto; CBLT-DT, Toronto; Global TV; CBC News, *Midday*;

CBC News, *The Journal*; CHAY FM, Barrie; CFOR FM, Orillia; and the *Packet and Times*. Like the opening salvo of a battle, there was a volley of questions lobbed at Joey from all sides. He did his best to answer as many of the questions as he could, as politely as he could, thanking everybody for their support throughout his ordeal. He expressed his thanks to the people who built the house for him. He said he couldn't wait to get settled and to start living a normal life again. The reporters then turned their attention to Linda, who did her best to answer the questions as politely as she could, while masking the overwhelming exhaustion that could be seen in the darkness wrapped around her eyes.

After what Joey and Linda believed was enough time outside, in the rain, answering questions, they started making their way to the front door of the house, but the reporters and the cameras accompanying them wanted more. The crowd of onlookers remained where they were, as well, still applauding, still shouting, still smiling, and still cheering. Meanwhile, those most responsible for the construction of the house were mostly absent from the homecoming. Only a few of the volunteers showed up and they kept their distance, preferring to watch the celebration from afar. Even Ken McCann and his wife, Dellsi, were conspicuously absent that day. They refused to come, despite requests to do so by several of the media outlets. In an article published the following day by Jim Wilkes in the *Toronto Star*, when asked why so few of the volunteers who built the house chose to show up for Joey's homecoming, John Palmer, the mayor of Orillia, said that was typical of small-town folk. "We're a pretty modest bunch," he said. "People up here like to do things, but don't go after the credit."

Once inside the house and out of the rain, the family was even more amazed by the interior than the exterior. The house looked even bigger inside than it did outside. There was a den to the right as soon as they walked in, and a staircase leading to the second floor

"The house that love built" following its completion and several of the people responsible for its construction in a photo from the *Packet and Times* on April 17, 1989. Photo by Vik Kirsch.

on the left. As they proceeded down the hall, on the right was an enormous kitchen, wide and spacious with an island in the centre, and to the left was the living room. There was no furniture, not a single piece, which made the interior look even bigger. But with that size came worry, as Mike and Linda immediately started wondering how they were going to furnish such a huge space.

The family was about to make their way upstairs when, through the enormous windows at the rear of the house, which would have brought an ample amount of sunlight into the kitchen and living room if not for the pouring rain, they were blinded by far more bizarre rays of light. Mike and Linda stepped back incredulously when, through the windows, they saw a small group of reporters taking pictures of them.

Mike and Linda tried to politely gesture for the reporters to leave them alone, to give them the peace they desperately craved, but the reporters didn't budge. They continued taking pictures while moving around constantly, trying to get the best angles they could, not caring in the least that they were getting soaked by the rain.

Mike's aggravation grew more intense when he saw the discomfort on Linda's already drained face, along with the exhaustion on Joey's. Danny remained indifferent to the snapping pictures, instead focusing on the enormity of the house he could now call home. Mike approached the windows and aggressively waved his hands, while sternly saying loudly enough for the reporters to hear that they were all very tired and just wanted to rest, and asking if they could respect the family's privacy. The reporters ignored Mike's requests and continued snapping picture after picture, positioning their lenses around him in attempts to get the best pictures of Joey they could. Their appetite for more photographs grew even more ravenous whenever Joey or Linda made eye contact with them.

Fed up, but not wanting to do anything drastic that could cause a scene that would surely be recorded and published for the world to see, Mike walked to the side of one of the giant windows and closed the blinds he was thankful had already been installed. But the reporters just moved to the next window, forcing Mike to repeat the process again and again until every window in the house's first floor had been sealed off. Finally, the flashing lights had ceased, but looking around the darkened interior of the house's first floor, the spacious dimensions seemed different. While the comfort those dimensions presented remained intact, the sudden absence of natural light made him feel eerily boxed in.

Danny, as he often did, smashed the tension that had momentarily taken hold by asking to see the basement, to go upstairs, to see his bedroom, to see the Jacuzzi, to see everything, especially the elevator, which, as soon as he used it once, he couldn't stop using. Up and down, up and down, he couldn't get enough of it. During every trip he laughed and shouted loud enough for his voice to be heard throughout the house. He couldn't believe there was an elevator in his new home!

Succumbing to the same eagerness the youngest member of the family had so openly and joyously expressed, the rest of the family proceeded to explore the entire house from the basement to the second floor. Just like the main floor, on the second floor there was no furniture to speak of in any of the rooms except Joey's, which in addition to being the biggest and most well-lit room had a specially designed bed, a pair of dressers, a chair, a big TV positioned perfectly for him to watch, and other pieces of equipment he needed. It was a magnificent set-up, and a stark contrast to the sparse milieu of the rest of the house.

When asked about the lack of furniture, Ken McCann said that aside from the fridge, stove, washer, dryer, drapes, and blinds, all of which were included, donated, and installed by the volunteers who helped build the house, the rest of the furniture should be the responsibility of Mike and Linda. "I feel they have to do something for the house — that's only fair," he said.

In 1998, ten years after winning Orillia's citizen of the year award for spearheading the construction of "the house that love built," Ken McCann was elected mayor of Orillia. Whether or not his role in the conception, construction, and overseeing of the house had anything to do with his victory is for those who voted for him to say.

•

Mike worked as much as he could, finding whatever jobs he could, and with the weather getting warmer, his focus after moving into the new house was on construction, mainly roofing. Through his roofing work, he was able to get the furniture he needed by forgoing his pay in favour of discounted furniture. And in what seemed like no time at all, Mike, Linda, Joey, and Danny (who had just turned twelve a week before they moved in) were able to turn the new house into their home. Soon, the interior started looking more personalized. There were framed family pictures on the walls and food filling the cupboards and fridge. There was also an army of VHS tapes of the finest horror and action movies the 1980s produced, from *The Texas Chainsaw Massacre Part 2* and *A Nightmare on Elm Street 3: Dream Warriors* to *RoboCop* and *Rambo: First Blood Part II*, left all over the living room and kitchen, often by Danny and his friends who came over and watched them. Danny even left his Rambo-style serrated knife with the removable compass at the hilt on the couch or the kitchen table. He and his friends also played in the elevator, laughing the entire time, shouting messages to each other with the intercom, and playing in the large, mostly empty basement. For Danny, the house was a playground. It was also the first time he could be somewhere that he could call home since March 9, 1988.

Meanwhile, Mike and Linda were discovering how much work it took to care for Joey outside of a hospital setting, and how exhausting that work was, despite the trained professionals who were almost always present to assist. And despite the beautiful, wonderfully intentioned surroundings given to him by the people of his community, Joey's life remained every bit as gruelling, stressful, and painful as it had been in the Shriners Burns Institute and the Hospital for Sick Children.

At 7:00 a.m. every day except for Sundays, when he got to sleep in, Joey had to have his morning bath. However, bathing for Joey, like everything else, was not like it was for other people. Wearing a mask and gloves, Mike had to carefully lift Joey from his bed to his wheelchair before taking him to the large bathroom in Joey's bedroom. Afterward, he had to remove all of Joey's clothes, and carefully lift his nude body from the wheelchair to a specially designed chair in the Jacuzzi, while the tub filled up with lukewarm water. As the tub filled, Mike inspected Joey's body, which was covered with open sores that were always leaking pus and blood, along with the collection of spiderweb-looking skin grafts. His body smelled like rotted flesh. The pus was the most pungent. The rancid scent was overwhelming enough to make Mike gag the first few days, but in time he got used to it.

Once water filled the tub, Mike had to gently scrub Joey's entire body with a washing pad and soap, giving the most attention to the open sores while making sure he didn't tear the new skin or worsen the existing wounds. The process of cleaning Joey's body usually took between forty-five minutes to an hour. By the end of the bath, the water was dark maroon. As the ghastly water drained, Mike had to quickly scrub the tub until there were no traces of the old water. Afterward, he carefully dried Joey's body before transferring him from the tub to his wheelchair, then brought him back to his bed. Before he could transfer Joey from the chair to the bed, however, he had to place special pads on top of the bed to ensure Joey wouldn't stain it. He then lifted Joey from the chair and placed him gently on the pads.

It would be about 8:30 a.m. by this point, and that's when the dressings had to be applied. Each part of Joey's body had to be dressed individually, depending how his open sores looked that day. Sometimes Mike used 4" x 4" gauze to wrap a specific limb, be it an arm, leg, or the torso, while other times, if the open sores were especially hostile, he had to apply special creams to treat them before dressing them with gauze. The dressing process usually took between one and a half and two hours. It would be about 10:00 to 10:30 a.m. by this point. The creams were extremely expensive, and Mike used jar after jar day after day. The gauze, which was used just as much as the creams, was also costly. Luckily, the Ontario Health Insurance Plan (OHIP) covered the costs of those items.

Breaks also had to be taken throughout the dressing process because it was painful for Joey, but it had to be done twice a day, once in the morning when he woke up and once at night before he went to bed. And if the open sores were particularly bad on any given day, Mike had to give Joey a second bath before his nightly dressing.

In between baths and dressings, Joey had to be fed all of his meals by either Mike or Linda. Each feeding took between thirty and sixty minutes. When Joey had to defecate, a specific pad was placed on the bed. He would then have to be positioned on the pad and rolled to the side so he could defecate on it. The pad would then have to be immediately disposed of, and Mike or Linda would have to clean him. To urinate, Joey would go in a jug that had to be constantly emptied and cleaned.

When it came to taking Joey anywhere, from appointments, which were constant, to getting some fresh air, the process of getting him dressed, while relatively short, was always painful because it involved a great deal of bending just to get into regular clothing like track pants and T-shirts. The pain had become so intense that specially designed articles of clothing had to be made with a lot of Velcro and patches. After he was dressed, Mike lifted Joey and put him in his wheelchair. They took the elevator to the first floor, proceeded out of the house, and got into a new red-and-grey van, paid for with forty thousand dollars from the fund. The van had a specially designed lift that got Joey and his wheelchair inside.

When Joey was not enduring baths, dressings, and a constant barrage of appointments, he was working with the eleven different professionals who were always coming to see him, treat him, and exercise him, which was always painful.

In the evenings, because sleeping remained a struggle, Joey stayed up very late. He usually watched TV while constantly asking Mike, Linda, and even Danny (whoever remained awake, as somebody always had to, until Joey finally fell asleep) to bring him food, water, and whatever else he might need, including emptying his urine container and helping him defecate.

That's what the days in "the house that love built" quickly came to be, and those days started blurring into one long hot summer that blurred into the following autumn, and winter, and spring, until the next summer arrived.

Once the constant routine of caring for Joey had been established, there wasn't much room for anything else for Mike or Linda, and with Mike also having to work during whatever time he wasn't required to care for Joey, finding time just to be alone was virtually impossible for a couple who had only been married for a few years.

Mike and Linda's love after the fire became a spoil of war, something they both had to fight for, and if neither was as up to the task as the other, victory would have been impossible. But fight they did, under almost impossible circumstances, but as in any war, the longer the fight, the tougher the toll and the deeper the scars. The price for the prize of the love they saved was high, and mere weeks after moving into "the house that love built," Mike and Linda were starting to pay it.

Following the fire, and throughout 1988 and the first four months of 1989, they were in a constant state of turmoil, often apart for days and weeks at a time. Linda was always by Joey's side at the Shriners Burns Institute and the Hospital for Sick Children while Mike, when he wasn't able to be at those hospitals, was either working or tending to other important matters. While that physical separation was difficult for both of them, it was also understood, but when that physical separation was no longer an issue they quickly discovered that, despite being in the same home day after day for the first time in more than a year, a distance still existed between them.

In the days following the fire, Mike was faced with a decision: to stay or to leave. It was the kind of decision that ultimately paved the way for the rest of his life. And despite his relative youth at the time, he was conscious of the magnitude of the decision and made it in the same amount of time it took to conceive it. He wasn't going anywhere. He had married Linda and he loved her, and he would continue to love her and support her until the very end, and that was that. But like the battle to maintain their love, the battle to continue down the path of unconditional support through the hardest of times took a toll on him.

When he married Linda, he already knew her kids came first. That was a foregone conclusion he understood and accepted. He was okay with being ranked below Linda's kids, knowing that position still entailed plenty of time for the relationship between him and her. But after the fire that time was severely reduced, and in the new house it was reduced even more.

Mike started feeling that he didn't matter. He cared for Joey at all hours, worked to make whatever money he could when he could, was there to support Linda while also being a father to Danny, and felt like he was getting absolutely nothing in return. He could no longer have conversations with his wife about anything other than Joey, and if they did manage to start talking about something other than Joey they always ended up right back at him. How was he feeling? Was he okay? What if this happens to him? What if that happens to him? What will Joey do in two years, three years, ten years? What about Joey? What about Joey? WHAT ABOUT JOEY?

It was suffocating. And whenever Mike brought up that he just wanted to talk about, think about, live for, something other than Joey, if only for a short time, Linda responded angrily. She snapped at him, yelling that Joey was her son, that she thought she had lost him more times than she could count, that she had given every ounce of her energy, her mind, her heart, her soul to him, and all she wanted was the support of the man she loved most.

Mike felt sick to his stomach when he'd hear his wife's passionate replies because they were all true and all valid, but that validity also brought forth its own set of questions as to what his position in the relationship had become. Was he a husband, an equal partner to his wife? Because he didn't feel like that anymore. Or was he just a tireless means of assistance that was around just to do whatever was needed, always on call, no questions asked and no complaints made?

He had a life of his own, dreams and ambitions of his own. Weren't they every bit as deserving to be fulfilled as anybody else's? Yet every time he contemplated that question, every time he thought about himself, he always felt like it was wrong to do so. He felt guilty, as if he had no business ever thinking about himself, knowing that Linda also had her own dreams and her own ambitions, and yet was able to erase them for the sake of Joey. It was a sacrifice Mike found astounding. He admired it and respected it deeply, seeing first-hand how selfless her decision to virtually eliminate herself was, allowing her to reach a point of fanatical obsession over her son's welfare. But — and this is what Mike wrestled with every single day — while Joey was Linda's first-born son and she took the responsibility beyond seriously, he wasn't Mike's first-born son. He wasn't his son at all.

Eventually Mike stopped telling Linda how he felt about anything to do with himself. He knew she loved him and did truly care about him, of that he never had a doubt, but that love, that caring, had been buried too deep to express. The weight of Joey proved too heavy, too consuming. Her unconditional love for her son, as awe-inspiring as it was, had alienated anybody outside their bond, including Mike.

As well, Linda's drinking had started becoming an issue in Boston. The few nights she wasn't with Joey at the Shriners Burns Institute and couldn't bear the cries from grieving parents in the Halcyon House, she and Mike would visit one of the nearby bars. The first few times it was enjoyable, a few drinks and even a few laughs shared between the couple whose lives had experienced a shattering detonation. But soon a few drinks turned into a few more, and a few more after that. Like so many people enduring a dramatic increase in stress, Linda quickly realized the more she drank, the less she felt, and the less she hurt. The worst nights were when Joey had just been through one of his major surgeries and his survival was impossible to predict until the following day, or, when he was scheduled to have a major surgery the following morning. Either way, the anxiety was often too much to bear, so she tried to drink it into submission.

Linda was not one to ever back down from a conflict. When she drank too much and somebody looked at her the wrong way, Linda aggressively addressed it. On one occasion, after she had been drinking excessively at a bar in Boston, she was told to leave, but on her way out she got into an argument with the bouncer who was twice her size, a fact that didn't affect her decision to yell at him. Growing more impatient with her, the bouncer threatened to call the police, when Mike interfered and told him about Joey, about the Shriners Burns Institute, about the fire, about everything, firing off the long list of traumas his wife was shouldering in rapid succession.

The bouncer looked at Linda. Her eyes were blurred with anxiety, confusion, pain, rage, and disorientation. In a soft voice, he urged her to calm down. He told her he wasn't going to call the police but she had to leave. He turned to Mike and told him to get his wife to a safe place. He told him that, regardless of what she had endured, he feared if she acted that way with the wrong person she would be putting herself at great risk. Mike thanked the bouncer and convinced Linda to come with him back to the Halcyon House.

Occurrences like this, while not constant, happened often enough to let Mike know that Linda's drinking was becoming a problem he couldn't fix, or judge. He had his own vices, his own dependencies that helped him ease the tightened grip of stress, fear, and anxiety that never seemed to let go since the fire. There were no other ways they could think of to deal with the avalanche of crises that seemed to pummel them on a daily basis. Therapy? There was no money for that and even if there had been, neither Linda nor Mike had time to actually do it.

When they moved into the new house, Linda stopped getting drunk to the point of getting kicked out of big-city bars and picking fights with bouncers, but the drinking itself continued. She often had a hangover in the morning, which was why Mike always had to wake up early to assist Joey with his baths and dressings. The hangovers became so consistent that Mike and Linda made an agreement that when she finally did wake up, it was her responsibility to feed Joey his lunch and dinner, as well as getting him dressed and bringing him what he needed throughout the afternoon. And at night, when she started drinking again, Mike took over and assisted Joey with his evening baths and dressings.

Homemade B-52s were Linda's go-to drink. She made them much stronger than any bar would serve. She'd prepare big batches of the milky cocktail and freeze whatever was left over, ensuring she always had some around whenever she wanted. They were just like the ice cream always available to the kids in the Halcyon House, and just like that ice cream, Linda's B-52s were a treat that made her feel better. It wasn't long before those treats became a daily occurrence, a dependency, something she didn't just want but needed, especially when the routine of caring for Joey had become as overwhelming as it was monotonous.

Occasionally, Linda drank until she passed out in the backyard.

•

Nia spent a lot of time with Joey in "the house that love built." Her presence was always welcomed not just by him, but also by Mike,

Linda, and Danny, because it was clear from the very beginning that she had no ulterior motives and no ambition to cling to his celebrity. A sweet, caring, compassionate companion, she liked Joey, and he liked her, and that was that. They went outside a lot where they talked, laughed, and enjoyed each other's company. Inside the house they acted like teenagers, whether that involved sneaking a few drinks of alcohol when the opportunity presented itself or, in some instances, physically enjoying their relationship, which was not the easiest thing to do, but they managed, and would often laugh about it afterward, especially when they were caught by either Mike or Linda.

The attention and affection Nia showed Joey during that period was every bit as critical to his recovery as the pints of blood he received during his routine transfusions or the daily cleanings and dressings he endured. However that blissful time did not last, as the attention, praise, and worship he received upon his arrival at

Joey sits in his wheelchair in the living room of "the house that love built" with his girlfriend, Nia Herhily (right), Danny, and Nia's sister.

the house not only continued but increased dramatically. The more attention he got from strangers, including several famous ones that most people could only dream of meeting, the less time Joey had to enjoy with those who really knew him and genuinely cared about him, including Nia. Over time, as Joey's celebrity continued to rise, so did Nia's discomfort. She couldn't handle the constant attention and the pressure that came with it, so they broke up, and while she continued to care about him, and continued wanting to be his friend, they started seeing each other less and less.

At first, Mike, Linda, Joey, and Danny thought the photographers who harassed them the day they moved into the house would linger for another day or two after they moved in, taking as many pictures as they could before getting their fill. However, even after weeks and months went by, the photographers continued coming around day and night, positioning their camera lenses through the blinds whenever they were opened just to snap a picture of the hero, Joey Philion.

One Sunday morning at 8:00 a.m, a van filled with seniors from Cambridge, Ontario, arrived at the house. The tour guide proceeded to knock on the door, waking everybody up, including Joey who, like the rest of his family, enjoyed sleeping in that day. Groggy, wiping sleep out of his eyes, Mike answered the door in a housecoat and was shocked at the sight of a dozen elderly citizens standing outside of the door, their bulky cameras raised, the straps wrapped around their necks.

"Can I help you?"

"We want to meet Joey, and get a picture of him," one of the group members replied. "He's such a hero."

Shocked at what was going on, he told the group that Joey hadn't even woken up, let alone had his bath.

"We really want to meet him," another group member said.

Looking at the enthusiasm on the faces of the group members, and sensing their insistence, Mike told them to wait a few minutes, then went upstairs and told Linda what was going on.

"Are you serious?" she asked.

He nodded.

"Can't you tell them to go away? It's Sunday morning, for Christ's sake."

"You want me to tell a dozen senior citizens to piss off?" he replied with a chuckle.

Mike went to Joey's room, woke him up, and told him what was going on. Joey, as he often did, agreed to see the people who travelled to see him and take his picture.

The family had a good laugh about the whole thing, except it started happening again and again, with a different group of senior citizens arriving each time, eventually leading to Mike and Linda having to put a stop to it. As a result, they endured harsh criticism from many people in the community. How dare they deny people the chance to see the hero, Joey Philion, at eight in the morning on a Sunday!

One night, when Mike and Linda had a sliver of free time, they went to a bar in the centre of Orillia. They sat and ordered a couple of drinks, but before the drinks even arrived a guy sat next to them and immediately started asking about Joey. How was he doing? What does he do with his days? How is his life? Annoyed, Mike asked the guy who he was, and bound by his profession the guy replied that he was a reporter from the *Packet and Times*. Linda told him to go away, while Mike called him an asshole for bothering them when it was abundantly clear they were spending some time alone, not hosting a press conference.

Everywhere they went in Orillia they were asked about Joey. They were pointed at and gossiped about behind their backs. They were constantly stared at with the kinds of looks that indicate that the onlooker was just talking about you or was about to talk about you as soon as they stopped looking at you. Everybody had opinions. Everybody seemed to know exactly what they were supposed to do. When Mike and Linda were out, people openly opined as to why they weren't at home taking care of Joey, and when they stopped going out, people opined as to why they thought they were too good to associate with the community. The whispers, the gawking stares, the constant opinion pieces about them in the *Packet and Times* were overwhelming. While they thought adding some humour to the tension whenever they were approached by somebody might lighten things up, it often had the opposite effect, as people openly and sometimes viciously criticized them for daring to make jokes about anything to do with Joey. The expectations placed upon them from the community were as impossible to live up to as they were ridiculous to impose.

While concentrated mostly in Orillia, attention followed the family wherever they went in Ontario. Joey was asked to participate in different media events in Toronto, from television and radio broadcasts to honorary award ceremonies during which he was showered with praise, to press conferences detailing his progress. Each event required the usual few hours of preparation prior to the nearly two-hour drive to the city.

While getting to and from these events was gruelling, especially for Joey, it was equally hard for Linda, who was obsessed with making sure he was properly and safely secured in the van. Her attention to her son's well-being during those constant trips to Toronto (which as soon as they entered the city limits often involved police escorts) was so intense that on one occasion on Bloor Street, not far from Yonge Street, following a radio interview, while Linda was buckling Joey into the van, an unannounced visitor entered. Joey was overjoyed at the sight of him. Linda was annoyed. While the van was large, its interior space was not abundant, and every additional person made it more cramped, especially for her when she was crouched down trying to secure Joey as perfectly as she could. Meanwhile, Joey and the visitor started talking. Finally, after saying goodbye, the visitor left, granting Linda a little more space to check one last time that her son was as safe as possible. Satisfied that Joey was secure enough for the trip home, she got out of the van, stretched, and asked him who the visitor was.

"Wayne Gretzky."

"Who?"

"You don't know who Wayne Gretzky is, Mom?"

"No."

Joey laughed. Moments later Mike arrived.

"Do you know who Wayne Gretzky is?" Linda asked.

"Of course," Mike replied. "Why?"

"He was just here, talking to Joey."

"Are you serious?"

Mike looked at Joey, who was smiling widely and nodding. He then started looking around, hoping to catch a glimpse of the legendary hockey player, but to no avail.

"Shit," he said. "I missed the chance to meet Wayne Gretzky?"

He looked at Linda, who just shrugged and said, "Can we go home now? Joey needs to rest."

Like any young celebrity, Joey started buying into the flattery constantly lavished upon him. Who could blame him? It would be difficult, if not impossible, to resist believing that you were, as Joey was constantly told, an inspiration, a miracle, a warrior, a hero, when sports legends like Bobby Orr and Larry Bird, actors like Christopher Reeve, singers like Elton John, Michael Jackson, and Phil Collins, and even the prime minister of Canada, Brian Mulroney, were saying it. But with that inescapable belief came the entitlement and attitude to match.

At the onset of the 1990s, after living in "the house that love built" for over eight months, Joey started getting more demanding. He had a bell that he rang whenever he wanted something and it didn't take long for everybody in the house, even Linda, whose

Linda, Danny, and Cherie Tuohy, outside "the house that love built."

patience knew virtually no bounds when it came to Joey, to cringe whenever they heard its constant dinging. He openly stated that the house was his (which was technically true, as Ken McCann and the majority of the volunteers insisted heavily, and publicly) and he never failed to make that clear to Mike and Linda whenever he thought they weren't acting the way he wanted them to.

Was he being petulant? Yes. Did he act like an entitled jerk? Yes. Did his ego grow enormously in an incredibly short period of time? Absolutely. Was such behaviour unusual for a teenager in his position? Of course not. Was his behaviour compounded by the abrupt blinding from the worldwide celebrity spotlight? Definitely.

In a report from the *Toronto Star* that was published in late 1988, Joey was asked to talk about how much he valued life after surviving the fire. He was quoted as saying, "The kids in Orillia, all they do is drink and do drugs, they don't really think about life at all."

Because of Joey's celebrity status, his comments were immediately picked up by every newspaper in Toronto and throughout Ontario and were even picked up by several newspapers in different provinces. Soon his words went national, and not long afterward Orillia was tagged with the nickname "Dope City."

While it was miraculous that he survived his ordeal, Joey didn't magically become more in tune with the sociological complexities of a small Ontario city. He was fifteen and under the influence of potent pain medication. Yet the vitriolic response from many members of that city's community, including children his own age, got so intense that Joey ended up having to issue a public apology.

ESCAPE

IN THE SPRING OF 1973, MR. BROWN, AN ENGLISH TEACHER AT BENDALE
Secondary School in Scarborough, showed his students several
slides from a trip he took to Vancouver Island. He drove there and
back, stopping numerous times along the way to admire everything
the vast Canadian landscape had to offer. He showed the students
pictures of everything from the seemingly endless water of Lake
Superior near Thunder Bay and the army of silos on farms stretching across the flatlands of Saskatchewan to the snow-capped peaks
of the Rockies of Alberta and the Ogden Point Pier in Victoria,
British Columbia.

Some of the students were bored by Mr. Brown's presentation,
constantly glancing at the clock, hoping it would tick faster so
they could leave and hang out with their friends outside, while
others feigned attention and enthusiasm, hoping it would endear
them to the teacher responsible for their final grades. Meanwhile,
a couple of students were genuinely enthralled by what they
were seeing. Their minds were blown by the extravagance of the
scenery that only grew more magnificent when transferred from
the strict parameters of the images to the limitless capacity of

their imaginations. One of those students was thirteen-year-old Michael Robert Hawkins.

The seed was planted. Mike was going to do what Mr. Brown did. He was going to make his way west until he saw the waves of the Pacific Ocean caressing the beaches of Vancouver Island. It was a journey of more than 4,300 kilometres. He had never left Scarborough, however, let alone the province of Ontario, and he was too young to drive a car, at least legally.

Mike's grandparents lived in Huntsville, Ontario, a little over two hundred kilometres north of Scarborough. He liked it there, and while it lacked the majestic beauty of British Columbia, it still offered him the natural surroundings that felt right to him. His grandfather often took him fishing when he visited. However, he didn't get to visit Huntsville as often as he wanted, since he only got to go when his mother drove him. Seeing an opportunity, he decided that was as good a place as any to start learning how to travel on his own. As soon as summer vacation started, a month after seeing Mr. Brown's life-altering presentation, Mike hitchhiked for the first time, all the way to Huntsville.

When he reached Huntsville and told his grandparents what he had done, he was immediately asked how his mother had permitted it, to which he shrugged and said he had told her what he was going to do and she didn't say no. With his grandparents not putting up an argument, Mike enjoyed a few days in Huntsville before heading back to Scarborough, hitchhiking the whole way.

Just a few days later, he was already getting the itch to hitchhike again. His friends thought he was crazy but his mother didn't seem bothered by it, so he did it again and again all summer, travelling back and forth between Scarborough and Huntsville. By the time school started again in the fall of 1974, Mike was already planning where he was going to hitchhike next. He knew if he was going to hitchhike across Canada he was going to need money for food and other supplies, so he got a job at a Christmas-tree plantation where during the warmer months he pruned the trees and in the winter months he helped with the harvest. He was so invested in his dream of hitchhiking across the country that he managed to convince his school to let him take his Christmas vacation a month earlier than everybody else, just so he could work more hours at the plantation.

By the time he started the eleventh grade, Mike had hitchhiked all over Ontario. He mastered all the little things he believed he needed to know to make it across the country. He knew the rules of hitchhiking like it was a sport and he was a pro. He knew that if you saw somebody hitching on the same stretch of highway you kept your distance, at least half a kilometre, and whoever got there first was allowed to go in front so they could be the first person seen by passing cars. He learned to read people as quickly as possible to gauge if it was safe to ride with them, to stretch his money, to sleep with one eye open, to talk confidently to and befriend every kind of personality. He became a master at "reading the roads," as he would often say, knowing where the best spot to catch a ride was, when the best time to catch it was, when it was best to walk a few kilometres, or when it was best to stay put. He was ready to go to Vancouver Island, and a few months shy of his sixteenth birthday, he started his journey.

It took him almost the whole summer to get to the island and another month to get back, just in time for school. Over the next few years, when he wasn't at school or working to make money for his trips, he was hitchhiking back and forth across the country for no other purpose than to bask in the freedom and the enjoyment of it all. The things he saw, the people he met, the drugs he took, the parties he attended, the lunacy of some of the situations he found himself in, would have been enough to satisfy the most ardent of adventurers. But for Mike, as soon as he got back home all he kept thinking about was the next ride he was going to catch, what the driver might look like, what type of person they might be, and what kind of conversation he was going to have with them.

He often lost himself in the abundance of memories he had accumulated, from how the stars looked above empty stretches of the Trans-Canada Highway in a remote part of Manitoba to a pair of fun-loving hippie girls he met near Wawa, to the salty scent of the air while riding the ferry from Vancouver to Nanaimo.

During one of his trips, he was picked up at around 7:00 a.m. on the Trans-Canada near Sault Ste. Marie by a young man named Oog, a German out of Edmonton. Oog told Mike about how he hadn't seen his parents in eight years when once, driving east from Edmonton, he spotted a familiar car going in the opposite direction on the highway. He turned around, followed the car, pulled up beside it, and confirmed what he believed: it was his parents' car. Just as shocked as he was, his parents pulled over at the next rest stop and they talked for about twenty minutes, hugged, and went their separate ways; Oog east to Toronto and his parents west to Edmonton.

Mike told Oog a story of his own.

Along the highway, with no light to speak of, feeling the chill of the night air, he was walking briskly to keep himself warm while figuring out where to sleep until the sun came out. He stopped to light a cigarette and jumped when the light from the flame illuminated the face of a man. Keeping his cool, Mike asked him what his name was.

"Dusty," the man said, before explaining in an unsettling tone that he was from Wyoming and had just been discharged from the army two weeks earlier. He had served during the Vietnam War and was hunting a man from Winnipeg he claimed had stolen his wife while he was away. Dusty then pulled out a big knife and asked Mike what he thought of it. Shaken, but still keeping his composure, Mike said it was a nice knife, but his attention was focused on Dusty's eyes, which through the light of the flickering flame looked wrong. Mike said he was going to walk ahead, in hopes Dusty wouldn't follow, but before he got any distance away, Dusty lunged at him and cut his throat with the knife. Mike managed to fight Dusty off before running into the darkness, where he hid in a ditch and tended to his wound. Luckily it wasn't too deep because if it had been, there wasn't much he could have done about it.

"That was a little less than four hours ago," Mike told Oog.

Oog shook his head, commented on the wildness of the road, and offered Mike some LSD. Mike gladly accepted the acid and laughed when Oog took some himself, and together, while continuing east on the Trans-Canada, they told more stories from the road, laughing hysterically throughout the trip.

When Mike met Linda in the autumn of 1982, he knew he had found the right woman for him. She was attractive, genuine, and took absolutely no shit from anybody. What drew him most to her, however, was that she truly liked him for who he was, making it clear early on in their relationship that she had no interest in changing anything about him, in domesticating him, or having him abandon the adventurous spirit she found so intoxicating.

Weeks after they first met, Mike wouldn't stop talking about Vancouver Island. He told Linda all about his travels criss-crossing Canada but the island was always the highlight, the pinnacle of it all. He spoke with vivid detail about the air of the island, the green, the water, the fishing, the bears, the deer, the endless trails, and the sloping mountains. It was a heaven he got to enjoy in life, and it would have been an absolute deal-breaker if she showed no interest in it. Fortunately for him, she showed eagerness to see the place the man she loved described with so much passion and reverence. And when Linda's young sons, Joey and Danny, heard about the island, they were just as eager to see it as their mother.

Just one week after their wedding, Mike contacted Canada Drive-Away, a company that sought drivers to deliver new motorhomes great distances away, drivers who in return got all expenses paid, including gas and food, along with a decent but not extravagant per diem. It didn't take him long to get offered the chance to drive a brand new Glendale motorhome from London, Ontario, to Vancouver. As soon as he received the offer, he told Linda. As giddy as a little kid on Christmas, he was barely able to contain his excitement. She told him it was a great idea. She then told Joey and Danny, who showed the same enthusiasm as Mike, which was no easy feat. A few days later he went to London, picked up the motorhome (which still had plastic on the seats), drove to Linda's parents' home on Pape Avenue in Toronto, where she, Joey, and Danny were waiting, picked them up, and they started their journey west.

The whole trip to Vancouver Island took ten days. Following the Trans-Canada, the family got to see Canada the way Mike had during his prior journeys. After encountering a tornado not far from Thunder Bay in northern Ontario, they made stops in Winnipeg, Brandon, and Regina. After leaving Saskatchewan they went to Banff in Alberta, where they enjoyed a thrilling gondola ride to the top of Sulphur Mountain. From the top of the peak Mike showed Linda, Joey, and Danny the beautiful Banff Springs Hotel, where he had worked for a short period during one of his trips across the country and celebrated his eighteenth birthday. They went on to Lake Louise, where Mike didn't know he wasn't allowed to fish and was caught by a stern game warden, who let him off with a warning but kept the fish Mike had just caught, a giant trout he was looking forward to cooking for himself and the family.

Near the end of the trip, Linda was starting to get homesick. It was her first time away from home and while she initially thought she was going to enjoy the adventure just like her new husband and two sons, she realized her attachments to her family, friends, and the city of Toronto ran deeper than she expected. Meanwhile,

Joey and Danny were loving the adventure of it all, acting just like Mike every time they encountered a new attraction or indulged in another experience.

Once they reached Vancouver, Mike delivered the motorhome. Afterward, the family was picked up by Mike's mother, who drove them to the Tsawwassen Ferry Terminal where they took the scenic, two-hour boat ride to Nanaimo. From there, Mike's mother drove them to the home in Campbell River where she had been living for the last few years with her parents. The reason for Mike's grandparents' relocation to the island was simple: after seeing pictures Mike had taken during his hitchhiking trips, they were so enamoured with the scenery and the stories their grandson told them that they decided to move there from Huntsville.

Mike and his family ended up living in a trailer next door to Mike's grandparents' home in Campbell River much longer than any of them anticipated, but they were having such a great time the thought of leaving never occurred to them. The town was a vibrant tourist attraction during that time, enticing visitors from all over the world, from hunters and sports fishermen casting their lines from the edge of the pier at Fisherman's Wharf to high-profile celebrities, many of whom owned or rented summer homes there.

The family explored every area the beautiful island had to offer, especially during the summers when they spent days, sometimes weeks, camping everywhere they could. They marvelled at legions of pink salmon forming glistening waves as they stampeded through the rivers during spawning. They got to see black bears, deer, and elk during long hikes where time didn't matter. Along the island's never-ending coastline, they gazed up at mighty eagles resting on the highest treetops or soaring through the air before diving down for rodents or even small dogs. They saw pods of orcas cruising through the bays and along the capes demanding respect from every boat in the vicinity while spraying clouds of mist into the salty air. They enjoyed the short ferry ride to Quadra Island and the long drive north along hilly roads to Sayward, and then southwest to Port Alberni and Tofino, where they played in the enormous waves made famous by surfers around the globe. They took a trip to Coombs, where they went to a farm on the highway that had a large fruit and vegetable stand with a roof where several goats lived, joyously bouncing around any time people approached. They drove south to Duncan and on to Victoria at the southernmost tip of the island. And whenever they were in and around the Comox Valley, they saw snow-capped Mount Washington, which always appeared in the distance yet seemed close enough to touch.

While Joey and Danny were in school, Linda worked as a dispatcher for Tony's Taxi on Quadra Island. Mike drove a cab, an unbelievably unsafe light-blue 1966 Volvo with the words "Star Wars" painted on it, while also doing roofing for some extra money. While Linda and Mike weren't making great money, they were making enough to get by, and during that time that was more than enough for them. Mike loved living on the island and, despite her early bouts of homesickness, so did Linda, as well as Danny and Joey.

Due to a massive recession throughout British Columbia in the spring of 1987 that abruptly made keeping and finding work virtually impossible, Mike and his family had no choice but to go back east to Ontario. Linda and Mike knew they couldn't afford to live in Toronto, nor did they want to after spending two years in the tranquil, natural environment of Vancouver Island. So, after some research, they found out about Orillia, a small, rural city that offered the same peace and quiet they had grown to love so much. In addition to the quieter life that Orillia offered, it was also affordable, and growing.

Mike found a plot of land with a small house, which was nothing more than a summer cottage, for sale at thirty-four thousand dollars. Knowing they didn't have that kind of money but also knowing that with some work, the house would easily sell for double that price after a couple of years, Linda called her father. That same day Linda's father arrived with thirty-four thousand dollars in cash. It was an interest-free loan to Mike and his daughter for their first home. Overjoyed at the opportunity, after buying the home Mike immediately got to work on it, knowing every improvement he made only made it more valuable, so when they sold it, after paying Linda's father back, they could take the profits and go back west.

Less than ten months later the house would be reduced to ash, and all of the plans the family made would be burned with it. However, the idea of moving back to Vancouver Island, while dealt a devastating blow, was far from dead.

•

Not long after the first envelope arrived at the Shriners Burns Institute containing cash and a short message offering best wishes and hopes, Linda and Mike had become overwhelmed with similar donations. Not sure what to do with the money they were receiving, and far too stressed and preoccupied with being there for Joey to even think about it, Linda and Mike sought help, and in May of 1988 they found it with Willson McTavish, the Official Guardian for the Province of Ontario. Working alongside a board of trustees, who like Mr. McTavish worked voluntarily, his job was to take responsibility for trust funds set up for minors like Joey. Mr. McTavish was a thorough man who truly believed in what he was doing, and after receiving permission from Linda to be in charge of the fund, he took the lead when it came to receiving, organizing, and managing the distribution of the money Joey was receiving.

MAY 22

One of the first things Linda, Mike, and Joey wanted to do after receiving letter after letter from people wishing him a successful recovery was mail them back a message of appreciation. However, when the letters quickly reached the thousands, an issue came to light that worried the family: stamps. Buying a few stamps, even a few hundred, didn't come with a debilitating cost, but when it came to buying thousands, even at a few cents each, the amount of money needed became substantial. Initially, the family thought that was a perfect example of what the fund was for, but when they contacted Mr. McTavish and asked for money to buy the stamps they needed to reply to every letter Joey received (he planned to respond with a simple thank you along with his modified signature), they were told that wasn't possible. After angrily asking why, they were told the money from the fund was to be used solely for Joey's medical expenses.

JUNE 21

When the fund reached sixty thousand dollars, Linda thought the money was best suited toward building a home for her family, but when she brought that up with Mr. McTavish, he told her no. When asked why, Mr. McTavish repeated what he said before: that the money from the fund was to go only toward medical expenses for Joey. When Linda protested, saying they all needed a place to live, including Joey, Mr. McTavish suggested the family live in a geared-to-income Ontario Housing apartment. She refused, saying she didn't want landlords, that they wanted a house, a place they could have a dog. They wanted what they had lost. She then suggested the money be split, half for Joey's medical needs and the other half toward a new home. Her request was refused.

JULY 15

A convenience store in Cumberland Beach, which Linda, Mike, Joey, and Danny frequented before the fire, had a collection tin. Over time the tin had accumulated a modest amount of money that the store owners intended to give to Mike and Danny after learning about the financial hardships they were enduring while Linda was with Joey in Boston. They told Mike he could collect the money they had received. Overjoyed at the generosity, Mike and Danny entered the store and were met with a sombre response.

"I'm so sorry, Mike, but I can't give you the money."

Mike asked why and was told it was because they were using Joey's name, so the money had to be given to Mr. McTavish and the board of trustees. As a result, while Linda remained in Boston with Joey, Mike and Danny ate sparingly for the next three days until Mike was able to find some roofing work that only lasted another few days, since he had to return to Boston to be with Linda and Joey.

AUGUST 18

During a brief break away from Boston, the Shriners Burns Institute, and Joey, Linda found a private lot in another part of Orillia, as she and Mike talked about not wanting to live in the same spot where so much had already been taken away from them. The lot was near the lake, and near the airport, which was important to Linda so that if anything happened to Joey, it would be easy for him to fly to Toronto, or even Boston if necessary. When she brought up the lot to Mr. McTavish, however, he once again reiterated his position that no money would be released for any other reason but Joey's medical expenses.

AUGUST 28

Linda continued fighting with Mr. McTavish, saying a new home in a new area should be the priority for Joey and the family, but Mr. McTavish remained steadfast in his position, and told her the family should continue raising money. He also told her that for their next home, they should stay on the same street where their last home burned down. If they didn't, people would think they were trying to better themselves with the money being donated. Linda told him none of the money was going to a new home anyway, so why should it matter where they chose to live? Mr. McTavish told her perception was important, and if people believed that the family was upgrading their lives, the donations would dry up. Linda said it wasn't fair, that she never asked to have her life, or the lives of her family, put in the hands of other people.

SEPTEMBER 27

Mr. McTavish refused to send any money to Mike for basic expenses in order for him to remain in Boston with Linda while Joey was at the Shriners Burns Institute. Linda pleaded with him about how important it was having Mike there with her, but Mr. McTavish said Mike had to return home and work to support his family.

SEPTEMBER 30

Linda again brought up the issue of a new home with Mr. McTavish, and he started considering the possibility of allowing some of the money from the fund (which by this point had grown to over one hundred thousand dollars) to be used for a new home, but only if the ownership was placed under the name of the fund itself. Linda didn't understand why such a step was necessary and why they were so insistent on it. She replied that she would agree only if, after three years, the ownership would revert to her name and Mike's name, as they did not want the fund to be in charge of their home, and while Joey would be eighteen by that time, she didn't believe it was wise to have him owning the family home at such a young age. Upon hearing Linda's counter-proposal, Mr. McTavish was upset and told her if she insisted on her demands, he and the board of trustees he represented would quit and all of the money in the fund would be frozen until a new board was set up.

OCTOBER 3-6

Linda and Mr. McTavish continued arguing about using the money from the fund for a new home, and Linda was now being told there wasn't enough money for a new home, and even if there were, it was too cold to start building one. Linda and Mike were completely unaware that during this time, Ken McCann was putting together the pieces necessary to begin construction of the "house that love built."

Meanwhile, Linda and Mike were receiving hundreds of follow-up letters from people who had sent money requesting tax receipts so they could write off whatever amounts they donated. Linda and Mike were unable to afford all of the stamps needed to send the tax receipts requested of them. They didn't bother asking Mr. McTavish to release any money for those stamps either, thinking it absurd to use the same money donated to them to pay to send tax receipts to the people who donated it. That decision ended up creating animosity between them and the thousands of strangers who had offered their help through donation.

APRIL 18, 1989

After hearing that the friction between himself and the board of trustees and the Hawkins family had made its way into the newspapers, Mr. McTavish made a public statement that the money from the fund was not going to sustain Joey for life and wasn't even going to last that long. He made it quite clear the family were not lottery jackpot winners, but despite his best efforts to paint the most realistic picture possible of the fund, the public had already made up their minds. They believed that Mike and Linda and Joey and Danny already had a new house, a new van, a new specially-built electric wheelchair, and millions in the bank, and they didn't feel the family had shown enough appreciation for all they had been given.

•

During the spring of 1990, people kept coming to "the house that love built" to see the hero, Joey Philion. They brought cameras and tape recorders. They came with questions and opinions. Sometimes they knocked on the door and other times, when any member of the Hawkins family was outside, they just approached and started snapping pictures and conducting amateur interviews. It became overwhelming for every member of the family, even Joey, as the constant questions about how he was doing, and how it felt to be such an inspiration to so many, were getting exhausting.

In early June of 1990, the family, desperate for a break from the relentless attention, decided to take a trip back to the place they had long dreamt of returning: Vancouver Island. After consulting with several physicians and receiving the okay that Joey would be fine for a trip of that length, they took the van and drove across Canada.

One stop was particularly memorable for Joey.

The family arrived at Moose Jaw, Saskatchewan, late at night, in the middle of a brutal storm. The rain poured, lightning struck, thunder rolled. The whole family was disappointed at the awful weather, but none more than Joey, who was visibly crushed. They had arrived eagerly anticipating an air show the following day, headlined by the famed Snowbirds, and after having waited hundreds of days, Joey was overjoyed that he would finally be seeing the "Philion Roll" performed in person. He had even been invited to the show by the Snowbird pilots themselves. However, with the air show scheduled to commence less than twenty-four hours after they had arrived at the grounds, there was little hope the show would go on.

Despite the darkness of the starless, cloudy night, it was obvious that the viewing grounds had been reduced to a muddy swamp. With all hope of seeing the show the next day lost, the family planned to hit the road as soon as they woke up the next morning. When they did awaken, however, they couldn't believe their eyes. Not only had the rain stopped but the sun, shining in spite of some stubborn clouds, had dried up a great deal of the mud. Mike immediately went to the office where tickets to the show were being sold and asked if it was still going to happen. They told him the chances were fifty-fifty.

When Mike returned, he told the family what he had learned, and just like everybody else who had arrived, they stood in hopes the show would proceed. The waiting was torturous. The air was still, hot, and muggy, and as the morning turned to early afternoon it got even hotter, but everybody continued waiting. That's when the first plane started dancing in the vast sky, the sound of its jet engines booming like an echoing scream for attention. The crowd cheered as the plane's dazzling performance left behind trails of white smoke that looked like enormous silk ribbons waving gently in the air.

At the finale of the show, the Snowbirds roared overhead. Consisting of nine CT-114 Tutors, each plane identically painted white and red with a streak of blue on both sides and the word "Snowbirds" inscribed near the front, they flew in perfect formation, each plane less than two metres away from the other. When the pilots performed the "Philion Roll," Joey was in a state of euphoria. He couldn't believe it. Seeing it right before his eyes brought him joy in ways that could never be explained. After the show, still feeling the rush from the display they had witnessed, the family had the opportunity to meet the pilots, who joked and laughed with them as if they were old friends. When they asked Joey if he liked the roll named after him, he said it was amazing, and thanked them for the unbelievable gift.

When they finally arrived on Vancouver Island, Mike and Linda explored the possibility of moving there permanently. They started looking at properties, getting prices, gauging how realistic a move there could be. The results were promising. The prices were affordable and the plots of land were gorgeous, especially in Sayward. The discussion about whether or not they should move there was as quick as it was definitive. Every member of the family enthusiastically agreed that was where they wanted to live. They thought it would be as easy as that.

Linda and Joey returned to Ontario in September of 1990, while Mike and Danny remained on the island. After their arrival, they asked the Shriners if they were interested in using "the house that love built" as a home for kids rehabbing from burn injuries and their families. The Shriners declined the offer to assume control of the house, due to its relatively isolated location. A report of the family's plan to leave Orillia and move to Vancouver Island, along with their intentions of giving the house to the Shriners and the Shriners' subsequent refusal, was published in the *Toronto Star* on September 15. Near the end of the article, local Orillia resident Jodie Wilson stated her dissatisfaction with the family's decision to leave. "I think it stinks. So many people did so much. There was such an overwhelming sense of community spirit."

Orillia's mayor at the time, John Palmer, was also quoted in the article. "Total shock. I just find the whole thing unbelievable. A slap in the face is a minor term for how people feel."

He continued, "The thing that worries me, what happens if somebody else needs help? People may not be as willing."

Things only got worse when it was revealed that the family hoped to use the money from the fund as a down payment for the property they found in Sayward.

Linda tried explaining in a brief article in the *Canadian Press* that her family hoped, in addition to making a home for themselves in Sayward, to create a rehabilitation centre on the property as a way to help people who had endured what she, Joey, and the rest of the family had. The response was far from positive. People immediately started criticizing the details of such an endeavour, while loudly questioning how the family could afford such a thing. Ken McCann expressed his opinions about the family's plans, saying it would cost at least five hundred thousand dollars to build Joey a new house on Vancouver Island, which was much more than what was in the fund, and wondered openly as to where the rest of the money was going to come from. Linda tried making it clear in other interviews that it was just an idea; that no ground had been broken, no land purchased, no concrete plans made, but several newspapers wrote articles that made it appear as if the rehab centre was on the verge of construction.

In an effort to clarify things further, Joey was interviewed by the *Packet and Times* in an article published on September 20, where he made it clear he had given his parents permission to seek approval from Mr. McTavish and the board of trustees to use the money from the fund to buy the property. "It's not like they are taking it. It was a decision we all made. I always have the last word in everything. I gave them permission."

Elsewhere in the article, when discussing his frustration with the media attacks on his family, Joey was quoted as saying, "We aren't doing anything wrong. Why can't people understand that?"

The attacks continued, culminating in a petition spearheaded by Ken McCann that quickly gained over a thousand signatures.

The petition was then presented to Mr. McTavish and the board of trustees in charge of the fund in an effort to prevent the family from using any of the money to purchase property on Vancouver Island.

When made aware of the petition, in an article in the *Packet and Times* published on September 27, Linda stated that using the money from the fund to buy the property was every bit as much Joey's idea as it was hers and Mike's. She also stated that to make things easier the home would be in Joey's name, not theirs, and she would even add her own signature to the petition, as she was quoted as saying, "If it is a petition to stop Linda and Mike Hawkins from getting the trust fund, I'll sign it."

In addition to the petition he started, on September 29 Ken McCann released a letter to the media. It read as follows:

> Mr. Wilson [*sic*] McTavish, the official guardian, is the only qualified person that will decide on whether or not Joe Philion's trust fund or house is to be tampered with. I will be presenting Mr. McTavish with correspondence received from concerned citizens which is their opposition to the Hawkins' request. We all have Joe's best interest in mind, and I know the Guardian will make the right decision.
>
> This is my final statement on the matter.
>
> Thank You
> Ken McCann

Just before Joey was scheduled to leave Ontario and go to Boston for a surgery involving his legs on October 2, Linda heard a knock on the door of "the house that love built." It was after midnight. She opened the door, but nobody was there. When she stepped out and walked onto the front lawn, she was jumped from behind and assaulted by Lynda Young, who, like so many other citizens of Orillia, had been riled into a frenzy as a result of the dozens of articles, opinion pieces, and news reports circulating over the last month.

This was the same Lynda Young who, not far from the spot where she was assaulting Linda, had rushed to Joey's aid and doused the flames consuming him two years earlier. Joey was upstairs, hearing the assault but unable to see it or do anything about it. Shaken by what had happened and completely shocked at the degree to which media-fuelled anger could be manifested, Linda was happy to leave Canada for Joey's surgery in Boston.

•

After Joey's recovery from the surgery, which took nearly two months, he and Linda made their way back to Vancouver Island. Once there, they reconnected with Mike and Danny. The reunion had been long awaited, and once they were together the Hawkins family felt relieved. They finally felt free. Joey, in particular, often acted just as he did when he had first seen the island five years earlier. He was cheerful, inquisitive, talkative, and amiable. He marvelled at the abundance of nature, from the endless forests and ocean to the mountains and wildlife. And with the much-improved weather, Joey spent far more time outdoors. However, the bliss came with thorns. There were many times when he became moody and irritable, petty and insulting. He snapped at people and bullied them, often at random. And while much of that attitude could be attributed to his youth, there were other reasons for his bouts of ill temper.

As much as he loved the island and preferred it over Orillia, Joey's confinement to his wheelchair, his inability to run through the forests he adored, to jump into and swim freely in the ocean he was in awe of, and to just go outside in the morning without having to endure an hour of dressings and other preparations, took a heavy toll on him. His situation felt sadistic at times. He had finally made it to the place of his dreams only to be forced to sit and stare at it instead of enjoying it the way he truly wanted.

Sometimes Joey's frustration led him to act out, as all teenagers do, and he would run away. Except Joey didn't "run away" as other teenagers did. Instead, after his irritation boiled over, he picked a direction on a nearby dirt road, pointed the joystick on his wheelchair forward as hard as he could, and sped away at the chair's top speed. On one occasion, after an argument with Mike, Joey said he was leaving. Equally frustrated, Mike told him to go ahead. He travelled about seven or eight kilometres until the battery of his chair died, leaving him stranded in the middle of a wooden bridge. He sat stewing, hearing the sound of the river below but unable to look down to see it. Less than an hour later, Mike pulled up beside him in his old, salmon-coloured pickup truck and asked Joey if he was okay. Instead of answering, Joey just stared into the distance, his thoughts a mystery. He kept quiet while Mike replaced the batteries on his wheelchair, allowing him to move once again.

•

When winter arrived and the calendar year flipped to 1991, the family found their new home in Sayward, British Columbia. It was 160 acres and had a small house and three cabins, which they hoped could become the foundation of the rehab centre they still wanted to put together. The price was three hundred thousand dollars and, with Joey's permission, the family was still awaiting authorization from Mr. McTavish and the board of trustees to use the money from the fund to make a substantial down payment. Mike had no doubt he could do a lot of the work on the house and cabins, while making enough money to slowly pay off the balance owed. In an act of generosity, the owners let them live in the small house while the deal to buy the entire property was coming together.

They believed they were finally going to be left alone, as the house they lived in did not even have a phone. But reporters from the CBC tracked them down and asked to interview them, with their focus on Mike. He reluctantly agreed, hoping he could use the interview to make it clear how much he and his family wanted to be left alone. The interview took place on the bank of the nearby river. The reporter asked Mike to sit on a pile of wet logs, which he refused to do. The reporter insisted, saying sitting on the logs would put him in the best light, making for a better shot. Mike refused again, saying he was fine right where he was. The reporter relented, and immediately started questioning Mike as to why he had taken Joey away from "the house that love built." Before he could answer, the reporter started questioning him about where the money for the property in Sayward was coming from. Then he asked if Joey was getting the proper care, and why they would leave Ontario when it had better medical facilities. The reporter came closer, his tone growing more accusatory.

Mike got angry. When the reporter got even closer and fired one last question that made Mike even angrier, he shoved the reporter, who toppled over the same collection of wet logs he had asked Mike to sit on. After crashing to the ground, the reporter, appearing shocked that anything he said could possibly elicit repercussions, asked Mike why he shoved him, to which he replied, "You were pissing me off," before he turned and walked away. The interview never aired.

A few weeks after the failed interview, a massive flood swept through Sayward. Linda wasn't home at the time but Mike, Joey, and Danny were. Members of the local fire department arrived and told them that the nearby river was overflowing, and they had to leave the property immediately.

There was a wooden bridge that acted as the only way in and out of the property. Knowing it wouldn't withstand a flood for very long, Mike heeded the warning from the fire department, who made their own rapid departure, and started driving to safety in his old truck. The flood was aggressive. The water levels rose quickly, reaching the windows of the truck in an instant. Mike made a beeline toward the bridge that he could already see swaying while the rushing water battered it relentlessly. There was no road to see, just water. The property had been completely swallowed by the flood, but the bridge still remained. Mike knew it wouldn't last for much longer. He saw logs and other debris darting through the water like aimless torpedoes. He drove faster, keeping his fears subdued and his focus sharp, knowing all it would take to wash them out was a single strike from a log or anything else of similar size.

Joey and Danny were screaming, terrified of the rising water. Mike drove even faster, powering his way through the water, fearing the bridge would give way any second. Once he reached the bridge, Mike carefully but rapidly drove across, knowing a single jerk of the steering wheel could take them over the edge. Moments later, staring at the rear-view mirror, he gasped when he saw the bridge collapse and wash away.

Once they were a safe distance away, Mike, Joey, and Danny caught their breath and gazed at what was left of what they thought was going to be their new home. The small house they had been living in was gone, consumed by the water. The cabins they hoped to turn into a rehab centre were also gone. Of the 160 acres, only fifteen remained above water. When they finally met with Linda, she was relieved to see that every member of her family was okay, but couldn't believe what had just happened. First fire, now water. Mike wondered aloud if a tornado was going to take away whatever home they decided upon next. Not long after the flood, local newspapers falsely reported that Joey was bravely rescued by a helicopter.

Once again left homeless, the Hawkins family started looking for another property, but with the flood devastating much of Sayward they had to venture farther south, where they eventually found a small place near Black Creek, less than forty kilometres away from Campbell River. They were unable to find anything remotely close to what they had found in Sayward, but they were desperate and anxious to find whatever they could for the time being.

Tensions between members of the family were high. Arguments broke out constantly and blame was thrown from one member of the family to another. They were beyond exhausted. Making matters worse, the media had once again found them.

In an article in the *Vancouver Sun*, the frustration of the family could no longer be restrained. When asked for what seemed like the thousandth time about why they left Ontario and "the house that love built," Mike first stated how much he and his family appreciated everything the people of Orillia did for them, then added, "But it doesn't give anybody the right for any strings to be attached to it. If Joe's well-being meant anything to them, and I mean really anything, they would go with what he really wants. It's got nothing to do with the trust fund. It's got nothing to do with the house. What they want is us."

At the end of the article, when asked if he could say one thing to the people back in Ontario, Joey replied, "Leave me alone."

WALLY'S WORLD

ANDY PHILION, DANNY'S BIOLOGICAL FATHER, ALWAYS APPRECIATED THE JOB Mike had done in raising his son, Danny, in his absence, but what Andy did not appreciate was seeing his name in every newspaper and news report as the father of not just Danny but Joey as well. While Joey bore Andy's surname, he was not Andy's son; instead, Joey's father was a man named Wally Herdman.

Wally and Linda got together in 1972. In 1973 Joey was born, and less than two years later, Wally left. Wally's disappearance, while devastating to Linda, who was left to care for her son on her own, was not surprising to her or anybody else. He had been addicted to heroin before Joey's birth and long after, spending more than twenty years in the world of drugs.

Andy didn't enjoy having to answer questions from random people about the state of a child who was not his own. He didn't bear any grudge against Joey personally, however; nor did he blame Linda for not revealing the truth about Joey's real father to the media. He understood Linda's reasoning. She didn't want to add more complications to an already chaotic situation, so she decided it best to just leave Wally's name out of it. It was a sensible choice, because while Wally was Joey's biological father and Joey knew that he was his father, they didn't know each other at all. They had no connection whatsoever. But that was going to change.

•

In 1991, when Joey turned eighteen years old, he was living in his own apartment, while Mike, Linda, and Danny lived in a nearby apartment in Black Creek on Vancouver Island. Meanwhile, Mike was working on a house for the entire family on Mccaulay Road. The living situation was not ideal but following the Sayward flood, and a spirited attempt to find a home like the one that had been washed away, there was nothing immediately available that fit the family's budget, needs, or wants.

For Joey, having his own apartment was an important step. While meagre, it did provide him with independence. And while he still had nurses providing constant care, and his mother often came around to make sure he was okay, and Mike came around to help with dressings, bathing, and whatever else was required when nurses were not available or money was too tight to pay for their services, Joey was granted freedom to do what he pleased. He enjoyed spending time outdoors, albeit with a thick lathering of sunscreen on his thin new skin. He liked going fishing and hunting with Mike and Danny, though the sounds from his electric wheelchair almost always scared off the animals. With temporary replacements for his amputated feet, Joey was even able to drive, which elicited plenty of odd looks from pedestrians and drivers alike.

Despite the appearance of Joey living a normal life, the residual effects from the fire still remained constant. Beyond the around-the-clock care he required and the countless visits to doctors whenever a new infection flared up or new issue came to light, Joey also had to continue taking an exorbitant amount of pain medication just to make it through the day.

Every morning when he woke up, Joey took six 20 mg oxycodone pills, which were designed to take effect quickly, and three 80 mg oxycodone pills, which were designed to take effect much more slowly. A few hours later at around noon, with lunch, he received another six 20 mg oxycodone pills and another three 80 mg oxycodone pills. At around six o'clock, with dinner, he took another six 20 mg oxycodone pills and another three 80 mg oxycodone pills. That was the schedule when things were going well and the pain he experienced was at its most tolerable. When he was experiencing severe pain his dosages doubled, sometimes even tripled. The incredibly high amount of medication he was consistently taking never really eliminated the pain; they just took the edge off. And when it came to the euphoric effects that often lead people to abuse the painkillers he was taking, Joey never experienced those.

He took Ativan (lorazepam) to relieve anxiety. It is impossible to state accurately how many pills he took because it varied depending on how he was feeling, but it was common for him to take six pills at once. He was prescribed as many as he needed whenever he needed them, which was all the time.

He took an unknown amount of Flexeril (cyclobenzaprine) for muscle relaxation because the muscles throughout his body often spasmed, causing him extreme pain each time. As with Ativan, and every other medication he received, he was prescribed as much Flexeril as he needed.

He took eight 4 mg Dilaudid (hydromorphone) pills for pain, and that was when it was tolerable. If he was in extreme pain, he took however many pills he needed to attain a semblance of relief. He also took 200 mg morphine pills whenever he needed them, which was often. At night, when he couldn't sleep, he took at least four Zopiclone pills, but took more if that's what he needed to fall asleep on any given night.

In addition to the aforementioned medication Joey was taking daily, doctors constantly asked him to try new pills for pain relief, anxiety, muscle relaxation, and insomnia whenever the opportunity arose. Sometimes they worked. Sometimes they didn't.

Whenever Joey was in the hospital and nurses unfamiliar with him saw the staggering amount of medication assigned to him, they refused to give him the dosages listed, believing there was some kind of mistake. As a result, he would be in bed suffering while the nurses went to get the necessary confirmations from the doctors, fearing that if they gave him the amount of pills listed, they would kill him. He always felt better whenever he went to a hospital and saw a nurse who knew him.

It was widely speculated amongst the Canadian medical community that nobody in the entire country during that period, regardless of their medical condition, was taking more painkillers than Joey. And nobody — no doctor, no psychiatrist, not even Joey himself — was able to fully comprehend, let alone properly diagnose, the toll that incredible amount of opioid ingestion took on his physical, emotional, and mental state.

When Joey turned eighteen on June 4, 1991, the expectation was that he would be granted control over the money remaining in the fund, while Mr. McTavish and the board of trustees stepped aside. However, Mr. McTavish and the board of trustees sought an extension, wishing to maintain control of the fund for an additional year. Joey didn't oppose the decision, and neither did Linda.

Despite the family's relocation to Vancouver Island, and the time that had passed since their arrival, Joey's celebrity had not waned. People were still very much interested in the lives of him and his family. As a result, Mr. McTavish's extension of control over the fund was reported in newspapers throughout Canada. It also made national news when on June 4, 1992, on Joey's nineteenth birthday, he was finally given complete control over what was left in the fund, which was nowhere near as much as what the public still believed it to be.

•

Less than a week after Joey's nineteenth birthday, he and Linda had to go to Boston to see various specialists who were deciding on another possible surgery, while Mike and Danny remained at home on Vancouver Island. The drive took several days. Unbeknownst to Linda, while she was on the road with Joey, Wally visited her parents' home on Pape Avenue in Toronto with a bible in one hand and a bouquet of flowers in the other. He asked to see his son.

Linda's parents, thinking it would be a good idea for their grandson to be reacquainted with his biological father, told Linda that Wally had come by and wanted to see Joey. Linda wasn't sure if she wanted to see Wally again, or if she wanted Joey to see him either. Her parents told her he looked much different. They said he looked, spoke, and presented himself in a much better manner than what they remembered from years past. They also told her that Wally said he was a born-again Christian and had been sober for eight years and was working as a drug counsellor on the streets of New York and, most recently, Toronto.

Before leaving Vancouver Island, Linda was in great spirits. She was happy and excited about the future. Joey had been doing better than ever over the last few weeks prior to their departure, and Mike and Danny were enjoying themselves while working on their latest attempt at a family home they could finally have all to themselves. With the family's positivity at a point they hadn't experienced in years, Linda thought the unexpected appearance of a seemingly reformed Wally would potentially yield even more joy. So she agreed to a meeting with Wally at her parents' home a few days later.

When Linda and Joey met with Wally, he was joined by three members of the church he attended. The meeting involved plenty of intense conversation and lasted several days. Linda did not sleep or eat during that time. When it was over, Linda, Joey, Wally, and the three members of his church all went to Boston together for Joey's appointment.

A week later, at around 4:00 p.m., while he was working on the new house in Black Creek, Mike answered the phone.

"I am no longer married to you," Linda said. "I am married to God."

"What the fuck are you talking about?" Mike replied.

"Wally is here with us in Boston. He is very special with the church, and he tells me that Joey is the Messiah, and he is going to grow new feet and heal people and be healed himself. He wants us to go to the Times Square Church in Manhattan, then we're going to Mexico before going to Israel, and that's what we're going to do. Goodbye."

"I'll see you soon," Mike said.

Knowing he had no time to spare, Mike immediately started preparing for a journey to Boston. He didn't tell Danny what was going on, figuring it would just upset him, and also because *he* didn't yet understand what was going on, so there wasn't much he could explain anyway. Instead, he just told Danny that he had to go to Boston to get his mother and Joey. After that, he dropped Danny off at his mother's home in Campbell River.

Later that day, with no bags to check or even carry on, Mike caught the first flight he could from Comox to Vancouver. He arrived at the Vancouver International Airport at around midnight. There were no direct flights from Vancouver to Boston so he had to fly through Toronto, but the earliest flight was not until 6:00 a.m. Left with six hours to wait, Mike sat in the airport, stewing and raging. Unable to sleep for a single second, his mind racing, his nerves on a razor's edge, Mike paced throughout the nearly empty, cavernous airport, drinking cup after cup of coffee and going outside every few minutes to smoke a cigarette. When it was finally time to board his flight, his adrenalin was still surging. He dashed to his seat, sat, and expected the plane to start moving immediately. But it stayed where it was while passengers slowly packed their luggage into the overhead compartments, chatting with each other, oblivious to the stakes Mike was dealing with. He was infuriated at every wasted minute the plane remained idle. When the plane finally took off, Mike glanced at his watch continuously throughout the flight. He could barely contain his anxiety, and he was left without any relief from cigarettes, sleep, or marijuana.

The plane landed in Toronto at around 3:00 p.m. Eastern Standard Time. He had hoped he could catch a flight that same afternoon to Boston but there were none available, so he had no choice but to wait until 7:00 a.m. the following day. He considered other options from taking a bus or calling a friend or family member in hopes of getting a ride, to renting a car and driving himself, but he knew that if he took a bus, with all of the stops, he would probably arrive at the same time as, or even later than the flight. He also knew he was in no condition to drive himself and he couldn't think of anybody who would drive him all that way either. He was stuck. And just like he had done in the Vancouver airport, he walked throughout Toronto's Pearson International Airport stewing and raging throughout the afternoon and night, while chain-smoking cigarette after cigarette and drinking cup after cup of coffee.

He called Linda's parents, who were able to tell him the name and address of the motel in Boston that Wally was staying in with

Linda and the church members. Initially, Mike was upset at them for setting up the meeting between Wally and Linda in the first place. He wondered how they could let a man like that anywhere near their daughter after what he had done to her in the past. But when he heard the worry in their voices when they expressed their regret at what they had done, his hostility softened. He shared their worry for Linda, whom he desperately wished to see, to talk to, to hold, and to get back to those who loved her most.

While in Pearson airport, Mike didn't call anybody else. He didn't yet know enough to say much, but also he didn't trust anybody enough (including members of his own family) to not say something to the media or to somebody else who might say something to the media. Whatever was going on, he wanted to keep it as private as possible, and he wanted to handle it himself because it was nobody else's business.

When it was time to board the flight, there was little chit-chat amongst the passengers as they packed their bags into the overhead compartments with the efficiency of those who had done it many times before. It was an early morning weekday flight to a major hub city in the United States and the majority of the passengers were clearly travelling for business. That suited Mike just fine, as he too was going there with determined purpose.

The plane arrived at Boston's Logan International Airport at around 8:40 a.m. Despite not having slept for nearly forty-eight hours, Mike was alert, and with plenty of experience getting around Boston, he had no trouble finding the motel where Linda's parents had told him their daughter and Wally were staying. By 9:30 a.m. Mike arrived at the motel. It was trashy, the kind of place where police cars are common. Nonetheless, he knew he was in the right place when he saw Joey's red-and-grey van outside one of the rooms. He approached the van and looked inside. All he could see were "Jesus Loves You" stickers and other Christian paraphernalia, including an abundance of pictures of Jesus and an assortment of his sayings covering every inch of the vehicle's interior.

Mike approached the motel room's door. He turned the knob. It wasn't locked. He opened the door and walked in. There was no sign of Joey, who he assumed was in the hospital, but he did see Linda sitting on the couch. She looked pale, gaunt, and exhausted. As tired as he was, she looked even more sleep-deprived.

"Come here," he said. "I want to talk to you."

She got up and they went outside. Seeing Linda, despite her appearance, alleviated much of the worry that had been plaguing Mike throughout his journey, allowing his anger to breathe free.

"I want my wedding ring back," he said.

"No," she replied. "I just want the best for Joe, and Wally is the best for him."

Powered by the combustible mixture of anger, frustration, and exhaustion, Mike started shouting at Linda, swearing at her, while trying to take the wedding ring off her finger. She resisted. At that moment, Wally, who had a large beard that made him look like an aged Charles Manson, came out of the motel room and said, "God loves you." Without uttering a word, Mike punched him in the face, dropping him to the pavement. On the ground, blood pouring from his nose, Wally repeated, "God loves you." Mike punched him in the face again. "God loves you." Mike punched him again.

With more blood spilling from his nose and his face starting to swell from the blows, Wally kept repeating the same phrase, and every time he did, Mike punched him in the face until he finally said, "If you keep saying God loves me, I'm going to keep hitting you."

Before Wally could say it again, and before Mike would have punched him in the face again as surely as the sun came up in the morning, the cops arrived. Linda told them Mike was going to hurt her. They threw Mike against the hood of their car before putting him in the back seat and driving away.

By 10:30 a.m., less than two hours since his arrival, Mike was in jail. He spent the night there but did not sleep. There were forty other men inside the holding area. By giving away most of his Canadian cigarettes, Mike was able to befriend many of his fellow prisoners who, just like him, were awaiting their time in front of the judge.

The following morning, beyond exhausted as he hadn't slept in nearly three days, Mike stood in front of the judge who sentenced him to one year for assault. However, the prosecutor said the judge had agreed that if Mike left the country within twenty-four hours and never returned, he could go free, but if he remained in the country beyond those twenty-four hours, he would be forced to serve the entirety of the one-year sentence in prison.

Mike turned and saw Linda, Wally, and several members of his church seated in the audience area of the courtroom. While Linda stared blankly, Wally openly taunted Mike by making childish faces at him. After walking out of the courtroom, Wally approached Mike and said, "You better stay away, or you haven't seen anything yet."

"Fuck you," Mike replied.

Knowing he had twenty-four hours to leave the United States of America, Mike immediately went to the hospital where he knew Joey was, knowing Linda would be there too. He made many attempts to try to see her, just to talk to her, to try to get her to see the lunacy of what was going on, but he was unable to get near her. She always had at least one of Wally's church members with her.

Mike ended up staying in Boston for a week, sleeping inside the hospital, regaining his energy and his mind while biding his time, waiting for an opportunity to see Linda alone. He tried to get into Joey's room to speak to him, but as with Linda, there was always a church member with him. Unsure what other options were available to him, Mike turned and walked toward the elevator and was shocked to see the judge who had ordered him to leave the United States step out. As soon as the judge saw Mike, his eyes bulged and he pointed at him before shouting, "You!"

Mike turned and ran to the administration office and said, "I'm checking Joey out, NOW." After that, knowing he had precious little time, he returned to Joey's room and whether by providence or bladder requirements, there was no church member inside. Joey looked at him and asked what was going on.

"Shut up," Mike replied, "we're going home."

With years of experience, he managed to get Joey out of bed and into his wheelchair in seconds, and they got to the van, which was parked in the garage. Luckily, Mike still had a set of keys for the van. Afterward, with Joey waiting inside the vehicle, in spite of the incredible risk, as there was little doubt the judge had already called for officers to apprehend the man who blatantly ignored his order to leave the country, Mike went back upstairs and found Linda in the waiting room. There was a church member beside her.

"We're leaving," he told her. "We're going home."

Linda said no, then told him he was going to get into trouble.

"I have Joe," he replied.

After hearing those words, she reluctantly got up and followed Mike, while the church member went to get Wally.

As soon as Mike got Linda into the van, he said, "We're leaving. We're going home. Right now."

He pulled the van out of the garage and deftly made his way through the Boston traffic, carefully avoiding doing anything that would garner attention from the police officers that he knew were looking for him. He just hoped the van had not yet been flagged.

Throughout the nearly six-hour drive to the Canadian border, Linda only talked about all of the great things God was going to do for Joey. She repeated what Wally had told her: that Joey's feet would grow back, and he would walk again and be the saviour, the

Messiah he was destined to be. Joey remained quiet throughout the entire drive.

Meanwhile, Mike, freaking out the entire time, managed to keep his focus on the road. Every time he encountered any kind of minor slowdown, he squeezed the steering wheel even tighter, while frantically looking through every window and at every mirror for signs of police. Regardless of how desperately he wanted to get out of the United States, he never drove above the speed limit. He knew the risk was too great and that if he saw any flashing lights in his rear-view mirror, he would not only lose his wife but would spend at least a year in prison.

When they finally reached the Canadian border, Mike assumed he was going to be arrested on the spot but, to his amazement, he was waved right through. A few hours later they arrived at Linda's parents' home in Toronto. They were relieved to see their daughter and grandson, and thanked Mike for bringing them back. The joy was short-lived, however, as police soon arrived. To Mike's surprise they did not arrest him; instead, they just told him he could no longer drive the van because it was not in his name. It was in Joey's.

Afterward, believing that Linda and Joey were safe at Linda's parents' home where they could properly recover, and needing a break from the turmoil and wanting to get back to Danny, Mike went to stay with a long-time friend named Vern Morris. He had spent nearly every penny he had to get to Boston as quickly as he could, and only had enough money left to purchase a Greyhound bus ticket back to Vancouver Island. Vern, who decided he didn't have anything better to do, as well as wanting to be there for his friend, went along with Mike on the gruelling five-day journey across the country. Mike had lost count of how many times he had travelled from Toronto to Vancouver Island, but what he did know was that this bus trip was the worst of them all. The bus was uncomfortable, he was barely able to sleep, and didn't even have enough money to eat properly during the trip. By the time he finally arrived back on Vancouver Island, Mike was beyond exhausted. But he was given no chance to rest because as soon as he arrived at the apartment in Black Creek where he, Linda, and Danny were staying, he saw Wally and Linda standing outside with every dish, every piece of furniture, every picture inside a moving van.

With Vern standing next to him, Mike approached Wally, who looked back at him with a smirk on his face and said, "You're too late."

Without uttering a word in reply, Mike punched Wally in the face, sending him to the pavement. He pounced on him and started pummelling him while Vern stood by, making sure none of Wally's church members interfered. Linda was screaming at the top of her lungs and the ensuing chaos led to the swift arrival of police, who arrested Mike and took him to jail in a scene of déjà vu that even he had to laugh at while sitting in the back seat of the police cruiser.

That same day, while standing before the judge in a courtroom in Campbell River, British Columbia, Mike explained exactly what was going on: that Wally had brainwashed his wife and was kidnapping her and Joey, that he had followed them all the way to Boston to get her back, risking his freedom in the process, and that he had assaulted Wally for attempting to kidnap his wife again while also stealing all of his household belongings. The judge listened attentively and compassionately and dismissed the charges, but warned Mike to stay away from Linda, Wally, and Joey. After leaving the courtroom, Mike and Vern went back to the apartment. It was completely empty.

Mike managed to track down his family the following day. They were all, including Danny, who Linda had picked up from Mike's mother's house, staying at the Edgewater Motel by Willow Point in Campbell River. Mike went there and managed to talk to Linda after making it very clear to Wally and the members of his church that he had no problem punching each and every single one of them and burning the motel to the ground, if that's what it took.

"This has nothing to do with you, Mike, it has to do with Joe," she said.

"You can't do this to a family," he replied.

"I'm going to do what I'm going to do."

"It's fucking wrong," he said.

"I want to follow God."

Refusing to give up, Mike spent the next few months trying to get Linda out of Wally's grip, but she was constantly surrounded by members of Wally's church who told her day after day that she was the mother of the Messiah, and she would help Joey help millions of people, and the Christian faith would heal him completely. Mike also knew that if he got arrested again he would surely end up in jail, and there would be nothing he could do to get his wife back from there.

So he found a deprogrammer, a man from California who was experienced at getting people out of cults and other similar situations. The man charged five thousand dollars for his services — money Mike didn't have. Nonetheless, he agreed to the man's price, knowing he would find the money somehow. He didn't care what he had to do. He loved his wife and was willing to do whatever it took to get her and his family back.

Mike had abandoned the house he was building on Mccaulay Road and was doing whatever work he could to pay his own way. He knew that if he just stayed in an empty apartment when he wasn't working, he would eventually end up doing something drastic, stupid, or both. So he went back to school at the North Island College, where he planned on improving his high school grades so he could study to be a physiotherapist. Working directly with Joey since the fire, he had attained a wealth of knowledge about physiotherapy and grew to enjoy it. A teacher at the college, with whom

Mike developed a friendship, offered to lend him his property on Quadra Island, where Mike could bring Linda, along with the deprogrammer, to give her the help she needed.

With a person willing to help (for a substantial fee), and a place where the help could be administered, Mike was more determined than ever to get Linda back. He tried on several occasions to get her away from the motel where she was staying but was always thwarted by members of the church. On one occasion, however, while he was parked a short distance away, he watched Linda walking alone to the van. He slowly got out of his car, keenly watching her the entire time. He got closer, waiting for his chance to get her, and when he believed the moment had finally come, he ran up to her and grabbed her. She started screaming, as people tend to do during an attempted kidnapping. He managed to calm her down, but knowing he had only a few moments before members of the church came rushing toward them, he looked her in the eye and said, "I just want my family."

She said no.

A few days later, with something big in the trunk of the old, cream-coloured Dodge Polara that he had recently purchased for less than five hundred dollars, Mike went to pick up his friend Vern and they took a drive. After about twenty minutes of driving through an endless series of back roads where forest dominated the scenery, Mike pulled the car over and got out. Vern asked what was going on. Mike popped open the trunk and gazed down at what appeared to be a body tightly wrapped in plastic. He then called out to Vern who came over and saw what Mike was staring at.

"I killed Wally, and I need your help to take care of it."

Without any hesitation, Vern looked at Mike and said, "Okay."

Together the two men grabbed the plastic-wrapped corpse and lifted it from the trunk, and that's when Vern noticed a thin skinless leg with a hoof at the end slip out.

"What the fuck?" he shouted.

Mike started laughing so hard his chest hurt. He then told Vern it was a deer that had been hit by a car a few days ago and was since skinned with hopes the meat could be salvaged, but it was too decomposed, so he was going to toss it into the bush for the bears, cougars, wolves, and whatever other carnivores were in the area to eat.

Vern turned to Mike and with an enormous smile said, "You motherfucker," before dropping the deer carcass on the ground.

With neither man able to contain their laughter, Mike managed to catch his breath long enough to respond, "If I don't find ways to laugh, I'll lose my mind."

Vern nodded before walking back to the car, when Mike shouted, "Hey, come on, I still need you to help me take care of the body!"

•

The only way Mike was able to keep track of Linda was through Danny, who had no choice but to go where his mother went. Before Wally took Linda, Joey, and Danny back east at the tail end of the summer of 1992, where they resettled into "the house that love built" in Orillia, Mike saw Danny (now fifteen years old), who promised to call him whenever he got the chance. It was a promise young Danny kept, as he called Mike every few months, giving him updates about how things were going.

During one of his phone calls, Danny gleefully said, "Mike, I have something to tell you."

"What?"

"It's something I'm really happy about."

"What is it?"

"I think you'll be really proud of me."

"What is it, Danny? Tell me."

"I punched out Wally! I got angry at him for how he was talking to my mom, so I beat him up."

"Good," Mike replied. "So, how is your mom?"

Despite those brief moments of joy shared between Mike and his stepson, the phone calls were often heartbreaking. Danny told Mike that Wally was creepy with his wild hair and beard and that he only talked about religion, even speaking in tongues just to show other people how touched by God he was. Wally even told people that he was the father of the modern-day Jesus, and that Joey's feet were going to grow back, and he was going to walk throughout the earth healing people.

Danny also told Mike that Linda's niece, Tanya, who was around the family during that time, told Linda that she had been brainwashed, but Linda wouldn't listen. And when Linda's parents got angry and started yelling at her, telling her to get out, to get rid of Wally, she always refused. Danny said his mother cried a lot, and always looked so tired and stressed out.

Danny begged Mike to help him come back to Vancouver Island, that he hated being around Wally. Mike was only able to offer words of encouragement, telling Danny that he could get through it, that he was strong, and that it wasn't going to last forever. When he hung up after each and every phone call, he felt like shit. He hated not being able to help his family. But he could only do so much if the one he was willing to risk everything for didn't want his help.

Throughout the rest of 1992 and for the first few months of 1993, Mike tried to live his life as best he could. He mainly focused on finishing his studies at North Island College while also getting his tractor-trailer driving licence, which enabled him to get a decent paying job at St. Joseph's General Hospital in Courtenay doing deliveries. However, the burden of his absent wife, the void of not

Joe Philion, centre, says he's happy to be back at his Cumberland Beach home with his mother Linda Williams and his father Wally Herdman. His family arrived Monday at the house the community built after Philion's home was destroyed in a 1988 fire that almost claimed his life.

Jeff Day — Packet

Linda, Joey, and Wally Herdman in a photo from the *Packet and Times* on August 22, 1992. Photo by Jeff Day.

having the family that had been a constant in his life since 1985, was heavy. He was riddled with sadness and felt lonely sleeping in an empty bed, and found it difficult to feel energetic when he always woke up in and came back to an empty apartment. Every time the phone rang he hoped it was Linda telling him she was coming home, and every time he heard a different voice, he silently swallowed the disappointment.

By the end of February 1993, Mike's hope of ever seeing Linda again, let alone reuniting with her, started fading.

He considered how much better his life would be without ever having to answer another question from another reporter about how Joey was doing. He would never have to defend and explain every decision he made on behalf of his family to an anonymous public that had never spoken to him, seen him, or knew him in any capacity aside from what they read and saw in newspapers and interviews. He would no longer have to deal with Joey himself, spending hours every day bathing him and tending to his weeping wounds, lifting him, getting his prescriptions, listening to him complain, and sacrificing everything just to serve his needs. He would be rid of it all.

But to be rid of Joey was to also be rid of Danny, the young boy who had been through so much and showed such strength. And to be rid of Joey would be to be rid of Linda, for they were absolutely connected. Her love for her son, which had proven to be obsessive, irrational, and even fanatical, was also pure, permanent, and would never budge or crack, regardless of the pressure. To have one was to have the other, and that was that. Mike had long accepted that, but after being without Linda for the first time since they got married, he realized that he would happily continue to endure Joey and the enormous responsibilities that came with him, if it meant he could have her back. He missed her dearly and loved her deeply, and her prolonged absence only solidified those feelings.

In early March of 1993 the phone rang, and as he often did, Mike looked at it with hope before picking it up.

"You were right, Mike."

He almost dropped the phone.

"Do you want to come home?

"I can't," Linda replied. "They are trying to turn Joe against me."

Mike told her to keep in touch, to call him whenever she wanted and whenever she could. He briefly considered going to Toronto and getting her himself, just as he had done months before, but thought better of it, knowing he couldn't risk his freedom again. Linda agreed to continue calling him. While the call was brief, just hearing her voice made his entire body feel warmer. He was overjoyed at hearing from her, but when that joy dissipated he was left with sadness and anxiety, knowing there was nothing more he could do but wait for the phone to ring again.

Two days later, Mike was in Fort St. John in northern British Columbia. He had found a job installing kiosks in all the Kmarts throughout the province. It was an especially cold day, reaching minus forty degrees Celsius, forcing him to put cardboard on the radiator of his truck just to stay warm. To avoid the frigid temperature outside for as long as possible, Mike walked into the mall where the town's Kmart was located, passed by a newsstand, and saw a newspaper with Linda on the cover with Wally, Joey, and Linda's niece, Tanya. He read the article and grew more enraged with every word. Joey was openly accusing him and Linda of ripping him off and taking all of the money in the fund for themselves.

Mike had long accepted there was little he could do about the treatment he had been receiving from the public, and while he hated it and despised the people responsible for it, he quickly learned how the public's appetites worked. But to read about Joey making public accusations against his own mother was too much. Nobody, absolutely nobody, had sacrificed more for Joey than his mother. Nobody loved him more, thought about him more, lost more sleep, or had put themselves through more personal hell for him than she did. While he knew that Wally was behind what Joey was saying, and just seeing the man's face on the front page of the newspaper made Mike wish he had punched him even more when he had the chance, Joey, who often told Mike and Linda that he was an adult and could be responsible for himself, was still saying those words, and he was saying them publicly.

After the release of that news article, in addition to receiving sporadic calls from Linda, Mike was also continuing to receive calls from Danny, who told him what life was like in "the house that love built" with Wally and his church members. He told Mike that all Wally and his people were focused on was getting money, wherever and whenever possible, in order to expand their following, with Joey as their blessed symbol. He also confirmed Linda's words by saying she did want to come back to Vancouver Island but she was afraid that Mike would not accept her and would not love her anymore. He also said that his mother believed there was a possibility that Mike would take her out to the bush and shoot her if she returned — something that Wally and his people constantly told her.

Near the end of 1993, on the final day of his apartment's lease in Black Creek and with what little he owned packed in the trunk of his old Dodge Polara, Mike was ready to go. He had reached his breaking point. The stress, the sadness, the emptiness, none of which looked to have an end in sight, was proving too much. His friend Vern, who remained on Vancouver Island throughout the year, was in the car, as was a woman named Shelly. Mike had been seeing her for a few months, and while she was a great woman who did a lot to make him happy, she wasn't Linda, and Linda was all he wanted.

There was no real plan as to where they were going to go. Before leaving, however, Mike sat on the only piece of furniture remaining in the apartment, a rickety old chair. He was completely still and completely silent, staring out the window. He couldn't understand why he sat there yet he couldn't move, because to leave that apartment, to get into the car and drive away, was to close the book on a life he still wanted more than anything else in the world. After several minutes, and many honks from the car horn and shouts from Vern and Shelly to hurry up, Mike finally got up and made his way to the door. He took one last look at the apartment before turning around and grabbing the doorknob. He took one step through the doorway when the phone, the only other item besides the chair that remained in the apartment, started ringing.

"Can I come home?" Linda said.

Mike didn't answer right away, waiting a moment to be sure he wasn't hallucinating, before replying, "Absolutely."

"I can't come yet," she said. "I have to keep trying to get Joe. I can't leave him with Wally. I know there is a chance. I know I can get him back and we can all come back together so we can be a family again."

"As soon as you're able to come back out here, you just let me know."

He gave her the necessary information to contact him again. After hanging up the phone, he went outside, got into the car, and said to Vern and Shelly, "Linda is coming back."

Vern asked when. Mike said he didn't know. Shelly looked on.

•

On March 17, 1993, the *Toronto Sun* published an article stating that two days earlier, Linda had signed a peace bond forbidding her from communicating with Joey for one year. Joey was quoted in the article as saying, "I don't want her anywhere near me" to Judge Leonard Montgomery. He was also quoted as saying, "She would swear and scream and throw things at me. She needs a lot of psychological help. I'm just not going to let her walk all over me again."

If Linda broke the bond, she could face up to six months in jail.

In the article, Joey publicly accused Linda and Mike of draining all of the money from the fund, stating, "They just blew the trust fund money. They bought property in B.C. The property was signed back to my grandfather and now I owe him $100,000." He then said Linda and Mike moved him to B.C. against his will, stating, "I'm fighting to keep my house. I have to get some money but I'm not asking anything from the public, and I don't want another trust fund."

The article concluded by stating Linda had moved into a hotel a month earlier and quoted her as saying, "The money being questioned was withdrawn by Joe. I'm not out to steal my son's money."

In an article in the *Packet and Times* that was also published on March 17, Joey said he wanted to fit back in with the Cumberland Beach community in Orillia. He said that he wanted to return to school, hoping to pick up where he left off before the fire, when his education was interrupted midway through the eighth grade. He also discussed the court order against his mother before saying he was considering further legal action against both her and Mike. When asked what it felt like fighting against his own mother, he was quoted as saying, "It's not easy, but I can't let people walk all over me. It's not something I want to do … I'm just trying to restore what I had."

Joey did end up pursuing further legal action against Mike and Linda through his Toronto-based lawyer, Brett Tkatch, and an Ontario Provincial Police investigation was made into how the money from the fund was handled. An article in the *Packet and Times*, published on April 30, 1993, started with the sentence: "Joe Philion's parents did not illegally drain the burn victim's trust fund, according to police." The article also stated that there was no evidence to support the accusations made against Linda and Mike Hawkins.

Joey's quoted response to the results of the investigation was "There's nothing I can do about it. I know what she did, but they can't prove it." He also said the police could not find enough evidence to build a case, but that assertion was refuted by OPP staff sergeant Doug Shearer, who said, "There was no basis for a charge to be laid." Nonetheless, Wally stated in several newspaper articles that he wanted to see a provincial inquiry into the matter. Following the OPP investigation, however, such an inquiry was deemed unnecessary.

•

On March 21, 1993, an article in the *Huronia Sunday Staff* began by stating, "There's an eerie electronic beep echoing in the upstairs hall of Joe Philion's house north of Orillia. The battery in the smoke detector is running down and nobody has the money to replace it, says Philion's unemployed father, Wally Herdman, who moved in with his son in August."

The rest of the article dramatically described the deterioration of "the house that love built," now occupied by Joey and Wally, with Tanya coming around at times and various members of Wally's church being present most of the time. According to the article, the telephone was disconnected because of $1,700 in unpaid bills while the electricity, with an outstanding bill of $1,380, was about to be shut off as well. Nurses had to stop tending to Joey because of unpaid bills. There were also outstanding property taxes and there was no longer any home insurance. Additionally, the elevator that Danny and his friends enjoyed so much had an inspection sticker on the door saying it was unsafe to operate, while the sprinkler system installed throughout the house in case of fire was no longer functional.

The only money Wally and Joey were receiving came from Wally's social assistance cheques. For food, Wally stated that he made routine trips to the local food bank and was receiving credit at a nearby grocery store. Joey applied for social assistance of his own but couldn't qualify until he could prove that all of the money in the fund had been spent.

Joey reminisced in the article about what had occurred during the fire, pointing out the errors and embellishments made by numerous newspapers, including the story about him jumping from a second-floor window despite the house only having a single floor. He also

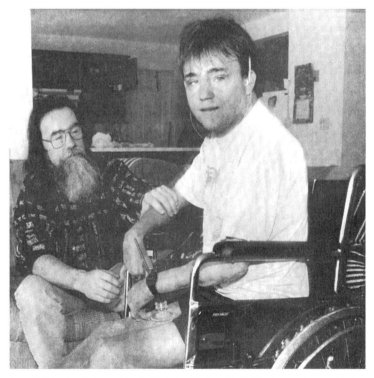

Joey, in his wheelchair, with his biological father, Wally Herdman, pictured in the *Orillia Sun*. Photo by Colin McKim.

detailed how he rushed Danny out of the house before sticking to the lie about running back inside to look for his mother.

Elsewhere in the article Wally, when asked about how he came into Joey's life after such a long absence, stated, "He asked for my help to get him out of the mess he's in. I do care about him and love him. I am his father. I've always been there. I've always been in contact with Linda."

When questioned about his relationship with his father, Joey replied, "For the first time in my life I've got somebody who's not into all the garbage."

.

After months of trying to convince Joey that neither she nor Mike were trying to rob him of any of the money in the fund, and that Wally was the one trying to get hold of whatever money he had left, Linda finally realized she had lost. She was not going to get through to him. So in the spring of 1994, with a heavy heart, she started preparing to return to Vancouver Island, to return to Mike.

She didn't have much money. All she had was a small, red late-'80s Suzuki Swift. She gathered everything she owned and stacked it on the roof of the car. The stack was higher than the car itself.

Danny and Linda's niece, Tanya, came along. Tanya was relieved to get away from Wally, who she found creepier and creepier as time passed. Meanwhile, Danny couldn't wait to get away from Joey's father and return to Vancouver Island.

While Linda still harboured regret for what she believed to be her failure to get Joey away from Wally and his manipulations, she couldn't ignore the hurt that came with her son publicly and privately accusing her of robbing him and telling the whole world he didn't want to see her. But as she got farther away from Toronto and its noise, Joey and his attacks, Wally and his brainwashing, the church and its followers, the newspapers and courts, the public's relentless opinions, condemnations, and gossip, the weight of her regret and her hurt, while still present, became more manageable with every passing kilometre.

By the time they left Ontario and started making their way through Manitoba, Linda, Tanya, and Danny were having a great time. They stopped in as many greasy spoons as they could. They laughed and joked with each other as often as possible. As they drove through the flat landscape of Saskatchewan, full of its enormous puzzle pieces of farmland, Tanya and Linda flashed their bare breasts at trains passing by, while Danny mooned those same trains. And as they drove through the mountains of Alberta, they played a new game of trying to convince every big rig truck to honk its horn whenever they passed. Some wouldn't play along while others happily obliged, blasting their horns as loud as they could. There were no fights, no long tense silences, no attacks or volleys of blame being tossed back and forth. They all knew what they had escaped. They all knew there was nothing more any of them could have done.

When they finally reached Vancouver Island, they coordinated things with Mike so they could meet him at his mother's home in Campbell River. They arrived at around four o'clock in the afternoon. Mike was waiting, and when he saw that little red Suzuki Swift driving up Lynnwood Road he couldn't believe his eyes. The car looked like it came straight out of a cartoon.

The first thing he said when they got out of the car was "How did you get all that shit on the roof?"

Mike suggested they go to a motel, where they could figure out where they were all going to live, since his apartment was far too small for all of them. Everybody agreed, and he drove there in his cream-coloured Polara while Linda followed in the little red Swift. The drive was short, and throughout the trip Mike constantly looked in the rear-view mirror, gazing at the mountain of stuff on the roof of the Swift, watching it sway from side to side, amazed that, despite how fragile it appeared and how much it looked like it was going to crash down, it managed to stay intact.

When they reached the motel, Danny and Tanya took a long walk to stretch their legs and soak in the ocean breeze. Meanwhile Mike and Linda, alone for the first time since the summer of 1992, went into the motel room. Linda took a shower, and when she came out Mike saw the exhaustion on her face and body. He saw the toll the last two years had taken on her, and he could tell by her eyes as they gazed back at him that she could see the toll that time had taken on him as well. Not many words were shared between them. They just stared at each other with relief. They were finally back together. A few moments later, Linda went to the bed, where Mike joined her, holding her gently, before they fell asleep in each other's arms.

A few days later, while he was sitting in the driver's seat of his car with Linda beside him in the passenger seat, Mike's girlfriend Shelly pulled up beside him, rolled down her window, and smiled. While they hadn't spoken for quite some time, she had told him on several occasions that she still had strong feelings for him. Mike panicked, thinking all hell was going to break loose. He turned to Linda, whose temper and aggressive nature he was all too familiar with. To his surprise, however, she appeared calm and cool. He told her who Shelly was, and without saying a word she got out of the car, walked over to Shelly's car, leaned in through the open driver's-side window, and said loudly enough for Mike to hear, "The wife's back. Get lost."

Linda calmly got back into Mike's car, while Shelly drove away and never attempted to contact him again. Afterward, Mike turned toward Linda. She smiled warmly at him, and the only thing stopping him from falling in love with her at that moment was realizing he had never fallen out of love with her throughout her absence.

•

Not long after Linda, Tanya, and Danny's departure, and after it became clear there was no more money left in the fund, Wally left too, never to be heard from again, leaving Joey alone in dire financial straits with nobody around to care for him. Not long after that, Joey got engaged to Lisa Bayev, a nurse who had helped tend to him in the past. They had developed a strong friendship over that time, which grew into a relationship that eventually blossomed into a marriage.

On August 30, Lisa's twentieth birthday, she brought Joey to her parents' home on Steeles Avenue in the North York area of Toronto because she needed help caring for him. In an article in the *Toronto Sun*, Celina Bayev, Lisa's mother, was quoted as saying, "Joe can't even go upstairs. He has taken over the living room. He can't even have a shower in my house. He needs more skin grafts, medical attention right now. It's a nightmare."

Meanwhile, Lisa's father said that he could not handle the massive responsibility of caring for Joey, nor did he want to, and that he wanted his life back.

Lisa stated in the same article that despite their best efforts to get assistance from the government to help with Joey's worsening wounds, they were constantly told to go through "proper channels," which were never clarified. She also stated that she and her parents petitioned welfare officials and politicians to assist them in finding a properly equipped subsidized home, along with palliative care. The article ended with Lisa stating, "He has to have full-time care. But nobody will do it. Nobody cares."

After just a few months at her parents' home and unable to find an apartment that Joey could live in, Joey and Lisa moved back into "the house that love built," which had become a shell of its former self. Joey finally started receiving the government disability benefits he had long been applying for, and while it was reported in various newspapers that he was receiving approximately $1,400 per month, what was not reported was that amount was reduced substantially because he was living rent-free, and that most of the money he received went to medical supplies not covered by OHIP. The debts he was unable to pay back slowly piled up, and by early 1997, Joey and Lisa owed more than one hundred thousand dollars. Making matters worse, they had defaulted on a seventy-six-thousand-dollar mortgage they had taken out on the house. As a result, sheriff's deputies were legally entitled to exercise a writ ordering Joey to move out of the house that had been built just for him.

A woman named Kathleen Keating was studying public relations at Fanshawe College in London, Ontario. She heard about Joey and Lisa's woes through the many newspaper articles being written about them and volunteered to help. In an effort to garner support for Joey, she set up a press conference a week before Joey and Lisa's scheduled eviction. It was to take place on the steps of the Wellesley Hospital and was to be broadcast on Citytv, a Toronto-based news channel. In addition to the press conference, Kathleen was able to convince the CBC's *The Fifth Estate* to rebroadcast a documentary they had made about Joey back in 1989. She also opened the Medical Home and Educational Trust Fund for Joey Philion as a means for people who wanted to help with donations. London lawyer Alan Patton agreed to act as administrator for the new fund.

The press conference started in the early afternoon of March 12. It was a chilly day, but Joey was not wearing a jacket. When asked why, he said he didn't feel the cold. Over the course of the conference, in his usual raspy voice, he asked for a temporary guarantor for another mortgage of approximately ninety-five thousand dollars, with the extra money after paying back the defaulted seventy-six-thousand-dollar mortgage going toward back taxes, an electricity bill that was in arrears, and other expenses. He said that if nobody was willing to help him, he and his wife were going to be homeless the following week. He added that if no guarantor was willing to come forward he hoped that somebody in Orillia or Toronto would provide him with a wheelchair-accessible apartment for about six hundred dollars per month. He said he just wanted to get his life together, that he wanted to finish high school and eventually study law and become a lawyer, so when the foundation he hoped to start for burn victims got going, he would be familiar with any legal issues he might have to deal with.

He also talked about Lisa's inability to find work, and how limited she was because she didn't have a driver's licence and they couldn't afford to apply for one. He then provided details about how tied down she was by the responsibilities of caring for him, from helping him bathe and doing countless other things most people never consider, to changing the dressings on the constantly seeping ulcers on the stumps of his amputated feet at least four times a day. He mentioned how he was supposed to have an operation to fix the ulcers at Wellesley Hospital, but they were closing it down and he had to wait until they moved the burn unit to the Sunnybrook Health Sciences Centre, which could take months.

In an opinion piece in the *Toronto Sun* published on March 17, 1997, an anonymous person wrote:

> Recently I saw Joe Philion on TV and just read a story about him in the Sun. I am one of Joe's neighbours in Cumberland Beach. I think he should stop asking people for help. People in our area have given enough already. He's twenty-three years old and has to start standing on his own two feet. The news says he gets $1,400 a month. And he and his wife can't live on that? At our house a good month is if we clear $450. Gimme a break. And if his wife, Lisa, is so willing to work, how

come she isn't busting her butt like other people to find a job? I've been searching for months, and my efforts finally paid off. They've got four dogs and their yard is littered with junk. People in the neighbourhood are indifferent to Joe now. They couldn't care less.

In contrast, in another letter addressed to Joey, which also included a money order for one hundred dollars, the author wrote the following:

Dear Mr. Phillion [*sic*],

I am writing to you in response to your news conference, which was televised on CITY-TV [*sic*] last week. Your situation touched me, as I can recall the first time I had heard your name due to your tragic accident. Your courage and bravery should be a source of inspiration to everyone.

I have enclosed a money order in your name, and hope that this can help ease your financial difficulties a little. I myself am not in a position to co-sign a loan, but I do hope that you get a response to your request.

I wish you and your wife all the best with your future endeavors.

D.

Nobody came forward as a guarantor and the new trust fund drew little money from the public. Joey and Lisa had no choice but to move out of "the house that love built." However, Advance Property Management of London did offer to rent Joey and Lisa a wheelchair-accessible townhouse in London, Ontario, as of April 30. It was an offer they gratefully accepted.

SHOTGUN

THE CEDAR WOOD COFFIN WAS CUSTOM BUILT BY THE DUCK BROTHERS: DAVE, Rob, and Steve. The lid had a beautiful carving of a wolf in the centre, done by John Baily. The plush interior was designed by Linda and her niece, Tanya. Hanging above the coffin were a blue-and-black plaid hunting jacket, a camouflage hunting jacket, a navy blue Umbro shirt, and a camouflage cap. There was a display featuring a 7mm hunting rifle, two small racks of 7mm bullets, and an assortment of colourful flowers.

There was also a fresh set of antlers from a deer Mike and Danny had been tracking for weeks. They had seen it several times, yet were never able to get a clean shot at it. But in the early morning of November 19, the day after Danny died, Mike went into the bush and couldn't believe his eyes when he spotted the same deer. He crawled to within forty yards of the beautiful animal, saw his opening, took a soft breath, and put it down with a single shot. The deer died before it hit the ground. When Mike reached the animal, he placed his hand on its soft fur and closed his eyes.

The three-day wake took place in the spare bedroom Danny used in the house where Mike, Linda, and Joey lived on Headquarters

Road in Courtenay. Visitors came at all hours. Friends, co-workers from the Diabetes Association, local homeless people, and old girlfriends all came to pay their respects. Many left gifts in the open coffin where Danny lay.

When the hearse arrived at the cemetery on November 21, Mike and some of Danny's closest friends took the coffin out. It immediately started cracking. Mike called for more people to help lift it and keep it from breaking. At first, Mike thought the coffin wasn't as sturdy as it appeared, but upon a brief inspection he confirmed that it was finely built, as tough and solid as Danny was. It was then he realized the cracking came from the additional weight from all the gifts placed inside.

There were many people at the funeral, but few words spoken. Heartbreak appeared on every face. As the priest spoke, Linda stood gazing at the sealed coffin. She did not wail. She did not utter a single word. She just stood there in a daze. Her eyes were dry, lifeless, and empty, as if she had already shed every tear she had. Mike stood silently beside her, holding her hand, staring down at the coffin. Joey was also there and, just like his mother, he didn't shed a tear.

Many people thought it was strange, even morbid, for Linda to insist on having Danny's body brought to her home and displayed for three days following his autopsy. She didn't care. She wanted to be with her son for as long as she possibly could before he was put in the ground. She didn't sleep for the entirety of the wake, refusing to forgo a single second of seeing his face. It was during those days, when nobody was around, that she cried for her youngest child, unleashing her tears so ferociously she looked and sounded as if she were being tortured. She had dealt with the possibility of losing Joey every single day since the fire, every single day for thirteen years, but losing Danny was a possibility she had never considered.

•

Daniel Gerald Philion was born on April 12, 1977.

Throughout his life, Danny fought to conceal a secret from almost everybody except for his immediate family and closest friend. Shortly after he was born, there were signs that something was wrong. His movements were uncoordinated, his muscle tone was uneven, and he was having problems moving the left side of his body, including his left hand. After several tests, doctors diagnosed him with cerebral palsy. They told Linda and Andy, Danny's father, that it was a debilitating condition that Danny was going to have to endure for the rest of his life. They weren't yet sure how severe it was, but considering how early they were able to identify it, they weren't hopeful.

As Danny got older, his symptoms worsened. Every time he tried to walk he ended up moving in a circle before falling, since he had no balance on his left side. He often cried and got angry. Linda told him to get back up and to keep trying. A few months after his third birthday he managed to teach himself how to walk in a straight line. He also had issues holding things and eating with his left hand, which was nearly paralyzed. Sick of constantly hearing from doctors that there was nothing they could do, Linda started tying his right hand. Danny was furious, demanding that she untie it and let him use it.

"Not until you learn how to use your other hand."

He argued, yelled, begged, and pleaded that his left hand didn't work.

"Then make it work."

Eventually Danny taught himself how to manipulate objects, including utensils, with his left hand. In time, he got so used to using his left hand there was little he couldn't do with it. However, despite his perseverance in teaching himself how to use his left hand, it was always difficult. He grew to believe that life was always going to be hard, always a challenge, always a battle he had to fight on his own.

When Danny started grade school, he altered his walk to conceal his limp and painfully forced his left hand to appear as if it functioned normally. But when the strain became too much and he could no longer hide his limp, or when his left hand started uncontrollably seizing, resulting in a dropped pencil or deformed appearance, his classmates laughed at him. He lashed out and fought anybody who mocked the effects of his condition. Danny didn't take well to school at all, nor did he take well to those who tried to tell him what to do within its walls. For students and teachers alike he was an adversary: a poor student, a problem child. As a result, he was always separated from others, always put in a state of isolation.

•

Hours after the fire, when he was taken to Lynda Young's home and left there while Mike and his mom went to Soldier's Memorial Hospital with Joey, ten-year-old Danny sat in the living room looking through the window, gazing at the black smoke billowing up from what was once his home. He wondered if his brother was dead and he feared he was responsible. He envisioned a scenario in which he could have prevented Joey from going back into the house after they both escaped unscathed. He regretted not grabbing his older brother and making him stay outside with him, believing that if he had, Joey would be right beside him in Lynda's living room, watching their house burn.

Days later, when Danny heard the news about Joey being transferred to the Shriners Burns Institute, and that his mother and Mike had to go with him, he was devastated. Since there were still months left in the school year, he had to stay in Orillia with his neighbours, Rick and Wilma. But he wanted to be with his mother and he wanted to be with his brother, and the idea of having to stay in school, a place he hated, instead of being with his family seemed stupid and wrong.

After joining Joey in Boston, Linda spoke to Danny as often as she could from the Halcyon House, but the long-distance calls were expensive, so she had to space them out while also keeping them brief. Danny tried to squeeze in as many words as he could during those conversations, talking at a rapid pace about how much he wanted to be there with her and with Joey. But when she wasn't able to respond quickly enough or show the attentiveness he wanted, he got angry.

On May 1, 1988, Danny was given the opportunity to go to Boston, where he could visit Joey at the Shriners Burns Institute. When he arrived and saw his older brother, he looked different. He was less frightening. His head was no longer swollen, and his face was more recognizable, but he also appeared more fragile than before as a result of all of the tubes connected to him. Joey gestured for Danny to give him a hug, but Danny hesitated. He was afraid to touch him, afraid to hurt his brother. A moment later, he watched a nurse enter the room and lift Joey, revealing the large skinless parts of his body. He stared at Joey's face, seeing the anguish. He gasped and backed up before asking his mother why she allowed the nurse to hurt his brother. She told him that any form of touching Joey hurt him, but it was necessary. After the nurse lowered Joey back down and left the room, he once again gestured for Danny to give him a hug.

In late June Danny was supposed to spend a week at a summer camp, but he didn't want to go. He wanted to go back to Boston with his mom and Mike so he could see Joey, but his mother told him no, that he had to go to the camp, that it was a gift. His mother drove him to the Yorkdale bus station and watched him get on the bus that was supposed to take him to the summer camp. However, as soon as his mother was out of sight, he got off the bus and started figuring out ways to get to Boston on his own. About an hour later, after being noticed by one of the bus station employees, he was forced to give them a phone number where they could reach Mike, who arrived not long after.

"I'm not going to the camp. I'm going to Boston with you and my mom."

When his mother saw him an hour later, she angrily told Danny to never do anything like that again, that something could have happened to him at the bus station.

"I'm not going to the camp," he replied. "I'm going to Boston with you and if you try to send me to the camp again, I'll just get off the bus again."

His mother and Mike glanced at each other before she replied, "Fine, you can come with us, but only for a little while, and when you come back here you're going to that summer camp."

Danny agreed. Keeping to his word, after spending a week in Boston to see Joey, he came back to Toronto and was once again driven to the Yorkdale bus station, but this time he stayed on the bus and went to the camp, where he ended up having a great time.

On the morning of September 7, 1988, when Danny was just a few days away from beginning the fifth grade, his mother, with an all-too-familiar pain in her eyes that he always hated seeing, brought him to the Children's Aid Society. He cried, yelled, fought, and argued, but she told him there was no other choice. She told him that Joey was going to have to stay in Boston for many more months, and she had to be there for Joey every day to help him survive.

"I know you want him to get better, Danny, and this is the only way," she told him. "Joey isn't doing well. He is losing weight. He's in constant pain and is getting depressed. He is giving up."

"What about Mike? Why can't I stay with him?" Danny asked.

"Mike is going to be in Boston with me, helping me take care of Joey."

"But what about me, Mom? Who is going to take care of me?"

When the possibility of being put into foster care was brought up throughout the summer, Danny listened, but didn't take it seriously, thinking it would never actually happen, but seeing his mother put pen to paper made it dreadfully real. While he stayed quiet, he was in a state of panic. After signing the forms, which seemed to go on forever, his mother said they were going to spend the day together. Before that, however, he was going to meet Marilyn, his new foster mother, who had just arrived at the office.

Marilyn was sweet, and made great efforts to comfort Danny, telling him she understood the situation and how upset he must be, but that it wasn't going to last forever, that he would be back with his mother as soon as it was possible. She then complimented him about how strong he was. But she was not his mother, and throughout their meeting he kept telling himself he would never call her mom. Even though he was mad at his mother for giving him up, she was still his mom, and nobody else was going to take her place.

Throughout the day with his mother, which they spent around Cumberland Beach, Danny made several last-ditch efforts to undo what he refused to believe was inevitable, but his mother was unwavering. He told her how unfair it was, and she agreed. As the hours quickly ticked by, he could see his mother getting sadder. He could see tears welling up in her eyes but never escaping. He thought it was his fault because of how hard he fought against her decision to give him up, but he was still upset with her. He couldn't understand why a mother had to give up one son to save the other.

At 5:00 p.m., Linda dropped Danny off at what was to become his new home. Marilyn welcomed him with a smile along with her husband, Buddy, who also welcomed him with a smile and warm words. Danny also met Marilyn and Buddy's son, David, who was around the same age as him. They got along almost immediately and started playing as soon as they met, but not before Danny reluctantly said goodbye to his mother while begging her one last time to let him go with her.

•

On April 17, 1990, less than a week after his thirteenth birthday, Danny moved into "the house that love built" along with Mike, his mom, and Joey. Believing the worst was over, that he no longer had to worry about living with other people, Danny thought life was back to normal. Back in Cumberland Beach he spent most of his time with his friends, especially during school breaks, while also helping his mother and Mike out with Joey. However, the stability didn't last and a little over a year later, he joined his family on their escape to Vancouver Island, forcing him to change schools from Sayward to Campbell River to Black Creek.

Despite the constant changes, Danny liked the attitudes of his peers on the island. All they wanted to do was spend time outdoors, which he loved, whether it was hiking, cliff diving, swimming in rivers and the ocean, riding on dirt bikes, or just doing whatever they felt like doing at the time. And while he did get into plenty of trouble, it was never anything serious, and usually just warranted a grounding, attitude adjustment with a belt, or the occasional visit by a local cop. By the time Danny reached fifteen years of age, he didn't want to live anywhere else. Vancouver Island had become his home, his new natural habitat. However, the comfort and stability of home was once again torn away from him when Wally arrived in the summer of 1992.

Not long after his mother and Joey were absorbed into Wally's world, Danny had no choice but to join them. He missed his friends. He missed Mike. He missed Vancouver Island. He hated seeing his mother always upset, always crying, always tired, and never paying him any attention. He hated seeing church members taking over a house he thought was built for Joey and his family, of which Wally, whom he hated the most, was not a member.

He couldn't stand the man with the nasty beard and obsession with Jesus who constantly issued demands and imposed ridiculous rules. That friction led to several arguments and a beating that Danny happily unleashed on him. Not long after that beating, however, Wally convinced Linda to send her youngest son to live with a foster family in Washago, south of Gravenhurst, twenty-five kilometres north of Orillia, where he remained for over a year.

In the spring of 1994, shortly after his seventeenth birthday, when his mother broke free of Wally and made the decision to return to Vancouver Island, Danny was overjoyed. He was finally returning to the place where he was happiest, while being rid of Wally and his madness. But the effects of that period had taken a toll on him.

While he enjoyed the trip back to the island with his mother and Tanya, once he arrived he was much quieter. Mike tried on several occasions to get him to open up about what had happened during the time he had spent around Wally, as well as the foster family he stayed with in Washago, but Danny refused to talk about it.

Over the next few years Danny got into a lot of fights. He fought people he didn't like. He fought people who didn't like him. He fought random people for trivial reasons. He fought people who rubbed him the wrong way. Some people he fought were the same size as him (which wasn't very big), others were bigger, few were smaller. Some fights he won. Some fights he lost. And when he lost a fight he always returned the following day, or even the same day, seeking a rematch, determined to settle the score. Fighting for Danny was about much more than the violence. The years of isolation and powerlessness created tension that needed to be released and if that meant forming a fist, then so be it. He didn't enjoy causing pain in others, but it was the only way he knew how to unburden himself of his anger. It was unhealthy therapy.

Despite his violent outbursts, in time Danny compiled an impressively long list of friends throughout the island, from Campbell River, Black Creek, and Courtenay to Comox, Nanaimo, and Tofino. Women liked him too, a lot. They were drawn to his strength, his impish sense of humour, and his direct, no bullshit demeanour, and he liked them just as much.

He became a huge hip-hop fan, revelling in the hits from the early and mid-1990s, from Goodie Mob's "Dirty South," Xzibit's "Papparazzi," Scarface's "I Seen a Man Die," and Raekwon the Chef's "Incarcerated Scarfaces" to Notorious B.I.G.'s "One More Chance (Remix)," Wu-Tang Clan's "Can It Be All So Simple," Snoop Doggy Dogg's "Murder Was the Case," Shaggy's "Boombastic," Bone Thugs-N-Harmony's "Mo' Murda," and Coolio's "Gangsta's Paradise." One of his favourite albums was Ice Cube's *The Predator*, a cassette he played over and over again until the ribbon eventually snapped.

Danny and Mike shared a bond that only grew stronger as Danny got older. They were each able to understand the toll the fire and its aftermath had taken on the other without ever having to discuss it. Mike also taught Danny about the value of marijuana during those years. He explained that it was an effective means to relax and ward off the demons created by the chaos. Danny heeded Mike's words and from the first time he tried it, he saw weed as a medicine first. He also found it to be a much better alternative to the prescription pills doctors offered him whenever he was brave enough to mention his troubled state of mind. It's because of that connection that Mike left a big, tightly rolled joint in Danny's coffin. He didn't put any matches or a lighter inside, however, knowing that would have hilariously pissed Danny off.

By the time he was in his twenties, Danny had matured a great deal. He became more responsible, while still finding time and reasons to have fun. He loved working for Diabetes Canada as a "swamper," which involved loading and unloading equipment and helping set it up. He was well liked by his co-workers, who always enjoyed his sense of humour and energetic presence. He also spent a lot of time hanging out at a soup kitchen in Courtenay where he handed out meals to homeless people, many of whom he became friends with as he neither dehumanized nor deified them. Instead, he just talked to them like he would to anybody else. He saw a lot of himself in many of them, knowing he could have been just like them, and by all accounts *should* have been just like them. On many occasions he asked them why he wasn't like them, considering the constant moving around, the multiple foster families, the exposure to people like Wally and his church followers, his propensity to fighting, the isolation. He asked them what made him so different, why was he the one giving the meals instead of receiving them, why was he lucky when they weren't, to which they usually replied that's just how life is: some win, some lose.

Another factor that helped Danny transition from the mayhem of his adolescence to his calmer, more productive and hopeful adulthood was his relationship with Joanne. She was an attractive, sweet, warm woman. She was much older than Danny, in her mid-thirties when they met, while he was only around twenty-one. She also had a sixteen-year-old son, who Danny immediately took to, treating him like a younger brother. He was fiercely protective of Joanne's son, while also showing an eagerness to teach him and help him whenever possible, which was at times awkward for the boy, considering that Danny was sleeping with his mother. Nonetheless, they got along very well. Danny genuinely cared for him, just as he cared for his mother, who cared about him a great deal, usually going out of her way to prepare him lunches that he took to work, making him the envy of all his co-workers at the Diabetes Association.

Danny also became a talented hunter. It was a testament to his toughness as hunting, especially for big game like moose or elk, required physical endurance, and for Danny that wasn't always easy. His cerebral palsy was still an issue, and there were many times when his symptoms were even worse than when he was a child, resulting in several grand mal seizures that involved a loss of consciousness.

As a result of Danny's hunting skills, which earned him the nickname "Shotgun," Mike started taking him to a place he rarely took anybody: his favourite hunting spot, Pink Mountain. Located about 180 kilometres northwest of Fort St. John on Mile 143 of the Alaska Highway, it is a little-known, beautiful peak in the foothills of the Canadian Rockies that gets its name from its pinkish seams. At Pink Mountain, Danny finally got to experience isolation in a way that didn't make him feel angry, neglected, or threatened; instead, he was able to appreciate its peace.

In the summer of 2001, during a trip to Pink Mountain, Danny and Mike managed to track and kill an enormous moose, the biggest either of them had ever seen. A few months after that trip, Danny and Joanne separated. He considered reconciling not long after the separation and she did too, but before he felt ready to give the relationship another chance, he wanted to have some fun first.

On the night of November 17, Danny was hanging out with two young women he was casually seeing in a cottage in Courtenay, right across the street from the home where Mike, Linda, and Joey lived. He wanted to party throughout the night but was starting to feel tired at around 11:30 p.m. He went to see Joey and, for the first time ever, asked if he had any pills to help him stay up all night. Joey said he did and gave him two 200 mg morphine pills, of which he had plenty.

Danny took the pills and went back across the street to the cottage where the young women were waiting, but less than two hours later, at around 1:30 a.m., Danny came back and told Joey that something was wrong, that he didn't feel right. Joey told him that to balance himself out he should take an ounce of methadone, of which Joey also had an ample amount. Danny took the methadone, returned to the cottage, and partied a little longer before losing consciousness on the bed between the two women. They thought he had just fallen asleep but his heart had stopped, and when they woke up later that morning there was nothing they could do.

The coroner concluded that Danny had died from a morphine overdose. In addition to the morphine and the methadone, there were only minor traces of marijuana and no traces of alcohol in his bloodstream.

He was twenty-four years old.

LINDA'S DIARIES

IN THE SUMMER OF 2001, WHILE LIVING WITH MIKE IN COURTENAY, BRITISH Columbia, Linda started writing a diary. The following is a series of paraphrased entries from that diary.

JULY 5

Her mother and father are both gone. Of her three older siblings, her brother Gary has been missing since December 27, 2000, after receiving fifteen thousand dollars; her brother Johnny escapes into himself and is batshit crazy; and her sister Debbie is depressed and may have stomach cancer. But she is happy. Joey is finally coming back home to stay with her and Mike after separating from Lisa. He arrives at 9:45 a.m.

She is worried about her oldest son, concerned he might become dependent on her. But he told her he needs her and she doesn't want to let him down. She isn't sure how much she can do for him, however, how much she can provide. She and Mike don't have much money and their debts are piling up. But she can't tell Joey that. She can't bear telling him how broke she is.

She is scared he is giving up. She is looking at the snow-covered mountains of the island. They look like heaven. There is a feeling in her gut that something is coming, that what she has been dreading for so long is soon to happen.

She wants to get healthier, to finally quit smoking, to drink less, to finally start taking care of herself.

JULY 7

She cleaned Joey's wounds in the morning. They looked worse than she had ever seen before. What remained of his left leg had been eaten away by infection. Green slime constantly oozes out. His wounds aren't exposed to enough air, only receiving it during his baths and dressing changes. They're festering. The nurses who occasionally visit him are only able to give him forty-five minutes a day. They are so overworked with other patients. Joey is not receiving the care he needs.

She has to change his drip pad every hour since he came back to live with her. It's great, though, because that means the poisons from his infections are leaving his body.

Joey hasn't been eating well for a while because he has no money. His spirits are low.

She and Joey went to Wolf Lake. His electric wheelchair was able to fit on the homemade raft she made for him. He was so happy when told they were going on their very own private booze cruise.

She thanked God he was back with her.

On the other side of the lake, she washed Joey's body and hair. He was kept afloat by a large flotation device. He loved the feeling of the water until he fell out of the floaty. She tried to hold him up, but the water was soon over his head. He started choking. With help from Mike and other family members, she managed to get him out of the water. She worried she'd have to give him mouth to mouth. Luckily, he started breathing on his own, then made a joke: "Mom, how about only one drowning attempt per week."

Even after thirteen years, he requires around the clock care. She and Mike aren't rich, so he can't get what he needs. It always looks so easy and so beautiful on TV and in the movies. People suffer accidents and everything is just magically taken care of. They usually end up solving mysteries, or writing books, or doing other amazing things. But in real life, with real people, that is not how it goes. It is a constant struggle. No longer famous. No more fund. Government assistance money being stretched like a rubber band begging to break. Hard times are hard times, even after surviving a horrible accident.

They still enjoy the little things, though. They can have campfires and roast marshmallows. They can fish.

JULY 12

Joey moved into his own apartment in Courtenay. It's empty. There is nothing but a bed and a chair. She can't bear having him stay there alone, staring at the four walls.

He still suffers so much and always needs his pain medication. The pills, the fucking pills. She is right back where she started. She suffers constant pain and anguish over Joey's pain. She barely sleeps. She always feels like she has to be there for him. She always has to make his pain go away. Like an eternal nurse, always on call. No days off. No rest. No life to keep what is left of his life going.

She works midnight shifts as a dispatcher for Comox Taxi.

Joey needs additional skin grafts, even after thirteen years. So many surgeries over the years. After the grafts he will need at least a month of bedrest.

He has to visit the welfare office. He tried to get into a computer class.

She writes again about getting healthier, about finally quitting smoking. But she is so preoccupied with her new chores. Constantly changing his dressings. Constantly massaging him with ointments and creams. She still has to work every night.

JULY 18

She is very sick. She can't stay awake. The doctor says she has a bronchial infection. She has to go on antibiotics and use a puffer. She got a note requesting stress leave from her job for one to three months. But she needs money. She tells the taxi company she can still work Wednesday, Thursday, and Friday. Next week is welfare week, too busy for a new dispatcher. Boss says she'll see; says, "The sooner you're off, the sooner you'll be back."

Nurses say it will take a year for Joey to get full-time services. She replies that it's too hard to take care of him, that she is too sick. Mike disrupts the meeting with the nurses, demanding the full-time services immediately. He tells them how hard his wife is working. They need help.

Next day a nurse comes and changes Joey's dressings, but gives no sponge bath. She has to do it herself. Seems like the system is done with Joey. He was a miracle survivor. But thirteen years later it is too much, too boring for the nurses and doctors. In their minds, maybe he should have survived for a year or two and then died a hero. But he kept crushing expectations. He just kept on living. She is the only one who didn't get sick of caring for him.

JULY 25

She no longer has the strength to lift Joey. She worries that Mike's privacy has been destroyed ever since Joey started living with them. She knows Mike hasn't forgotten or forgiven what Joey said about him, what Joey did to him. She can't hold anything against Joey.

She is happy Joey is back. She never wants him to leave again.

Mike is very angry. It stresses her out more than he knows.

The house is a constant mess. Joey sleeps all the time when she doesn't take him to work with her.

JULY 31

Mike went to his mother's. He is staying for two weeks.

Joey needs to get out on his own for a bit. He needs to live life without her for a while. He needs to know what it's like.

Time off is a godsend. She can take a breather. The nurses' help is so needed and so appreciated. God will get them through everything. She doesn't want Joey to feel like a burden. He is a gift.

AUGUST 18

Joey is teaching her how to live without him. He tells her not to stay overnight anymore. They talk a lot. They're going to write a book together about their experience. She is getting weaker. Instead of going home at 2:00 or 3:00 a.m. from Joey's, she leaves at 11:00 p.m. or midnight. Sometimes she skips entire days. She hates that. He tells her to do it.

She knows what he is doing. He is leaning closer to death. He seems so at peace. She can see the angels around him. It's breathtaking, but also scary.

•

Those were the final thoughts expressed in her 2001 diary.

•

In 2005, Linda admitted to Mike that she wanted Joey to die. She believed he had been through enough, and she had been through enough. She started working on another diary in the fall of that year in which she recollected what she felt after Danny's death on November 18, 2001, four years earlier.

NOVEMBER 15

She had started staring at Danny's coffin at 6:00 a.m. She only had seven hours left with him. She begs God in heaven to fill her with the Holy Spirit, to keep her strong. She wants Danny to be filled with the white light of the Holy Spirit. She doesn't want him to get lost. He needs to be guided to the angels above. She thanks him for choosing her to be his mother for twenty-four years, six months, and twenty-four days. She wants him to show her he is okay. She wants to learn how to be guided to him. She wants him to teach her how to communicate with him. She knows he can do this. She needs this. She isn't sure if she can let people take his body away in the coffin. She will always want one last kiss. One last touch. One last look at her youngest son.

She feels angry. She feels regret. She believes she should have spent more time with Danny. She tells God she should have been a better mother.

As the minutes tick by, she stays in front of Danny. It is gut-wrenching. Agonizing. Full of fear and pain.

Soon, Dan, they're going to put the lid on the box made of love and never will I get to touch you again.

She is scared. She begs Danny to help her through it. She doesn't want them to take him away. She wants him to stay where he is.

Five hours to go.

She feels like she is going to explode. It is ripping her apart.

Four and a half hours to go.

She believes she is giving up a part of herself.

Three hours to go.

People are showing up. They're preparing for his exit out of her life. She asks Danny if he knows he is dead, that he took some of Joe's pills and never woke up. She tells him that he needs to go to the light, to Grandma and Grandpa, who will meet him there. She says she, Tanya, and Joanne are going to a psychic and for him to please be there or come with her.

She hopes the psychic is real so she can see him.

Two hours and ten minutes to go.

She is learning to appreciate his music, to appreciate the meaning of the songs. It is his time to go to a better place but she can't come to grips with it. Was twenty-four years long enough? It is the hardest, saddest thing she has ever felt, even with Joe, because Joe didn't die. The pencil is heavy.

Dear God, they're taking you away.

DECEMBER 5

To bring a child into the world is painful — when a child is taken out of this world, your heart will truly break.

It's been seventeen days since Dan died. Her body screams for him. Her heart begs for him. She can't take it. She is on her knees. He has her attention. He has all of her emotions of love, fear, anger.

What the fuck do you want from me? Fuck, I've had enough.

She wants her son to tell her he is okay, happy, and safe.

She wants to see Sylvia Browne, the medium from TV, to find out. They spoke on the phone. Sylvia offered to help her for a fee of ten thousand dollars. She is willing to pay it.

She told Mike about Sylvia, the self-proclaimed medium who gained fame from numerous appearances on *The Montel Williams*

Show and *Larry King Live*, who was discredited on several occasions, particularly in the early 2000s when she provided false information about several missing children. She told him the fee Sylvia was charging and Mike said they didn't have that kind of money, and even if they did, they weren't going to give it to a fraud like her.

DECEMBER 14

It's the morning of November 18, 2001. A cop comes to the house. She and Tanya are getting ready to go to the beach. Mike is hunting in the bush. The cop asks if Dan was her son. Why "was"? She said he *is*. The cop says he is dead. She screams *no*. She grabs the cop and forces his body around the room. She tells him he is mistaken.

She suddenly feels calm. She sits in disbelief. She has to identify the body. She tells Mike when he comes back from hunting. He screams and cries before going into shock.

Joe is asleep. When he wakes up, she tells him Dan is dead. He is calm. She believes he isn't reacting because he is too busy worrying about her. He looks confused.

She still can't believe it.

It doesn't start to get real until she arrives at the hospital to identify his body. She opens the door to the room where he is supposed to be. She hopes it isn't him. She takes one look.

She doesn't celebrate Christmas that year. She helps at the soup kitchen instead. The same one where Danny used to spend a lot of his time.

She begs him to show her something. She needs him to send her something to reassure her that he is okay. She wants him to pull her hair, to mess with the lights. She just wants to know that he is okay, even in death.

•

Within the pages of that diary, there is a letter Linda wrote.

Well, here I am, 50 years old. I lost my dad then mom, Danny and knowing Joe may pass soon. I'm broke, no nest egg, on stress leave and scared to death knowing I'm going to bail on this next hurtle [sic], good possibility I may lose my marriage and lose the one and only person that will love and care for me the most on this planet. Since March 10th, 1988, I have been caring for Joe and watching him get to his full potential and watching his body grow weaker over the years, thinking of the amazing miracles I've seen on this journey.

The letter continues with Linda wondering why she was sent on the journey. She had seen one child in a wheelchair. She buried her other child. She saw a local psychic who said Danny sent her peace and she believed it to be true because she felt it. The letter finished in mid-sentence.

I feel my body falling apart with abuse for me ...

The rest of the tattered notebook is blank, until nearly halfway through a page filled with words written in blue ink appears.

The date has shifted from 2005 to early 2009.

MARCH 7

At around 11:00 a.m., while at work, she feels a pain in her chest, followed by another and another. She gets up, takes a few steps, and nearly falls. She thinks it's a heart attack. Somebody calls an ambulance. She spends eight hours in the ER. She has an X-ray. It wasn't a heart attack, they say. Must have been stress related, they say.

MARCH 10

She calls Mike from work at 5:00 p.m. and tells him they made it through another March 10. The anniversary of the fire is never a good day. An hour later the phone rings. It's the doctor. They found a spot on her lung. They want to do a CAT scan to check it out.

MARCH 17

She does the scan.

MARCH 21

She sits in the doctor's office. She begs her not to say she has cancer. She closes her eyes and holds them shut. She opens them. She stares at the doctor who says she is very sorry. The doctor says it doesn't look good. It has spread to the lymph nodes of her lungs. She leaves the office devastated. She believes she is a dead woman walking. She calls the office at Comox Taxi. She is crying. She asks them to send Mike to the doctor's office. [He was driving one of the taxis.] She calls her sister, crying. She tries holding it together when telling Mike. He can't grasp what is going on. He refuses. He says it can't be. He says they will fix it. He says everything will be okay. She tells Joe. He handles it well. He tells her paradise awaits her.

APRIL 14

Mike is going to drive her to her biopsy appointment tomorrow at 7:30 a.m. She is terrified. She can't relax. She doesn't want to write anymore. Time is going so fast, a far cry from how slow it went twenty-one years ago when she was caring for Joey. She is going to be at the table before she knows it, waiting for results she doesn't want to hear. There won't be good news. Life is over. She believes in

God. Paradise is waiting for her. She will be with God the creator. She will be with her mom and dad. She will be with Danny. She will be with all of the people who have passed away over the years. She will be with all of the beautiful pets. Dying isn't a bad thing. It's just scary getting there.

APRIL 27

She gets the biopsy results at 2:30 p.m. Fate awaits. She is scared. Very scared. Is the doctor going to tell her she is going to die? She sees the world for what it is: a mess. She believes in God. But she isn't sure if she is worthy enough for eternal paradise. She believes when it is her time to go God will take her home. She believes God will come for her before December 21, 2012, like it says in the bible.

On April 20, Linda had written a letter to Joey that was never given to him.

> *Hi Kiddo, I guess if you're reading this, I am in heaven with God and Danny, mom, dad and everyone else who has passed, all my pets, too. Paradise Joe, wow. I'm here right now, and I'm going to try to be with you when you read this letter. I will do whatever I can to show you I'm here right now. I'm not sure what I will be able to do but I will try everything available to me, or Danny can show me how it works.*

The letter continued with her telling Joey that he was a great son, and she thanked him for sharing his knowledge of God with her. She told him it was scary to know she would be dying soon, but her soul knew where it was going, and when she let herself hear that, she felt peace.

She wrote that she believed the journey she was about to take was the best journey of all. She would take all of her experiences over the years with her to heaven, where she believed she would need it, where she would be healthy and full of life and busy working. Maybe she would be helping people cross over. She told Joey she knew he was hoping to join God as well but he had to be patient, that he was very special and God had amazing work planned for him and he knew it. Everybody would be waiting for him in heaven and when he saw her, she wanted him to run into her arms with a somersault, but to make sure he didn't trip over all the pets. He had to remember to be prepared to be licked and jumped on before he reached his family.

She also assured him that Mike would pay his cable so he could keep watching TV and keep using the internet.

JUNE 10

She is told to do chemo, radiation, and surgery, then more chemo and more radiation. She will not do chemo or radiation. She will try her best to shrink the tumor with natural cures. She believes in God.

NO DATE, LAST ENTRY IN THE DIARY

Joe's body is getting tired of healing. He is getting weak. His wish is to come home and die. Living at an old-age home is taking away his quality of life. It is so short-staffed. He is at peace. He is ready to cross over.

Then Linda wrote down the combination of her safe, her cell phone password, her Visa credit card number, bank account information, Air Miles reward card information, and instructions for Mike to take everything. She wanted him to max out her credit card and transfer everything he could to the website where he liked to play poker. She wanted him to have everything, even though there was barely anything.

She told Mike her biggest fear was there was nothing after death. No God, no paradise, nothing but blackness. She couldn't bear that thought, so she refused to believe it. Instead, she chose to believe in God and paradise and the dream of seeing her parents, her youngest son, and her pets again. She refused to accept the possibility that all of the pain she had endured and all of the suffering she had seen and felt was for absolutely nothing.

•

The cancer that was first discovered in her lungs in 2009 eventually spread to her brain.

On June 12, 2010, early in the morning, while lying in the bed she shared with her husband, she shouted, "I can't handle the headache anymore. It's time." Mike gently lifted her and positioned her against a pillow, doing all he could to make her comfortable, but the pain in her head was too much.

He called for an ambulance. It arrived within minutes. While they waited, they said, "I love you," to each other as many times as they could. After getting her into the ambulance, Mike followed in his car to St. Joseph's Hospital. When they arrived, Mike realized he was parked in an emergency area. He told the paramedics that he had to move his car and would be right back, but to wait for him so he could talk to his wife and be with her as they took her in. However, when he got back, the paramedics and his wife were gone. He rushed inside the hospital and was told Linda had already been taken into the ER and was getting X-rays. He waited, hoping to say, "I love you," again, hoping to hear her say, "I love you," back. The image from the X-ray showed her entire brain as stark white. She never regained consciousness. At 6:20 a.m. on June 14, 2010, she passed away.

She was fifty-five years old.

•

It wasn't until a few years after Linda's death that Joey would reveal to Mike the lie he had been holding on to for decades: he was responsible for the fire that changed all of their lives. It is tragic that Linda died always believing she was the one responsible for what happened on that bitterly cold March morning. The weight that the feeling of culpability had on her for so many years was immeasurable.

THE EMBERS REMAIN

IN THE DAYS LEADING UP TO AND THE DAYS FOLLOWING DANNY'S FUNERAL, JOEY was in a state of absolute denial. He refused to believe his actions had anything to do with his brother's death.

Over time, just as Danny regretted not being able to hold his big brother back when they were both safe outside of the burning house, Joey regretted not holding his little brother back. He wished he had done something differently. In the weeks, the months, and the years following Danny's death that regret only grew, but the reality was even worse: the same medicine Joey was given to ease his pain ended up causing more pain than he could have ever imagined.

Shortly after Linda received her cancer diagnosis and made it clear she was going to forgo chemotherapy and radiation (a decision that angered Joey, as he believed that having asked him so many years earlier to go through absolute hell to stay alive for her, she was obligated to do the same for him), *CTV News* published a story on July 5, 2009.

"He's not afraid to die at all," Linda was quoted as saying. "In fact, he's looking forward to it."

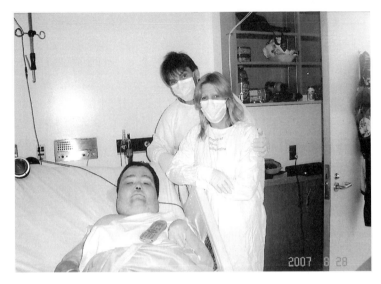

At St. Joseph's Hospital in Courtenay, British Columbia, on August 28, 2007, Joey is visited by Terry and Connie Hawkins.

The article described Joey's state as bedridden and bloated after enduring hundreds of surgeries over more than two decades. Catheters no longer worked, preventing him from emptying his bladder. Yet another surgery was recommended to fix the issue. It involved cutting a hole through his "cement-like" stomach to drain it. However, an anesthesiologist wasn't available to assist in the procedure.

"It's a very high-risk, high-infection decision that they're not sure they're going to make," Linda said, adding that without the surgery, her son wouldn't survive much longer. "His bones are in a lot of pain, and his back. He carries a lot of pain with him."

Near the end of the article, Linda was quoted as saying, "His soul's happy. His happiness is because he's at peace ... And he really is. He believes in God. He has a very healthy outlook on death."

An article published by the *Peterborough Examiner* on June 17,

2009, echoed the sentiment that Joey was ready to die, with a quote from Joey that stated, "I know my body. I know for a fact my body is ready to go. I've reached the end of the line."

Linda was also quoted as saying, "Joe's body has been trying to heal for more than twenty-one years and it's finally giving up. He's going downhill fast."

The article continued detailing the aftermath of Joey's survival and the meteoric rise of his celebrity, culminating in the establishing of the fund and the construction of "the house that love built," before summing up Joey and the family's precipitous fall from grace with the following lines:

> In the years that followed the family fought over access to the trust fund. A man claiming to be Philion's biological father showed up on Cleveland Avenue and moved in with his putative son for a while.
>
> Other people came and went and as the money disappeared, the house got more run down and one winter, according to a neighbour, the pipes burst because the heat and electricity had been cut off.
>
> The hope and optimism that had swept through the community began to sour and public opinion began to turn against Philion and his family.

In what reads as a final nail in the proverbial coffin, the article concluded with the following lines:

> Philion, now living on a disability pension, eventually had to sell the house built for him to pay off debts.
>
> The house has sold a number of times since and is neatly kept by the current owners, the lawn trim and a row of yellow and purple irises lining the driveway.

"The first few years after the fire, strangers would drive by the house to gawk," said Tamara McKendry, who lives directly across the street, "but people in the neighbourhood rarely mention Philion or his family anymore."

Joey's desire for death and ability to talk about its inevitability was no secret to anybody around him, including doctors and nurses. One day in late 2010, during a conversation with Mike, the question of what to do with his body after his death came up. A doctor and a few nurses were present and none of them, despite their best efforts, could hold back laughter when Joey, without missing a beat, said, "We already tried cremation and that didn't work, so that's out."

On several occasions Joey asked Linda to end his suffering, but she always refused, saying to do that would be admitting that he was giving up. After her death, however, he made it clear to Mike that he no longer wanted to live. And while he had asked him before to end his suffering, just as he had asked his mother, that day was different. On that day, with tears in his eyes, he begged Mike to end his misery.

Mike knew the life Joey was living better than anybody. He knew Joey wasn't doing anything except sitting in his room in the extended care ward at St. Joseph's Hospital. He knew nobody was visiting him anymore and that nobody cared about him anymore. Several residents in the ward, most of whom were suffering from dementia, would walk into his room and just take his things. Sometimes he was asleep when it happened but during the times he was awake, he begged them to leave his room and to leave his stuff, but unable to raise his voice, unable to move, he had no choice but to watch it happen. One day, while he slept, somebody walked right into his room and stole his computer, the only outlet he had to the outside world.

Mike considered doing what Joey asked of him, and that terrified him. He knew if he did what Joey was begging him to do he would end up in prison, where he would probably die because he couldn't live through the long sentence he'd be facing. Nonetheless, he went as far as speculating with Joey as to how it could be done. Several options were discussed, but no real planning ever took place. Mike was unwilling to sacrifice his own freedom to grant Joey his. To further distance himself from taking things any further, he didn't visit Joey again for three months, scared that in a fit of pity he might do what he knew he would spend the rest of his days regretting. Joey was left powerless, forced to live until his body, and his body alone, decided it was time to die, regardless of how much his mind and his heart wanted it to happen.

It was during this period of despair in 2013, on Joey's fortieth birthday, when Mike brought a fresh deer roast with potatoes, carrots, and gravy to his room at St. Joseph's Hospital, that Joey admitted he had started the fire by accident. Earlier that day, Joey had decided to get baptized, and Mike believes Joey's confession was a result of his baptism, that it motivated him to cleanse himself of a burden that he felt he had to bear because of the immense media pressure placed upon him.

Mike had always suspected that something didn't add up when it came to how the fire started. Even the physical evidence — including a log found two and half metres from the fireplace, a clear sign there was tampering of the fireplace by whoever was home and awake at the time, which was only Joey — had left Mike confused and suspicious. Linda also suspected something wasn't right but refused to entertain any further thoughts about it because all she cared about was her oldest son. When Mike finally found out the truth from Joey's own mouth, he was furious. He hated Joey at that moment, and since that conversation their relationship was permanently fractured. He couldn't speak to Joey for months afterward because he was too hurt that he and Linda had lived a lie they knew nothing about and had unknowingly supported for over twenty-five years, a lie that Linda never got to discover for herself but undoubtedly would have forgiven Joey for telling.

That same day, Joey also confessed to Danny's father, Andy, that he accidentally started the fire. The first thing Andy asked was "Why didn't you tell the truth?" Joey replied, "I was nervous, and scared of what people would think. I didn't want to be blamed for what happened." Andy, just like Mike, was furious at what he had heard, furious that everyone else had been blamed, while Joey got to be the hero.

MIKE

ON AUGUST 19, 2019, MIKE HAWKINS HAD A PSYCHIATRIC CONSULTATION AT the North Island Mental Health and Substance Use Services Collaborative Care Clinic. He was referred to the clinic by his long-time doctor who wanted him to get an assessment that would likely confirm the post-traumatic stress disorder he believed Mike had been suffering through for years.

The following excerpts are from the report written by the psychiatrist after the consultation they had with Mike.

> *Michael is a 60-year-old man who is living in Campbell River in a trailer with his partner.*
>
> *He states that he has had multiple losses over the years and recently he has not been able to handle the emotions that have come up and this seems to be worse since his wife died in 2010.*

Mike provided details about his childhood, from hanging out on Yonge Street in Toronto when he was eleven and twelve years old and his teenage hitchhiking adventures back and forth across

Canada to his strained relationship with his mother and the imprisonment of his father.

He had to put his dog down after his wife died, which was another trauma.

Yellow was a warm, gentle, extremely friendly golden retriever that Mike got as a puppy in August of 2001. From the moment he had her, they were inseparable. During the most stressful periods of the early 2000s, Yellow was always there to comfort him, whether it was licking his face to wake him up in the morning or bringing him one of her many toys and dropping it in front of him.

Yellow was well known around the Courtenay and Comox area of Vancouver Island. People always knelt down to pet her whenever they saw her, which she gladly accepted. Whenever she rode in the back seat of whatever car Mike was driving, she poked her head out of the open window with her tongue dangling whenever Mike shouted, "Look, Yellow, there's another dog."

Linda called Yellow her daughter.

Whenever Mike and Linda visited Joey at St. Joseph's Hospital, the staff let Yellow freely roam the hallways, despite that being strictly against the rules. The residents, most of whom were living their last days, loved it whenever she came around because she was always happy to sniff, lick, and shake a hand.

In March of 2014, Mike was told Yellow had cervical cancer. Despite his financial difficulties, he paid three thousand dollars to have her undergo emergency surgery. She was fine throughout the summer, but in the beginning of September she suddenly stopped eating. She couldn't walk very well and it was obvious she was in pain. Mike brought her back to the vet. They said they might be able to perform another procedure, but the odds of success were low and it was expensive. Mike wouldn't have cared about the money if he had it, but he didn't. The reality of the situation devastated him, but the vet told him, perhaps to ease his guilt, that even if Yellow had the surgery and survived it, she was already very old and would probably not make it much longer anyway. Nevertheless, Mike wanted nothing more than to keep her by his side. He needed her, but Yellow was suffering and even though it was going to crush him, he knew she had to be put down. He chose to do it himself so he could spend as much time with her as he could.

The following day, he took Yellow on a long walk along one of their favourite trails not too far from home. Despite her obvious pain, Yellow walked right next to Mike, who walked slowly, savouring every moment he had with her. She constantly looked up at him, her big expressive eyes peering into his own.

When they got back home, he laid out all of her toys in the backyard and watched her play with them. He then made her a steak dinner and gave her a big bowl of ice cream for dessert. Meanwhile, he kept his sadness hidden, fearing she would sense it. Afterward, he brought out her favourite blanket and they lay on it together. He held her close, but gently, not wanting to cause her any more pain than she was already feeling. She licked his face. He rubbed her ears and neck, the spots she enjoyed most, while she closed her eyes, soaking in his touch. Her breathing was laboured.

Mike had hidden a .22 calibre rifle underneath the blanket. Yellow knew guns were never good. She often went hunting with him and the sounds they made always scared her. He didn't want her to panic, not even for a single second, so he waited patiently for an opportunity when she was distracted and found it when she started staring up at the sky, her tongue out, tail wagging, looking every bit as beautiful, sweet, and loving as ever. He grabbed the gun, pointed it at the back of her head, closed his eyes, thought of nothing but her, and fired.

After he buried her, he finally unleashed the tears that had been building up ever since the inevitable became real. He couldn't stop. He cried until it physically hurt. He cried like an infant incapable of expressing his pain any other way.

He didn't want another dog, believing it was impossible to find one that would love him, and he would love, as much as Yellow. But in November of 2018 he believed he was finally ready to give and receive that same love again and he got a beautiful, energetic Labrador puppy. He named her Willow.

He states that he has a great deal of difficulty sleeping and he has nightmares and sleep walking most nights. Even with some Trazodone he only gets about 4 hours of sleep per night.

He has intrusive memories as well as flashbacks and multiple triggers including smells and hospitals.

To this day, every year, on March 10, with no set alarm, Mike wakes up at 6:14 a.m., just like he did in 1988.

Almost every other morning, feeling pressure in his chest, lungs, throat, and face, Mike wakes up screaming as hard as he can, but not a sound comes out. He never remembers the nightmares he suffers night after night and is thankful for that, believing that knowing the origins of such bloodcurdling, muted screams would reveal a horror he doesn't wish to see. Linda suffered from the same silent screams, often waking up with the same expression of terror.

When Mike wakes up from his nightmares, he is completely soaked to the point where his T-shirt, underwear, and pyjama pants need to be wrung out and dried in the still dark morning. The sheets usually need to be changed, as well, as if he were a child, but instead of urine from his bladder, it's fearful sweat his body can't contain.

Sitting awake in the early mornings, with the rest of the world resting peacefully save for the animals outside, he quietly drinks coffee, then smokes a cigarette and a joint back to back. The television is usually on, turned to a channel playing classic television shows, the kinds of shows he enjoyed watching in his youth, from *Gomer Pyle, U.S.M.C.; The Jeffersons*; and *All in the Family* to *The Twilight Zone* and *Alfred Hitchcock Presents*.

When he sleepwalks, Mike always goes outside, sometimes in nothing but his underwear when the nights are hottest. Once out there, he just stands in the darkness under the stars and moonlight.

He questions if his nightmares stem from being a prisoner of guilt. Despite doing all he could over the years, he feels as if it was not enough, that he failed. His only solace comes from the belief that he did not fail Linda, that he stuck with her to the very end.

While he can't recall the details of his nightmares, he can remember the smell: the indescribable stench of burnt flesh. He believes that unmistakable smell will eternally haunt him after hundreds of days spent in the Shriners Burns Institute and the Hospital for Sick Children. Whenever that smell invades his nostrils in the world of reality, even if only for a moment, he panics and attempts to flee, as if the smell is fire itself. He suffers the same bouts of terrifying panic whenever he smells bleach, as he immediately starts hearing Joey's tortured screams during every bath he was forced to take in the enormous tub. Even the sterile odour of a hospital itself makes Mike shudder, overcoming him with fear as soon as he walks in. He can't handle it. It sends him down a spiralling descent into memories he can never escape.

One night, when Danny was lying in his coffin in the next room, the day before he was to be taken to the cemetery to rest, Mike awoke from another nightmare and saw Yellow standing at the bedroom doorway, loudly barking into the open air. Mike stared, momentarily confused, wondering if he had even woken up at all because Yellow never barked. Nonetheless, he trusted her, and if she was barking in the direction of something he was convinced something was there. He believed it was Danny.

Current Medications Michael is on:
1. *Tylenol No. 3 PRN*
2. *Bisoprolol*
3. *Amlodipine*
4. *Trazodone 50-100 mg at bedtime*
5. *He was prescribed Citalopram 20 mg daily, but says he only took that for about 3 or 4 days then he stopped it.*

The psychiatrist recommended THC pills. Mike laughed before telling him that he had been smoking marijuana since he was eleven years old and that without it, he probably wouldn't have made it for as long as he has.

In the early spring of 2000, Mike broke his leg. He was prescribed Percocet for pain. He took the medication throughout his recovery, and while it helped ease the physical pain, the euphoric numbness against the mental exhaustion he had constantly felt made a much bigger impact. When his leg finally healed, the doctor told him he no longer needed the pills, but the feelings of escape and mental painlessness were too much to resist. He kept taking more Percocet despite the doctor halting his prescription.

Even when doctors were suspicious that other people might be taking some of Joey's pills, and even when Joey himself told the doctors he didn't need as much as he was receiving and they substantially cut down the amounts he was given, he still received an exorbitant number, resulting in plenty of leftovers for Mike. But when Danny died the following year, the pain of his loss was too much for Mike to handle, and the numbness he got from his daily dose of Percocet was no longer sufficient. He needed something else, something stronger, to help him escape from the pain.

During a hunting trip to Pink Mountain in 2002, Mike brought a bottle of OxyContin. He initially thought it would help him with the physical rigours of the trip, but once he started taking it, he couldn't stop. Known throughout Vancouver Island as hillbilly heroin, OxyContin was just as easy and just as free for Mike to get as Percocet, because he got them from the same source: Joey. At the house there was an abundance of the pills, just sitting there. Despite Joey consistently telling them he didn't need as much as they were giving him, the doctors kept on prescribing more and more OxyContin, just as they had Percocet.

It wasn't long before Mike knew he had a problem. He knew he had to stop. So he gathered all the leftover OxyContin in the house, which had continued growing month after month from Joey's excessive prescriptions (amounting to tens of thousands of dollars' worth), and flushed them down the toilet until there was nothing left. Afterward, he went cold turkey, resulting in weeks of withdrawal, a nightmare that caused him even more suffering than the pain that had led him to pills in the first place.

He lost his wife of 25 years in 2010 to cancer.

In the autumn of 1984, Mike and Linda were talking on the phone. She was at work at the Toronto Humane Society. He was at home. It was pouring rain. She brought up marriage and asked what he thought about it. He told her he would love to marry her. She said, "Okay," and then asked if he really wanted to do it. He said, "Yes." They decided to do it the following spring, during the Victoria Day long weekend in May. After their wedding on May 25, 1985, none of their family or friends thought they would last longer than a year.

The phone conversation Mike and Linda had when they decided to get married seemed banal, as if they were discussing what to eat for dinner that night, and that's because there was no thought required from either of them. The love they had for each other was already firmly established, so consummating a public, official confirmation of that love was as easy a decision as settling on chicken.

The moments most cherished between them were always the simplest ones, whether walking together along a trail in Vancouver Island, or just talking during a drive, or spending a night in a cheap motel in Orillia. It was that simple yet powerful love that guided Mike through the chaos following the fire. He loved Linda and he decided to stick with her until the end, right or wrong, and that was that.

When Linda refused to try chemotherapy and radiation for her cancer, Mike was angry, but when she told him she didn't want him to go through the same kind of pain and torment caring for her that he had gone through caring for Joey, he understood.

The worst pain came the morning after Linda's death, when he woke up without her next to him in the bed they had shared. It felt unnatural. It felt wrong. He had never felt sadder and lonelier in his entire life than he did at that moment.

After that, he couldn't sleep in their bed again. He wasn't even able to enter the bedroom he had shared with her, avoiding it as if there was a vicious contagion inside. He got fat, eating ice cream and anything else he could get his hands on, sitting on the same surprisingly comfortable couch where he also slept. He only saved himself from becoming obese by taking Yellow for walks in the bush that lasted for hours. When he was finally able to re-enter the bedroom, nine months had passed. Inside the room nothing had changed but there were cobwebs everywhere.

On the day of the fire, Mike's wedding ring, which he had left on the dresser because he couldn't wear it at work due to the heavy machinery he operated, was lost with the rest of his and the family's belongings, melted away in the heat of the blaze. A few years later, while they were living in "the house that love built," after managing to gather enough of her own money, Linda bought Mike a replacement wedding ring. He cherished it, and every year on May 25 he wears it all day to remember Linda, to honour her, before taking it off just before he goes to bed.

There has been a lot of financial stress.

Mike miraculously still has, and wears, the same light-blue jean jacket he acquired before the fire, before he got married, before the 1980s even started. He has managed to keep it clean but it does not look new, far from it. It still serves its purpose, however. It keeps him warm and the two inner pockets are still intact, one for his cigarettes and one big enough for a one-litre bottle of water. He never had the money to replace it. Whatever money he had went to Joey. Whenever there was a new procedure that wasn't covered by Canada's health care system that could potentially make Joey feel better, whenever the family had to travel across the country to accommodate his next appointment, whenever he needed supplies, whatever money Mike had accumulated through whatever jobs he could get would be used until there was nothing left. Whatever properties Mike had tried to purchase or build, maintain, and possibly sell over the years disappeared, one after another, first by fire, then by flood, then because of Wally. The next two properties he had were lost to Joey's needs.

Mike was never the kind of man to dream about riches but rarely having money, and never being able to keep it the few times he was able to make some, took an enormous toll. After the fire, he quickly extended the same view he had of his jean jacket to whatever vehicles he owned, the shoes he wore, and the guns he hunted with: if it still functioned, it was good enough for him. But that wasn't true. It wasn't good enough for him, nor was it a noble choice, or a repudiation of capitalism and greed. It was a mentality he had to adopt out of necessity. There was no choice in the matter. It didn't matter if he actually wanted something better or not, because there was no way to get it. Instead, he had to preserve what little he had — mend it when it ripped, fix it when it broke, and clean it to ensure continued performance, or else he would no longer have it.

There is nothing rewarding in not having anything, in never having money in your pocket or bank account, in not having a home in your name, in never being able to build any kind of savings. There is no freedom in financial frailty, only stress and pressure.

The reality of Mike's financial state was severely distorted by the media's constant coverage of the fund, a large sum of money the whole world could see but didn't care to understand. If that money was a reservoir of fresh water, the public refused to see the concrete dam encasing it, a dam that only gave access to a select few, of whom Mike was not one. Instead, they only chose to see the water and its shimmer from the constant light of cameras.

> *He is anxious all the time with easy startle and hypervigilance. He also has anger and irritability, although he is not an angry person.*

One early morning in the summer of 2020, somebody broke into Mike's car and stole his prized hunting jacket, three dollars in loonies, and his cigarettes. At around 4:30 a.m., not long after the break-in, with the sun still a few hours from rising, Mike went to a nearby drug den the local Campbell River police had no interest in shutting down. It was the kind of place that attracted people desperate enough to commit a robbery in the early hours.

Mike kicked the door of the den until four men came out. Unarmed, undeterred, and unafraid, Mike threatened the four men (all of whom were larger and much younger than him) with vivid descriptions of what he would do to them if he found out they had anything to do with the robbery. Terrified, they provided him with hints as to who the culprit was and the area where he could be found.

Less than two hours later, Mike tracked down the thief at a gas station not far from his home. He knew he had found the culprit because there was a decrepit pickup truck parked with Mike's beloved hunting jacket inside. It was one of the most precious and expensive items he owned, an item he took great care of, a necessity for whenever he went hunting, one of the few activities that brought him joy and peace. He opened the truck door and retrieved his jacket, which still had the cigarettes inside the pocket but no loonies. He opened the glove compartment and found thirty-two dollars in change, which he took, considering it a thievery tax.

Despite having his jacket and cigarettes back and more than ten times the amount of money initially taken from him, the anger he felt toward the person who had the audacity to steal what little he had and what little he cherished was too much to let go. So he walked into the gas station and proceeded to beat the shit out of the thief who, just like the four guys at the drug den, was bigger and younger than him. The beating was quick and bloody, and when Mike was satisfied the thief had got the message that he had robbed the wrong guy, he left. Meanwhile, the gas attendant looked on, appearing not that upset at what she had just seen.

Mike knew there was a strong possibility of consequences for his actions. He knew he might have to go to jail, where he would lose his freedom and lose even more time, but he didn't care. Somebody had stolen something he loved and it was unacceptable to have something else he loved taken from him. He couldn't and wouldn't stand for that. It was that simple.

A few days later, after seeing the security footage of the beating in the gas station, and already knowing who Mike was, local police went to his home, which didn't surprise him. The only surprise was how long it took for them to come. However, instead of arresting him on the spot, which he was certain was going to happen, they told him the man he beat up was even more known to them than he was. Additionally, being a big twenty-three-year-old "tough guy," he was embarrassed at getting his ass beaten by a sixty-year-old man and refused to press any charges. The police then asked Mike if he wished to press charges against the younger man for breaking into his car, a crime he had confessed to. Mike refused, saying that justice had already been served.

He has always dealt with the trauma in the past by trying to keep busy. However, he feels like it has really caught up with him at this point.

In addition to love, routine was the only thing that got Mike through the years following the fire. He stayed busy and blurred the days together, dealing only with what was in front of him, refusing to look too far ahead or glance back at what was left behind. The present was all that mattered, the now, the day-to-day in one single day.

In the years following the fire, monotony was a saviour that rarely visited, but when it did it brought calm, just as it had when he had been imprisoned in the late 1970s, and especially when he was kept in solitary confinement for brief periods. Despite the constant humming sound in a room where the lights never went off, he at least knew that day, and the next day, and the day after that would be the same. And when he was released from solitary, he focused on maintaining his routine, and when that was destroyed, whether it was due to a fist fight with another inmate over Jell-O, or when he caught himself looking at cars passing by through his small, barred window and wondered where they were going, what the driver was doing, and what kind of life they lived, he worked feverishly to restore order by continuing to shrink years, months, and weeks into a single repeatable day.

He reports that he has low moods and feels numb and detached and he does not have as many emotions anymore.

Ever since the fire and the coverage of the aftermath in the media, Mike had to endure opinions, most of which were negative, from every single person he encountered, from strangers on the street to people he loved, family members, people he thought would always stand by and support him. Even to the present day, there are members of his family who refuse to speak to him because of opinions they derived from what they read in newspapers or heard on radio shows.

Mike was often told he should have left, that Joey and Danny weren't his kids, not his responsibility. He was told what he should have done and what he shouldn't have done by people who had nothing to do with the situation, a situation that was constantly changing, requiring monumental decisions that had to be made in seconds because equally important decisions were to come moments later. And if he did one thing he was criticized for not doing the other, and if he did the other thing he was criticized for not doing something else. There was absolutely no winning in the eyes of spectators with no stake in the game.

He feels like now he is alone, and they have all died. He has a lot of grief. He is not really sure how to handle it all. He still enjoys things, but not as much as he used to.
It certainly sounds like Michael has experienced large amounts of trauma throughout his life and he currently meets the criteria for posttraumatic stress disorder with worsening of symptoms since his wife died in 2010.

The following is a conversation between Mike and the psychiatrist, based on Mike's memories.

"Have you ever had thoughts of ending your life, Mr. Hawkins?"

"No."

"Never?"

"No."

"Really?"

"No."

"Why not?"

"*Why not?*"

"My apologies, but are you sure?"

"Of course, I'm sure. Why? Should I have those thoughts?"

"I wouldn't say you should but considering all the trauma you've endured I'm surprised you haven't. Many people who have been in similar situations as you typically end their lives."

"I've never thought about ending my life," he replied to the psychiatrist. "I just want to *live* my life."

•

At the time of this writing, every day is a challenge for Mike when he wakes up: whether or not he is going to keep trying to live the life he wants to live or fall victim to regret about the life he was prevented from living.

He speaks softly, rarely raising his voice. He hates loud noises, especially yelling, and as much as he hates shouting himself, he hates hearing it from others even more. The loudness of other people's voices is often too much for him to handle. He immediately feels on edge, which can lead to aggression. He likes quiet. Every shout from a person nearby is a grenade exploding just a few feet away.

Mike's life in his early sixties revolves around only a few things, but all of them are important to him because they all bring him joy and peace.

As children look forward to their birthdays, Mike looks forward to the opening of hunting season. He gets giddy in the days leading up to it. He thoroughly cleans his trusted 7mm rifle and shotgun, ensuring they will work perfectly when the time comes to fire the shot he has waited months to take. He checks his hunting clothes for rips and carefully mends them. He makes sure he has all of his gear. He pre-walks his chosen spots, the same spots he has hunted in for decades, spots that span well over a hundred square kilometres, tracking the movements of the animals, getting a gauge on where they will be.

When hunting season opens, he is rarely home. He routinely wakes up as early as 3:00 a.m., has a smoke, gathers some joints for the day, double-checks he has everything he needs, and heads out to the bush. Sometimes he hunts with friends, but only the ones he respects as hunters: those who will not slow him down or disturb the tranquil concentration needed to bag a beautiful buck with as many points as possible. Most times, however, he goes by himself, regardless of the weather. If it's pouring rain, even better, as the falling drops make it harder for the animals to hear him move through the bush. And no matter if he goes alone or with others, he always makes sure to make a stop at Tim Hortons, where he buys his usual medium triple triple.

He comes back home in the mid-afternoon if he doesn't get anything; if he does get a deer, he could be in the bush well into the evening, depending on the hour and how far he has to drag the carcass. Either way, at the end of a hunting day he is exhausted, and usually takes a nap before getting up and doing what he has to do the rest of the day, then going back to sleep later that night, and waking up at 3:00 a.m. the next morning to do it all over again.

Hunting, and all of the adventures it has brought him — from discovering wolf dens, fending off an attacking mountain lion, and outrunning furious black bears to having friends accidently shoot holes in his new hunting pack, to having to sleep under a tree because he was too exhausted to get back to his truck only to wake up covered with frost — makes him feel alive. He adores the vastness of the bush, the quiet it gives him, the calm.

The thought of eating meat from a grocery store is ridiculous to Mike. The only meat he eats is the meat he personally hunts and kills, meat he takes to a trusted butcher who, for a fair price, turns his kill into kilos of chops, steaks, ground chuck, honey garlic breakfast sausages, roasts, and jerk. Nothing is wasted. The freezers in his home get full seemingly overnight, and what he can't eat himself he shares with those he cares about, those who know there is no gift more heartfelt from Mike than a package of his prized meat.

When hunting season ends, his mood shifts. He is already looking forward to the opening of next year's season. The tiredness comes and he starts feeling restless and bored. The ennui sets in quickly, like a rapidly approaching storm. The past comes back, grabbing and pulling him back to a time he will not only never forget, but in such times feels he is still living through. He panics, gets irritable, and is hard to be around. He occupies his time frantically, refusing to sit still. He must stay busy. He fishes in the island's vast collection of rivers and lakes, some of which don't even have any fish despite his stubborn insistence to the contrary. He gardens, taking great pride in whatever he chooses to grow, from tomatoes and lettuce to flowers. And since the legalization of marijuana in Canada, he enjoys planting his own weed.

He tries to be outdoors as much as he can, which usually involves long walks, often with Willow by his side, just as Yellow was years earlier. During the times he can't be outdoors, he likes to watch classic films, mostly about the wars of the past, a subject that has long captivated him. He plays online poker, winning some, losing some, but enjoying it all the same. And he plays pool, a sport he has played throughout his life; a sport in which he was once nationally ranked; a sport that took him from pool hall to pool hall throughout Toronto and various parts of the country during the 1970s, 1980s, and 1990s; a sport that saw him win large sums of money only to lose it all after insisting on playing just one more game. In his later years, when he managed to find the time, he played in several competitions and did quite well in many of them, even sharing a table with great Canadian players like Alex Pagulayan.

He also spends a lot of his time doing physical labour, the kinds of jobs that exhaust people half his age. It's a miracle that he is able to continue doing the kind of work he does, from block work in big landscaping jobs to driving trucks that he is tasked with loading and unloading throughout the province. He does the kind of work his physically battered body should not be able to handle because he needs to believe he still can, even though it has resulted in a long list of jarring injuries from a broken neck and several hernias to a shoulder in desperate need of reconstruction. There is still gas left in the tank, and that means more to him than he can ever hope to explain to those who openly question why he persists.

He likes to spend time with his friends, talking, playing music, and joking, always joking. To laugh is to live for Mike, and not to laugh is to die. Laughter is not just a medicine, it is a release and a reason to go on. Whenever he laughs, he appreciates that he can still do it, savouring it like a fresh elk burger with bacon, shredded cheddar, and homemade fries. For a long time, especially following the most tragic periods of his life, he worried if he would ever have the strength to laugh again, but he always did, and continues to do so, as often as possible, hoping in his final moments that his last words will be draped with as much laughter as he can muster.

•

I still remember the first and only time I called him Mike. It was during the family's escape to Vancouver Island in 1990. We were at a campsite near Campbell River. I was only eight years old. I called him Mike because everybody else called him that, and I was curious how it would sound coming out of my mouth. As soon as I said it to him, he knelt down, looked me in the eye, and told me sternly, almost angrily, "Don't ever call me that. I'm your dad. You call me Dad."

So from now on, I will refer to him by the name he prefers.

I was two years old when my mom and dad separated. A year later he married Linda. After he remarried, my dad would sometimes pick me up and take me to the house in Orillia. A few days before he came to get me, he usually told my mom to tell me he was coming. I eagerly counted the sleeps before his arrival. More times than not, however, he didn't come, and he would give my mom excuses that left her furious and me heartbroken. As a result, my mother stopped telling me when my dad told her he was coming to see me. She figured that if I didn't know he was coming, I wouldn't be disappointed if he didn't show up.

A few days before the fire, my dad called my mom to tell her he was going to bring me to his house that Saturday, which would have been March 12, 1988. He then asked her to pass the phone to me. As soon as I grabbed the phone, he told me we were going to spend the weekend together. I was overcome with excitement, which only grew when he said he promised he would come. As soon as I heard the word "promise" I was certain I was going to see him because promises can't be broken. That's what I was taught and that's what I believed.

My mother doesn't remember what time she received the phone call informing her that my dad's house had burned down and Joey was on the brink of death. What she does remember, however, was that the call came the same day as the fire, and it was brief. All my dad told her was that there was a fire, the house was gone, Joey might die, and he wasn't going to be able to see me on Saturday. After she hung up the phone, she broke the news to me about what had happened. I didn't ask her about the fire, or the house, or Joey. All I asked was if I was still going to see my dad. When she told me I wasn't, I got angry and demanded to know how he could break his promise. She got upset with me for only thinking about myself, before realizing I was just a five-year-old boy who wanted to see his father.

From 1988 to 1992, when I turned ten years old, I saw more of my dad in newspaper articles and on the news than I ever did in person. Whenever he was on TV, I would be sitting in the living room with my mother wondering if he was thinking about me. Whenever he looked directly at the camera, I naively said, "Mom, he's looking at me, right? He can see me, right?" And whenever he flashed a smile, I said, "He's smiling at me, right?"

From 1993 to 1998, I no longer thought my dad could see me through the television or was smiling at me, and I no longer wondered if he was thinking about me either. I didn't want to see him during those years, but I still did see him from time to time. I resented him, even hated him at points. It wasn't difficult to harbour such feelings either. They were constantly fed by the barrage of vilifying articles and reports routinely published by various media outlets. My spiteful attitude toward my dad was fuelled even more by members of his own family who told me negative story after negative story about a man I had rarely seen and barely knew. I thought I had a deadbeat dad who had abandoned his son.

While seeing my dad during those years after the fire was rare, when it did happen it was always memorable.

Since it was the only opportunity I had to see my father in the months following the fire, I was there at the Hospital for Sick Children in 1989, seeing Joey after he returned from the Shriners Burns Institute, talking to him, joking with him, all the while feeling terrified at the sight of somebody who looked like they had already died yet remained alive. I was there in "the house that love built," seeing Linda's homemade B-52s in large containers in the kitchen, thinking they were milkshakes. I was in the house, sleeping in the guest room upstairs, when Linda passed out drunk in the backyard. I was there during the escape from Orillia to Vancouver Island in 1990, sitting in the back of the red-and-grey van for days, watching the country pass me by. I can still viscerally recall the awful stench of cigarette smoke wafting throughout the van during the trip. I was there in Moose Jaw, standing in the mud watching the Snowbirds perform the "Philion Roll." Years later, I got to walk with, play with, and adore Yellow.

During the summer of the escape to Vancouver Island, I was ignored most of the time. My dad and Linda were too busy trying to set up their new home in Sayward to pay much attention to me. So I took long walks by myself along an assortment of trails. After a few weeks, I was told I couldn't take those walks anymore because there were bears around and I was just a child, but since nobody was really paying much attention to me, I took them anyway. I loved the adventure, the thrill of those walks, and I ended up seeing an array of animals including those same bears I was warned about.

I didn't like Linda at all during that time. She was almost always short-tempered with me, treating me like an annoyance, a nuisance that was in the way demanding to see my dad. She yelled at me and even hit me at times. I had no idea about the pressure she was under, the constant worries about Joey and finding a proper home, the traumas she had already dealt with and was continuing to deal with, and the relentless lack of sleep, but how could I have known? Why should I have cared? I was just a kid.

Joey was also impatient with me but, considering what he was going through at the time and how often he was left alone with a hyperactive eight-year-old who had no idea what was happening, it's hard to blame him. He treated Danny the same way, so Danny took out his frustrations on me whenever he got the chance, usually through playful tortures. Once he told me to drink from ponds on the slippery, sloping cliffs above Elk Falls and I ended up getting a mild case of beaver fever, which is Canada's version of Montezuma's revenge. Danny and I had a lot of fun together, though, from fights that involved swinging bulky pillows at each other like battle-axes and him teaching me how to do a proper sleeper hold, to watching in amazement as his uncle Johnny ate and drank things no human ever should, to shouting along with the chorus of the Beastie Boys' "Fight for Your Right" whenever it was on MuchMusic.

In the summer of 1996, when I was fourteen years old and Danny was nineteen, I came to visit the family on Vancouver Island, staying in one of the motel rooms the family shared, as they were between homes at the time. Danny had his own motel room, and I always hung out with him. He smoked weed my dad gave him, but always told me not to touch it because my dad threatened to kick the shit out of him if he ever found out Danny had given me any. A few days after my arrival, some kid tried to steal my bike. I told Danny and he jumped out of his seat, walked outside, went right up to the kid, and told him, "You see this bike. This is my little brother's bike, and if you try to take it from him again, I'm going to kick your ass."

As an only child, hearing him utter those words made me feel so protected, so connected, that from that moment on I idolized Danny and loved him.

That same summer I had a huge crush on Pamela Anderson. Knowing about my crush, Danny rented a movie she starred in called *Naked Souls* and surprised me with it. We watched it together and I was so happy, not because it was a good movie, which it definitely was not, but because it was the first movie she starred in where she exposed her bare breasts, which was the only reason Danny rented it for me.

I still vividly recall the day I got the call informing me that Danny had died. It was the early evening of November 18, 2001, and it was an ugly, grey day. There was freezing rain and slush. I was walking along Dundas Street in downtown Toronto. I was in a daze after I hung up the phone, heading to a class, unsure if I should even go or not. As soon as I walked in, although I didn't tell any of my classmates what had happened, they all approached me and asked if I was okay, saying that I looked terrible and should go home.

I was supposed to see Danny the following summer. The last time we had spoken, a few weeks before he died, he told me he was going to take me to the most popular strip club in town, the Courtenay House, and he was going to make sure I had a great time. He told me he was going to take me all over the island and take me to parties with all of his friends and that we were going to spend a lot of time together, like brothers. I miss him dearly, and even though I have already outlived him by many years, whenever I think about him I still see him as older, bigger, wiser, stronger, and tougher than me.

The last time I spoke with Linda was just a few months before she died, when the cancer had really started terrorizing her brain. She talked with slurred speech and wasn't able to remember much, not even what she had just said a few moments earlier, but she none-theless made it clear to me how much she cared about me. She told me I meant a lot to her and that she was very proud of me. She said she loved me, but I couldn't say it back.

When Linda died, I felt the same conflict I had when she was alive. On one hand, she had taken my dad from me, and despite her kind words later in life, words I genuinely believed, the way she treated me during that summer on Vancouver Island resulted in a resentment I was never able to relinquish. On the other hand, with age came understanding, and with that understanding I grew to respect her, knowing that everything she did, right or wrong, good or bad, she did for Joey, whom she loved so purely, so unconditionally, so fiercely, so fanatically that she was willing do anything for him, including giving up her own life. It would be too simple, too ignorant, and too reckless to dismiss her as a bad person or even as a victim of her own devotion, because I know my own mother would have been every bit as fierce if she had been in the same position. And Linda loved my dad deeply, of that there is no doubt. She made him happy for many years despite the tremendously difficult circumstances they endured, and for that I will always be grateful to her.

I still remember how horrible I felt reading a newspaper article about Joey's release from the hospital, just before his transfer to "the house that love built," in which my dad was quoted as saying, "This is probably the happiest day of our lives, the family's back together again. It's been a long time." Ever since the fire, I constantly read or watched my dad talk about how much he loved his family and how much he believed in Joey and how much he admired him. Just once I wanted him to look at the camera and say *my* name and say flattering things about me, just to let me know that I existed and he was thinking about me. But it never happened.

There was a good reason for that.

My mother had made it very clear to him that I was to be kept completely out of the news. She was having a hard enough time raising me on her own, barely making ends meet with government assistance cheques while living in Toronto Community Housing building #90 in the Mornelle Court neighbourhood of Scarborough, Ontario. She did not want reporters poking around asking questions, confusing me even more. My dad was happy to oblige. After seeing the media circus for what it was, he didn't want me anywhere near it either, so whenever a reporter dared to bring me up, he immediately shut down the interview, making it as clear to them as my mom had made it to him that I was off limits.

He thought about me every day after the fire, but he had to keep it to himself. In the burn wards of the Shriners Burns Institute and the Hospital for Sick Children, he saw a lot of kids die and families break apart and lose their minds. Despite all of that anguish, he felt relief that it wasn't me in those wards, that it wasn't me suffering.

I didn't know any of that.

All I knew was that I wanted a father, and for a long time I felt like I was wrong for wanting that, that I was being selfish, that others needed him more than I did, and I should accept it, but I couldn't. Meanwhile, Linda wanted a husband, Danny wanted a stepfather, and Joey wanted a constant caregiver. How could he be all of those things to all of those people at the same time? If he had left Linda, Joey, and Danny after the fire to be a father to me, he would have been crucified by the public, forever known as the man who abandoned the heroic Joey Philion, but more importantly, he would have hated himself for leaving his family at the time they needed him most. Yet choosing to stay with them through it all meant having to leave me, his only son, behind.

Since I saw my dad so infrequently during those years, regardless of the anger, resentment, and hatred I felt, I held on to every minute I got to spend with him and cried whenever it was over, because I never knew when I would see him again. That prevented me from ever saying what I really felt to him, from getting mad at him, from yelling at him, from even being myself around him, because I was afraid of doing anything that could jeopardize whatever little time we had. To this day, I still get irritated whenever I have to share my visits with him with other people, knowing that everybody else has had far more time with him than I ever did. I'm doing much better with that, however, since I've told him exactly how I feel. I've been mad at him and yelled at him, and I've refused to be anything other than myself around him. It is a new, still raw relationship, built from the ashes of all that was lost, but it is a relationship I cherish and am grateful for.

Not too long ago my dad told me that if I was to ever have the same kind of accident as Joey and be forced to experience the same pain he did, he would do for me what he refused to do for Joey: he would end my suffering as soon as he possibly could, and whatever consequences came as a result, he would happily accept.

I love you too, Dad.

THE HEROES WE WANT AND
THE HEROES WE GET

THIRTY-THREE YEARS, SEVEN MONTHS, AND TWENTY-FOUR DAYS AFTER THE fire, on November 3, 2021, Joey Philion passed away, alone, at the Vancouver General Hospital, from a urinary tract infection that reached his heart.

He was forty-eight years old.

Of those 12,291 days since the fire, not a single one was promised to him, and for every one of those days his ravaged body and mind had to fight to live. Nobody could understand how he was able to maintain that fight for so long. They never will. That's because how he continued living was secondary to *why* he continued living, which was inspired by his only goal since the fire: to live a regular life.

In his later years, accomplishing that goal meant living online, where he got to freely establish and cultivate friendships, liking, commenting, and connecting with the world around him while carefully controlling how he was viewed by that world. On social media he wasn't Joey Philion, miracle survivor of the 1980s, public punching bag of the 1990s, and forgotten tragedy of the 2000s; instead, he was just Joe Philion, single, Canadian. Digitally, he was free, unburdened by the stigma of his injuries from the fire and the baggage of its aftermath. On social media he was anonymous, a name with no weight. And what did he do with an outlet that neither he nor anybody else imagined at the time of the fire and in the decade following it? He posted cliché memes like "Golden Rule: Never Expect. Never Assume" or "I like people that I can trust with eyes closed and my back turned." Just like everybody else. And while some of those memes doubtlessly inspired sincere emotions — particularly the religious ones that said things like "The God behind you is stronger than the enemy in front of you" — they are memes precisely because he felt those sincere emotions just like everybody else.

Parts of Joey's personality did often shine through, especially his humour, as dark and sardonic as ever. In 2019, he wrote a post on Facebook stating that he had just been informed that according to several doctors he had survived the worst third-degree burns for the longest time of any person in the world. He followed that up by writing that it wasn't a record he was really interested in breaking.

To speak to Joey online without the enormous distraction of the accident he suffered was to talk to the person he would have been if the fire had never occurred. What so many people seemed to misunderstand was that the fire didn't suddenly turn him into a philosopher, a saint, or a sage. He wasn't a genius or a gifted, exceptional person before the fire, and he didn't become any of those things after it. People shouldn't have held him to an absurd Jesus-like standard just because he survived that fire, and he shouldn't have had to bear the ridiculous responsibilities of his miraculous survival either, but he did. He should never have been defined by the events of March 10, 1988, but he was.

When I last spoke to Jocy in the summer of 2020, I wanted to tell him that I was interested in getting to know the real him. But that wasn't exactly true. I thought about asking him what he was doing, but what was the point? I knew what he was doing: nothing. I also had to consider whether or not I believed the things he said. He told me he was living quietly and comfortably in a nice apartment in Vancouver and had medical attendants checking in on him, but was that true? In 2018, I had been told by close members of the family that he was broke, and living in a shithole somewhere in Surrey where homeless men who claimed to be his friends made copies of his house keys and robbed him while he had no choice but to watch it happen from his wheelchair. Was any of that true?

The reality versus the fiction of Joey's life had been blurred ever since the fire. He had lived so many lives since 1988 it is still difficult to know which parts of them were real and which weren't. During our conversations, he told me there was a movie in the works about his life. Was that true? I'll never know.

•

Dr. Zuker said that one of the many effects of severe third- and fourth-degree burns is that they completely knock out the body's immune system. Every disease-fighting cell is destroyed, but nobody knows why. Maybe it's the body knowing that after suffering that kind of extensive damage survival is not an option, so it ensures its own demise by destroying its only means of defence against disease — in a way, committing suicide. If that's true, does that mean that Joey's medical miracle may have been a monumental act of interference against the will of his own body?

For years, I've often wondered what would have happened if Joey had died in the fire. How would the lives of Linda, Danny, and my dad have gone? Would Danny and Linda still be alive today? Would my dad and Linda still be together? Or, if Joey had survived for only a few days, weeks, or even months before succumbing to his injuries, would Linda have gone with him just as she told him? Would he still have been viewed as a hero to countless people or would he have been written off as another sad story, another tragic statistic, another young victim of fatal burns?

In order to know if heart transplants, kidney transplants, lung transplants, or any other groundbreaking medical procedure work, people almost always have to die. But in Joey's case, he lived, and continued to live, granting the doctors at the Shriners Burns Institute the opportunity to continue experimenting and learning from him. For many months and many surgeries, Joey was like a living, breathing, feeling, organ donor.

All of those experimental procedures performed on him led to monumental progress in how to treat burn victims, especially when it came to cultured skin and the methods by which it could be utilized. Many of those methods are still used today, and over the last three decades they have saved the lives of countless severely burned people around the world. The benefits of Joey's survival for complete strangers have been staggering, but the price of that survival, including the tragic loss of his mother and brother, have been arguably just as staggering, raising the question: Was his survival and subsequent agony worth it?

The ravenous fire on that early March morning was determined not only to devour the house on Cleveland Avenue but the entire family residing inside, and even after the final flame was doused, the fire was never truly extinguished. It was an elemental beast that Joey openly challenged. Not used to such insolence, the fire did not give up its pursuit and eventually claimed both Danny and Linda. Still not satisfied, it tried to consume my dad as well. He, like Joey, managed to survive its wrath, but not without suffering immensely. Just like Joey, my dad has scars, but his are invisible.

·

A closeness between me and Joey never developed but I've always respected him. I've always been in awe of his strength and courage, of his refusal to live in this world on anybody's terms but his own, and of his utter defiance of death itself. Do I believe he is a hero? It's a question I've thought about for as long as I can remember, and the answer changes like the seasons. What doesn't change, however, is my only memory of Joey before the fire.

It was a grey day in October of 1987. Joey was babysitting me and, as was said in the beginning of this story, I was only five years old at the time. He took me for a ride on his dirt bike. I clung to his back with my tiny arms wrapped around his midsection and before I knew it, he was racing around the quiet roads of Cumberland Beach, Orillia, right by the house that was fated to burst into flames less than six months later. Because I was inexplicably wearing shorts, I was constantly raising my legs, as the hot metal of the bike's crude engine kept burning them. After about fifteen or twenty minutes, noticing the gas tank was leaking, Joey stopped the bike. With the supreme confidence of a carefree teenager, he reached into his pocket and took out two pieces of Bazooka bubble gum. He tore them open, gave me the little comics inside, chewed both pink pieces for a few moments, then took the wad out of his mouth and firmly pressed it against the tiny hole in the gas tank, plugging it completely.

After that, he noticed me gently touching the burns on my legs, wincing every time. He told me I'd be okay before revving the engine loudly. I told him the burns hurt. He reassured me that

I would be fine, that I would survive, then he smiled and asked me if I wanted to go back home or if I wanted to keep enjoying the ride.

Joey, before the flames.

ACKNOWLEDGEMENTS

I WANT TO FIRST THANK MY MOTHER FOR GIVING ME EVERYTHING SHE HAD and more, most of all for the freedom to pursue the life I always dreamed of.

To my dad, thank you so much for sharing your thoughts, memories, and feelings from such a tough time. I know how difficult that was for you. Thank you for providing me with so much of the material necessary to make this story complete. Without you, this book couldn't happen.

To Russell Smith for so many great suggestions to make the story better, and most of all for believing in this book. That means a lot to me. To the entire Dundurn Press team for their hard work and belief in this work, those I've had the pleasure of interacting with — Kwame Scott Fraser, Meghan Macdonald, Erin Pinksen, Laura Boyle, Alyssa Boyden, Rajdeep Singh — and those I didn't, you all have my deepest thanks. Thank you to Susan Glickman for such a thorough edit that made the story even clearer than I could have hoped.

To Charlie Franco at Montag Press for giving me my start. I will always appreciate you. And to all of the Montag authors for their help and support over the years, I wish you nothing but the best.

Lara Harb, thank you so much for your unwavering help, patience, and love, especially during those times I was consumed with doubt.

Nathan Whitlock, thank you for your time and your help when I was still trying to find this book a home.

Tanya Godard and Andy Philion, thank you so much for your feedback and help with the photographs.

To Paulina Castro, the incredible support you have given me throughout my life as a writer, from my first book to now, will never go unappreciated.

To my friends and family, thank you *y gracias* to all of you for your encouragement while I was putting this story together.

Finally, I want to acknowledge the memory of Joey, Linda, Danny, Pepe, Nanny, Terry, Connie, Kathy, Cochi, and Tolstoy. You are all missed.

ABOUT THE AUTHOR

Photo by Lara Harb.

WHEN JONATHAN R. ROSE IS NOT WRITING A NEW story, he's usually reading a new story, watching a new story, or walking around observing the world around him while putting together a new story in his mind. Like a mathematician thinks in numbers, an athlete thinks in physical movements, and a musician thinks in notes and verses, Jonathan thinks in story.

An avid traveller since he was eighteen, Jonathan has travelled to dozens of countries, all of which have exposed him to an array of perspectives from a variety of people. For Jonathan travel is an addiction, so when he's not somewhere else he's almost always thinking about being somewhere else. It's those travels, including living in Mexico for a decade and Argentina for two years, that have led to the creation of so many of his stories.

\